Annie Gray

From the Alps to the Dales

100 Years of Bettys

PROFILE
EDITIONS

First published in Great Britain in 2019 by
Profile Editions, an imprint of
Profile Books Ltd
29 Cloth Fair
London EC1A 7JQ
www.profileeditions.com

Copyright © Bettys & Taylors Group, 2019
10 9 8 7 6 5 4 3 2 1

The moral right of the author has been asserted.

A CIP catalogue record for this book is available from the British Library

ISBN 978 1 78816 243 2

Typeset in London by Charlotte Klingholz
Printed and bound in the UK by Gomer Press Ltd

Contents

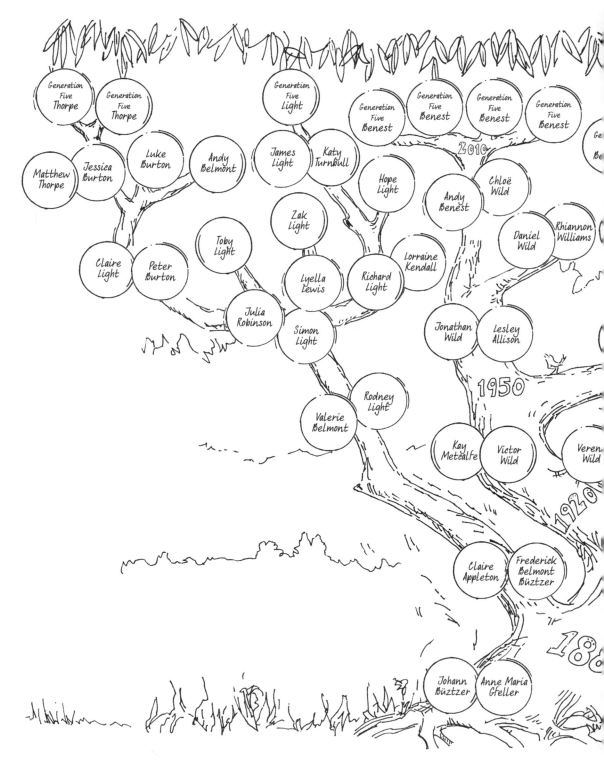

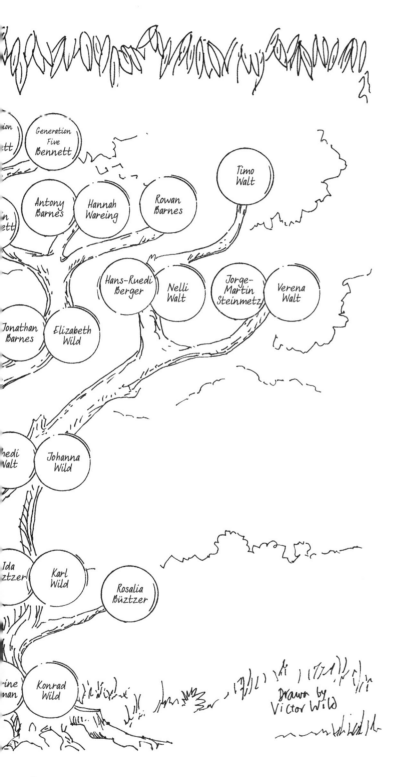

Generation
Five
Bennett

Timo
Walt

Antony
Barnes

Hannah
Wareing

Rowan
Barnes

Hans-Ruedi
Berger

Nelli
Walt

Jorge-
Martin
Steinmetz

Verena
Walt

Jonathan
Barnes

Elizabeth
Wild

uedi
Valt

Johanna
Wild

Ida
ztzer

Karl
Wild

Rosalia
Büztzer

rine
man

Konrad
Wild

Drawn by
Victor Wild

Bettys family tree based on an
original illustration created by
Victor Wild, the nephew of Bettys
founder Frederick Belmont

5

Foreword

by Lesley Wild,
Chair of Bettys & Taylors

As Chair of our Board and a third-generation family member, I am immensely proud to be leading Bettys & Taylors at the time of its 100th birthday.

I know that if our founder, Frederick Belmont, could see how the business he started a century ago has grown and developed, he would be bursting with pride too.

Looking back, it seems incredible that we have survived and thrived through so many challenges: world war, massive social change and technological revolution.

I believe the secret is that we have never forgotten Frederick's original vision – I like to think that if he were to wander into Bettys today, much of what he might see would be familiar to him – the handmade bread, cakes and chocolates from our Craft Bakery, accompanied by the finest teas and coffees, cosy and comfortable surroundings and delicious Swiss-Yorkshire food delivered with a smile.

I'm certain too that Frederick would regard the decision in 1962 of his nephew and successor Victor Wild to buy the Taylors tea and coffee business as a stroke of genius – creating the business we know today. But, above all, I believe Frederick would be thrilled that we remain an independent family business, owned by his descendants, continuing to serve the third, fourth and fifth generations of his customers.

I hope that you relish reading this wonderful book – Annie has brought our amazing story to life, setting it in the context of the times and uncovering more of our fascinating history. Our archive is blessed with an abundance of material which she has skilfully woven into the social history of eating and drinking through the last 100 years.

It is a truly heart-warming tale of determination overcoming adversity and of the amazing contribution a tenacious immigrant can make to the benefit of us all.

Lesley Wild

Introduction

by Annie Gray

9 a.m., and I'm by no means the first person through the doors of Bettys in York. The only one of the six Bettys cafés still occupying a site from the founding decades, it's an iconic building, its huge plate glass windows looking out onto St Helen's Square. Through the windows, besuited business types scuttle past, takeout coffee clutched in hands, and the clank of delivery vans forms a background noise. Inside, all is muted, and, as my breakfast arrives, I sip at my first drink of the day (Blue Mountain coffee) and surreptitiously dunk my cinnamon toast. I'm on a Bettys crawl, a rascal run: all six branches in a day, and I'm pacing myself.

Breakfast is a fairly quiet time, although later there will be queues around the art deco façade, and the shop will be bustling. At the table across from me, the waitress is laughing with a

gentleman who is clearly a regular. I catch his eye, and he ends up regaling me with stories of Bettys, from the surprising number of celebrities spotted in the Ilkley branch, to the rather posh manageress of the Stonegate branch, dropping back into her native broad Yorkshire when a tray was dropped in the corridor. Over the course of the day, I'll meet other long-time customers, along with staff, and, although their stories will differ, the joy with which they will tell them and the warmth they have for Bettys will be universal.

I head out into the rain, onto the square and down to Bettys Stonegate, which is all uneven floors and sudden doorways into hidden rooms. The atmosphere is quite different; the café upstairs with views onto the street below, and the shop downstairs fronted by a small-paned Georgian window, so characteristic of the historic streets of York. Here, I have a crisp apple juice and watch a lovestruck couple gaze in awe and delight as their afternoon tea arrives at 10.30 a.m. They Instagram each layer of the cake stand. On the way out I congratulate the shop staff on their amazing window display,

with a Bettys centenary cake in the middle. They tell me that the window regularly loses panes, from hens and stags leaning up against it to have their pictures taken.

Time is getting on, so it's into the car and a swift drive up to Northallerton, past the green fields and wide vistas of the A19. It's market day, and the high street is bordered with stalls selling fruit and vegetables, pies and umbrellas. Bettys

Northallerton is in an imposing Georgian building, and as I go through the shop and join the lunchtime queue, its origins as a gentleman's house are evident. Past the staircase, the back suddenly extends out into a set of joined, very open rooms, top-lit and full of light. This is the only place I've seen floor tiles as opposed to carpet, and the space is broken up with huge plants, which continue out into the terrace garden.

I'm famished now and order a chicken schnitzel with pommes allumettes. I can't resist adding a side of sugar snap peas with mint and hazelnut and a pot of tearoom blend tea. The portions are hearty Yorkshire ones, and I tuck in with glee. Most of the people around me are also having lunch, although I note that in the corner two enthusiastically chatting ladies dressed in vivid pink are sharing an afternoon tea, complete with champagne. It's quite a different set of people from those I shared my breakfast and elevenses with, fewer tourists, more low-key and local. The café manager, who has realised what I am up to (I'm met at every stage by members of my dedicated Bettys crawl support team from head office), asks if I'd like to visit the cellar, so we climb down the ladder and peer at the old wine racks, and I take pictures of the walls.

Next up is Ilkley, another drive away, this time through the edge of the Yorkshire Dales, past sheep peacefully grazing in the shelter of drystone walls. Yorkshire's industrial heritage is well represented too, with red-brick mills and chimney stacks, especially along the rivers. The colour of the buildings has gradually changed from the sandstone of the Georgian era to the smoke-blackened walls of the area around Leeds. The cloud has lifted a bit, and as I drive into Ilkley I can see why it is such a popular place for visitors who want to explore the countryside

beyond. It's crammed with impressive Victorian architecture, and the Bettys here is in an 1870s building, originally a grocery shop. I pause for a minute under the wrought-iron canopy, looking down the street before going in. Again, the shop is at the front and the café at the rear. My eye is immediately drawn to the huge window, with delicate floral stained-glass insets, and which forms the back wall. It feels a little like being on a luxury ship. There's a piece of marquetry, a work by the Spindler studio, to one side reinforcing the idea of solidity.

I'm in need of a pick-me-up, so I opt for a hot chocolate and an Engadine torte, a real hit of warmth and spice without being heavy. It also

stunning view of the gardens as they drop away below me. Another Spindler panel takes up the remaining wall, *Les Herbes folles*, which translates charmingly to 'mad grasses', and I spend a few moments admiring it.

I sit down to herbal tea, which seems apt, along with my favourite Bettys item, hot buttered pikelets. I'm not the last person there, thankfully, despite the late hour, and I smile at a family on another table. They have colouring books and crayons spread out among their cups and plates, and a chocolate-smeared toddler in a high chair is clearly having a great time. There's no sense of pressure to leave, and I revel in the buttery glory of my pikelets as the rain starts once more.

Finally, I come to Harrogate, the first of the Bettys towns, where the original shop and café opened in 1919, although the current branch is over the road from where it all started. As I walk up the hill toward Montpellier Gardens I look over, past the war memorial, to the original site, and give it a nod of recognition. Then I turn to admire yet another packed Bettys window display, before heading to my final meal of the day.

means taking a good look at the cake stand and having a chat with a couple on their way out – they regard themselves as almost-regulars, coming here whenever they are on holiday nearby. I also hear another Bettys story from my head office host, whose first visit was when she was pregnant and overdue, waiting to be induced that day, and had woken up to find her house flooded. Champagne with breakfast at Bettys seemed entirely apt.

I've hit the start of the evening rush hour now, and the short drive to RHS Harlow Carr seems to take forever. I make it at 5.25 p.m. with minutes to spare, running in, determined to complete the Bettys set. This is the only Bettys in a 21st-century building, a hard space to transform, being long and open and lacking the soaring light levels of the other branches. But, as I pass the shop and enter the café, I realise that the whole back wall is a window with a

Bettys Harrogate is a late Victorian building, built at the very end of Victoria's life, as the Edwardian era started. Known at one stage as the 'café under the clock', it shares with the other branches a sense of timeless elegance, but it is also very much a hub for the wider company. I've drunk tea in the offices and the main boardroom upstairs. I'm still full of pikelet, so I opt for a Yorkshire rarebit, accompanied by a glass of Swiss wine, which I'm eager to try. Seated in the middle of the restaurant, I've got a good view outside and in. It's a quiet, comfortable atmosphere, with live piano music forming a background ideal for chatting and eating as well as relaxing after a hard day's driving and drinking. My fellow diners are a mixture of business people in suits with their ties stuffed in pockets, locals enjoying the peace after the day trippers have departed and the occasional tourist looking gleeful at getting a table by the window. The waitress tells me to come back for breakfast and ask for the seat in the corner, the best vantage point in the house.

Throughout the day, in all the tales I've been told, and from the people I've watched, one theme has emerged strongly: a sense that Bettys is timeless, that it means so much to so many because it is so reliable and never-changing. At one level, this is absolutely true. The underlying values of Bettys – an emphasis on excellence, on service and an investment in its people – have never changed. Bettys has always combined a Swiss ethos, derived from the family that founded it, with a firm attachment

to Yorkshire, where they are settled. It has always valued craft skills, whether in the furnishing of the branches or the making of its products. But, as I look about me now, I can't help wondering whether those about me know how much, in some ways, what they think of as timeless is very much of its time. For Bettys is very much rooted in the now. It has always been a modern business, albeit one very proud of its heritage, and it has changed a great deal over the last 100 years.

This is the story of a business – Bettys – of how it was founded, flourished, lost its way, but came through to rise stronger and more prepared for the future than ever. But a business, even one as personable as Bettys, does not build itself: this is about people, from the family who founded and still run it to the many thousands of people who, over 100 years, have shaped dough and dipped chocolates, poured tea and packed boxes (and the many millions who have eaten and drunk the

products of the Bettys and Taylors craftspeople). It's also about changing consumer tastes, social trends and the nature of the high street. The story goes back beyond the day the doors in Harrogate opened, and will go beyond the celebration of the Bettys centenary in 2019. We start at the end of the 19th century, 750 miles and 134 years from my breakfast coffee, with a boy called Fritz.

Before Bettys

1885–1919

What's on the menu?

Long before Bettys opened, its founder was learning the trades of confectionery and sweet-making in Switzerland, France and the UK. When he was in Paris, Fritz Bützer also worked as an 'entremétier'. In the modern kitchen brigade, this term refers to the chef in charge of starters and side dishes, but, at the time, the word could also refer to the chef in charge of sweet entremets, which today we'd call desserts, sweets or puddings (the corresponding modern term is *pâtissier* or pastry chef). In Edwardian Europe entremets were a category of sweet foods eaten as part of a separate course which came after the savoury courses – which in particularly grand meals involved a choice of soup, fish, intricate meat dishes with complicated sauces, roast meats and vegetables and showpiece large joints, served in an endless procession – but before the ice creams, delicate biscuits, nuts and fruit which formed dessert.

An entremétier had to be able to make cakes and biscuits, be a master of pastry, a whizz at creams and custards and jellies, and an expert in meringues, jams, jellies and curds. Some entremets were served hot, others cold. Edwardian food fashion was for highly elaborate dishes, often moulded, coloured with food dyes and garnished to the extent that the basic ingredients were unrecognisable. Sugar was cheap, and Fritz's clientele would have expected his work to show skill, time and talent, all worth paying for.

By the 1930s, when Bettys had four branches plus a bakery, Fritz was no longer cooking. However, his nephew Victor remembered that 'he showed me how to do an apple charlotte'. This classic entremet dates back to the 18th century and was a recipe which could be found on tables up and down the social scale. By the 20th century it had become a working-class favourite too, by now a truly democratic dessert. This recipe comes from a book by Charles Herman Senn, one of London's most influential chefs as a writer and educator. Like Fritz, he had been born in Switzerland but trained in Europe before finding success in the UK.

Charlotte de Pommes
(Apple Charlotte)

Cut a stale, fine-grained sandwich loaf into quarter inch-thick slices, cut these into strips about one and a half inches wide and of the same length as the charlotte mould which is to be used for this dish. Cut also a sufficient number of triangular-shaped or narrow kite-shaped slices to cover the bottom of the mould. Grease the inside of the charlotte mould with clarified butter. Now dip the shorter pieces of bread into the oiled butter and place them, one by one, in the form of a circle at the bottom of the mould; it is best to allow the slices to overlap each other, the points always meeting in the centre. Next, arrange the long strips in a similar fashion, by dipping each into oiled butter and fixing them closely against the sides of the mould with a well-made, fairly stiff apple purée flavoured with sugar, lemon and ground cinnamon. A small quantity of cake-crumbs can be added if liked. Trim off the strips of bread that overlap the edge of the mould and bake in a fairly hot oven for about forty minutes.
Turn out onto a hot dish and pour hot fruit syrup around the base of the dish. Serve quickly.

In 1885 the Belle Époque, or Gilded Age, was in full flowering across the capitals of Europe. Successive waves of industrialisation had led to the growth of cities and the urbanisation of countries such as Britain, where around two thirds of the population lived in towns. A highly affluent, mobile elite moved freely between London, New York and Paris (overwintering in the south of France), where they patronised the new exclusive restaurants, where meals were cooked in the fashionable French style, with kitchens staffed by teams of male chefs often drawn from France, Germany, Italy and Switzerland. The urban middle classes were also thriving and were increasingly visible in city centres, for a long time mainly the province of workers, but now filling up with department stores and restaurants, cafés and tea rooms. There was a buzz in the air, and even the ageing British queen Victoria was embracing such modernities as electricity, telephones and gas cooking apparatuses.

The buzz, however, was limited. When Fritz Bützer, the founder of Bettys, was born in Switzerland in April 1885, his parents would never have foreseen the future that lay ahead of him. Switzerland was overwhelmingly rural, with very limited social mobility. Emigration levels were high, as workers of all levels sought to escape the lack of opportunity, together with the deprivation which led, inevitably, to high infant mortality and low life expectancy. Starvation was never far away, and life was hard: the tourists who came in increasing numbers enjoyed the clean air and good winter sports, but to most of Switzerland's residents the luxury hotels and restaurants of Lucerne and Zurich were as far removed from their reality as could be.

It was into this Switzerland, rather than that of cuckoo clocks and chocolate, that Fritz was born, in a hamlet called Lindenbach. It was in a German-speaking area, about 50km from Bern, and its residents spoke with a thick local dialect.

Opposite The Mill at Wangen-an-der-Aare, Switzerland

Above Fritz Bützer as a young child in 1888

Fritz's family were respectable professionals; his father, Johann, was a miller and master baker, and his mother, Anna-Maria, Johann's second wife, was a teacher. She died of tuberculosis when Fritz was aged one, leaving his father with four young children: Fritz's sister Ida was three, Hans was seven, and Rosalia was eight. Hans died a few years later, and just a few months after that, Johann married again, a wife being a necessity both to look after his children and to help run his business. Karoline Kummer quickly added two more children to the family, and Johann invested heavily in a new business, a mill at Wangen-an-der-Aare, another small village carved out of the forest that covered most of the area. In 1890, when Fritz was five, a fire broke out, fires being not uncommon in bakeries and mills, where flour dust could easily and explosively combust. It was the middle of the night. Karoline carried her two babies while Johann grabbed Fritz and Ida by their hands, Rosalia clutching his nightshirt tails as they fought their way down the stairs and out of the door. At some point, Rosalia, overcome by smoke, let go. Johann, having saved the other two, plunged back in. His unconscious body was brought out by what passed for the emergency services – probably local volunteers with basic equipment – but he died a few days later from smoke inhalation along with burns. Rosalia was already dead. Fritz would barely remember his father, and Karoline never remarried.

Karoline had worked as a housekeeper before her marriage, but now, with four dependent children and another on the way, she moved back in with her family in Niederönz. There, she gave

birth to a son just a few weeks after the fire. He died a month later. The Bützers had life insurance, and now a protracted court battle ensued to gain a proper payout. The family was very poor, and while Karoline's mother looked after the babies, Ida and Fritz were growing older and more able to work. They stayed with their stepmother for four years, but eventually entered the Swiss care system as *Verdingkinder* or 'contract children'. Now renowned for the endemic abuse and maltreatment which children suffered in it, the contract children system was in place until the 1960s in some areas. The children became the responsibility of their *Heimatort*, a significant concept under Swiss law and in Swiss culture, which referred to an individual's ancestral home – in this case, the village which Fritz and Ida's father came from, Teuffental, a small farming village of around 200 inhabitants. Under the *Verdingkind* foster system, children were effectively auctioned by the local authorities to the lowest

Opposite, top The old bridge in Wangen-an-der-Aare

Opposite, bottom Johann Bützer and Anna Maria Bützer, parents of Fritz Bützer

This page An illustration of child labour. This was commonplace within the Swiss care system up until the mid-20th century

bidder, the person who wanted the least from the state for their upkeep. Usually this meant someone who wanted cheap labour, and, although these children were supposed to be fed and cared for, as well as schooled, in practice they were often neglected, their names forgotten in favour of the all-purpose '*Bub*', or boy, sleeping in barns with little clothing and emerging from the system barely literate – if they emerged at all. Fritz bore scars on his face for the rest of his life: whether from the fire or from his subsequent treatment is unclear. His mental scars went deeper: a lifelong search to belong, and to be loved.

Ida and Fritz initially stayed together, with a family whose grandson was, according to official records, 'uncontrollable', but they were quickly separated: Ida went to learn to knit with a Mrs Röthlisberger who needed an assistant (there were worries that she was too harshly Christian, but it was a trade), and Fritz became a farm worker with a Mr Schiffmann, a local court official and farmer. Karoline tried desperately to reunite the family, and Ida moved back as soon as she could pay her way. Fritz joined them for a few months, but the local court reported that the new school wasn't suitable: his previous one was 'deemed entirely sufficient for being a craftsman … the boy displayed not enough eagerness to learn to rise to a scholarly profession'. There were reports that the siblings were 'malnourished and often appear to be hungry'. He was returned to the Schiffmann farm and the local school, where he was learning reading, writing, maths plus manual skills, gymnastics and singing. His school reports show that he read better than he wrote, and he was marked for orderliness and cleanliness along with his academic studies.

In 1899, aged 14, Fritz left the *Verdingkind* system behind. His childhood had been brutal, and neither he nor Ida spoke much about these years in later life, but they did have one thing many other *Verdingkinder* did not, and that was a family. Karoline, however, could not be relied upon for financial support, and, although she was now working, she was an emotional and financial burden. In 1902 she had an illegitimate child, Ernst, by her employer, whether through an affair or rape is unknown. Ida later wrote that 'even though she failed me bitterly, she has had to do heavy penance'. Fritz agreed that 'she hasn't had much of a life'. Her siblings, though, provided a network through which

Fritz could find a trade, and, although the money for official apprenticeship fees was lacking, he started work with one of Karoline's brothers, Gottfried, as a trainee baker. In 1903 Fritz took his bakery exams – the Swiss system was rigid and relied on official qualifications. His scores were entirely average, except in dough-making, and he seemed destined to become a small-scale baker, scratching a living as his father had before him. The family couldn't afford for him to sit more exams, and so he followed the usual track of working in various small bakeries as he learnt on the job. When he was 19 he was examined for the obligatory Swiss military service. His record shows he was unsuitable for training due to astigmatism, as well as the physical effects of childhood deprivation: he measured only 1.66 metres (5 feet 4 inches), far shorter than average, despite his bakery-honed biceps and strong upper body. A photograph of the time shows him proudly erect, sporting a small – but carefully waxed – moustache and with the bushy eyebrows which make him easy to recognise in many subsequent pictures.

In 1904 Fritz made a brave career decision, switching from baking to confectionery. Baking revolved around yeasted goods and careful management of ovens (all solid fuel in small bakeries at that time). Confectionery was a harder, more prestigious and

Opposite Fritz Bützer as a teenager, c.1902

Top Schiffmann's Farmhouse in Teuffenthal, by Victor Wild

more competitive profession, whose practitioners were often more literate, and definitely more artistic, with a wider range of skills than bakers. Today the term 'confectionery' has come to mean sweets, especially chocolates, but in 1904 it covered a much broader range of foods, all centred on sugar but encompassing everything from sugarcraft (pulled sugar and pastillage) to decorated cakes, biscuits, meringues and the foods commonly found on the dining tables of the well-to-do: soufflés, tarts, jellies, mousses, pastries and so on. It was highly specialist, and, even where households kept their own cook, they would often buy in confectionery items, and shops and caterers flourished in towns with an established middle class. Fritz couldn't, of course, afford the official training, but nevertheless he gained positions in several shops, eventually moving to Lausanne in French-speaking Switzerland. He had learnt basic French at school but now became fluent enough that the next move, which came via recommendation from either a relative or a colleague, was out of the country, to Marseille. One of his aunts wrote approvingly: 'that you want to criss-cross the world at such a young age I find commendable, it will broaden your horizons and increase your knowledge and skills!'

A typical scene in a working bakery, c.1900

'... that you want to criss-cross the world at such a young age I find commendable, it will broaden your horizons and increase your knowledge and skills!'

In France, where formal qualifications were far less important than in Switzerland, he could progress much further, developing his skills in line with the flair for artistry he already possessed. He worked at the Confiserie Probst, almost certainly a Swiss firm (*confiserie* was the French term for a confectioner's). He was already planning the next move, however, and his postcard collection from the time shows how spread out his network of connections now was. Cards came – and went – from Paris, including from another of Karoline's relatives, Adolf (or Adolphe) Kummer. In 1907 Fritz joined him. By now Fritz was occasionally using the French form of his name, Frédéric, especially with his French-speaking friends. It was as Frédéric that he joined La Saint-Michel, a mutual society and labour exchange for pastry chefs and ice cream makers, which secured him a job as an entremétier (chef in charge of side dishes, in particular sweets) in a restaurant on the Boulevard Sébastopol. He almost certainly had one or more chefs working under him. It wasn't enough, and only a few months later he was on the move again, with a new recommendation for a job with a Swiss-run business in Bradford, England.

In 1907 Fritz wrote a wonderfully tongue-in-cheek letter to Ida, his 'proud Bernese lady', detailing his journey from Paris to Bradford: 'The dumbest people always fare best. How I managed to travel right across France and across three-fourths of England as well was more a matter of luck than good judgement on my part.' Later the story grew in being retold, to the extent that it's hard to entirely tell fact from fiction. Certainly, the trip was eventful, starting at 8.30 p.m. from Paris with Fritz rather the worse for wear, meeting a fellow Swiss on the train, being severely seasick on the ferry and arriving abruptly in London with no real clue where he was going and no English – worse still, unlike the multilingual culinary world he was used to, 'none of these asses understood French or German!' He recalled shouting out 'Bratwurst, Bratwurst', and finally someone who spoke a little French put him in a cab to catch the train to Bradford. In later accounts he claimed to have lost the address of the business he was going to, and possibly even to have forgotten the name of the town, but in the original letter it appears he knew exactly where he was going: a Swiss firm called Bonnet's, a caterer and confectioner on Darley Street, which also 'hosted balls and soirées'.

It's unlikely that Fritz would have gained entry to the country without his letter of recommendation: Britain was in the grip of an anti-immigration movement, which had resulted in the passing in 1905 of the Aliens Act, the first piece of major legislation intended to curb immigration into the UK. Aimed

Top French postcard received by Fritz Bützer from his relation, Adolphe Kummer, 1908

Opposite Fritz Bützer as a young confectioner in Friborg, Switzerland, c.1904

Makers of the famous Bonnet's Chocolate,

At 2/6 Per lb.   By Post, 2/10.

LUNCHEON AND TEA ROOMS.

THE FASHIONABLE RENDEZVOUS OF BRADFORD.

44, DARLEY STREET, BRADFORD.

Starving in a land of plenty

mainly at Russian and Eastern European Jews, who had been fleeing increasing persecution at the end of the 19th century, the Act insisted that would-be workers must prove they had the means to support themselves before being allowed to land (they also had to be mentally sound and without a criminal record). There were no figures for immigration, and no one was sure how many people the new Act would apply to, only that there were lots of 'destitute aliens' of 'a low type of civilisation' coming in and that measures were needed to stop them. Fortunately, Fritz was safely Protestant, Swiss, and he had a job to go to.

Bradford was a wool town, whose size had exploded off the back of technical innovation during the first industrial revolution in the late 18th century. It had been granted city status in recognition of its importance – and size – only 10 years before Fritz arrived. Over the previous 30 years the population had nearly doubled with around one third of its 400,000 inhabitants working in textile manufacturing. It had a substantial middle class along with very rich industrialists and workers, both in its mills and in the various support trades such as transport and

Opposite Bonnet & Sons, Bradford, where Fritz Bützer was first employed when he arrived in Yorkshire

Top Postcard sent to Fritz Bützer, 1908

utilities, whose circumstances ranged from comfortable to dire. The area around Bonnet's was packed with substantial late Victorian buildings, marks of civic pride and wealth, the pride of which was the Wool Exchange of 1864, an exuberant example of neo-Gothic architecture which celebrated Yorkshire, using local builders and decorated with statues of local heroes. It emphasised Bradford as a place that produced goods, not services. Fritz was a producer too, now the foreman chef leading a team of five plus three apprentices, all Swiss. He told Ida it was 'the most beautifully furnished and noblest place in town', adding: 'I quite like it here.'

However, as ever, money was on his mind, providing as he was for Ida, now a seamstress, and Karoline, back in Niederönz, and he now realised he could earn far more in an English firm, where he'd be something of an exotic novelty. He was a driven man, and he'd arrived with great expectations for a country which at that time still ruled a vast empire and was thriving. Shopkeepers could become rich: one of Fritz's colleagues had advised him clearly that 'England is the land of opportunity. They are years behind there in developing sophisticated sweets of all kinds.' He found that Yorkshire worked well for him: there was limited competition but great demand, and despite his initial lack of English, he learnt fast (although he always retained a thick Swiss accent and a dry Swiss sense of humour). By 1910 he'd gone freelance, working for confectioners both large and small in Bradford, Wakefield, Halifax and, on and off from 1908, Harrogate.

Throughout his travels, Fritz remained in constant contact with Ida through letters and postcards, and they supported each other emotionally as well as practically. As a man, he had more freedom than his sister to move about and enjoy all the various pleasures the cities he visited had on offer, and she told him: 'every time one of your letters arrives, it is a cause for celebration!' Ida was forging her own identity, which included fighting off undesirable male approaches. She was well aware of the differences gender imposed: 'I do like to have fun, just like you, but I need to maintain my decency.' He urged her to get out of Switzerland, to come and join him, but she wrote back: 'England is not on my mind at this time. Let's talk about that some other time, agreed? Here I have a very good clientele, so

Left Fritz Bützer

Right Fritz's sister, Ida Bützer

why go to a foreign country and fish in troubled waters, as they say. There I would be a servant: here I am my own master.' He replied that he was 'really proud of my sister'.

He was now earning enough to propose to Ida that they meet up in Paris, still hoping to persuade her to then come to England. She considered it, writing: 'I thought of maybe going to the French-speaking part of Switzerland for a year so that I could at least get fluent in French before daring the jump to England.' The meeting didn't come off though, and a few months later she instead proposed that he visit her: 'We shall also go and see the Lindenbach creek where we first saw the light of day, shall we not? … We shall walk a lot, I think, with packs on our backs like tourists, and we shall take food with us and have picnics so that it will not be as expensive. And in all of Switzerland there will not be a happier brother and sister pair travelling the country.'

Fritz's new life in England was one of opportunity, if he could take advantage of it. Confectionery was as prestigious a profession as it was elsewhere in Europe, with a particular cachet attached to French, Italian and Swiss men. The French had long since taken over the upper echelons of cooking and were to be found leading all of the grandest restaurants. The French language was in everyday use for upper-class menus. The Italians were more divided: on the one hand there were businessmen such as Gaspare Gatti, owner of a string of catering concerns in London, and on the other there were those who lived in slums in many big towns, working in dank basements turning out cheap ice cream for the masses (and causing occasional outbreaks of cholera or other diseases due to the conditions in which they worked). Then there were Germans, heavily represented in the baking and butchery trades. The Swiss, neither French nor German nor Italian, but able to harness the reputation of all three, were surprisingly commonplace in the culinary trade. Fritz worked out early that the best way to sell his services was to play on his French connections, for his business letterheads read 'F. Belmont, chocolate specialist'. The name 'Belmont' may have come from his 1910 lodgings in Harrogate, which were at 26 Belmont

Fritz Bützer with his sugar sculpture creation, c.1904. This was replicated by hand to feature in Bettys' centenary celebration windows

Avenue, where the daughter of his landlord was a toffee packer – Farrah's of Harrogate, famous for their toffee, were one of Fritz's clients.

Fritz described Harrogate in a letter to Ida as 'a first-rate resort town'. In 1910 it had a population of around 88,000, but this figure included a large number of visitors, and the population swelled enormously during the summer months as the wealthy flocked to use the Royal and Victoria baths or the Pump Room and enjoy the other facilities on offer. For those who came to take the waters, the day started with an orchestra playing in the Crescent Gardens, followed by gentle exercise. Walking gently up Parliament Street, just on this one street a person would pass shops offering almost everything he or she needed. There were a few practical tradespeople, such as seedsmen and ironmongers, but otherwise the street was replete with chemists (unsurprising, given the ostensible motivation for visitors was their health) and every possible item to wear or carry. There was even a specialist

Early 20th century postcard showing Parliament Street and Cambridge Crescent, Harrogate, later to become the home of Bettys

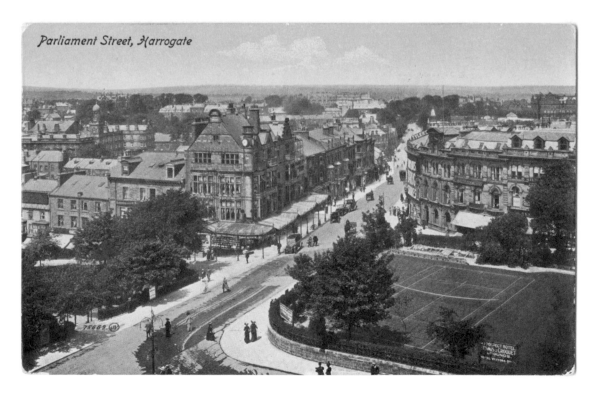

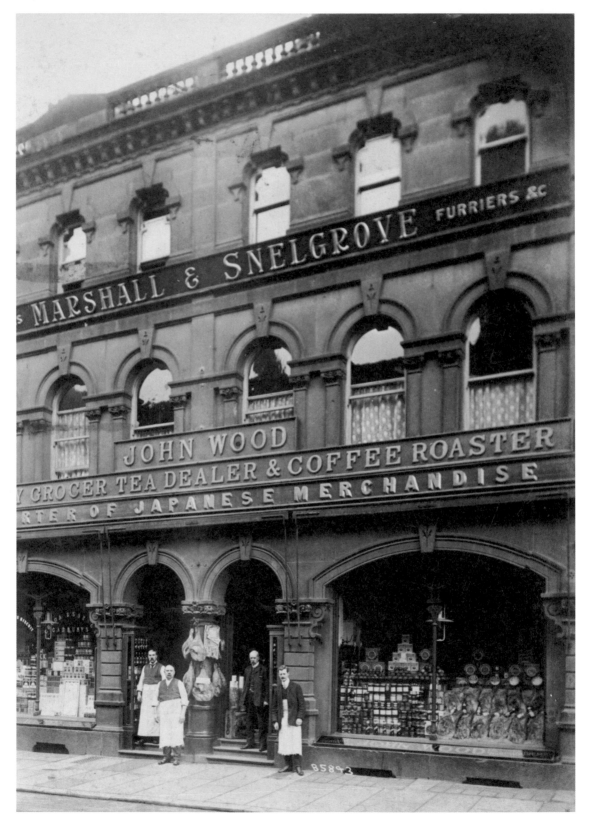

Opposite John Wood's grocery store, Bank Buildings, James Street, Harrogate, 1880–1910

Top View of Harrogate looking toward No 1 Parliament Street. This shows Bettys' current building under construction in the background, c.1900

in cycling and athletic wear, in case the multitude of hat fitters or hosiers didn't appeal.

More pertinent, there were confectioners – Fritz worked for a while for Semadeni's, at 14 Parliament Street – and cafés. Parched promenaders could choose from the Scotch Bakery and Café in the Royal Arcade, a Taylors' Kiosk and the resplendent Taylors' Imperial Café on the corner of Parliament Street facing Cambridge Crescent, where another park would provide benches and respite. If they did carry on further, the shopping got even better: Cambridge Crescent had a branch of Ogdens (a jewellers and Harrogate institution) at no. 9, and there was another branch on James Street, which led down to the station and was the most prestigious street in Harrogate. There, the walker would find more cafés, including Harrogate's best: Standings. The interior had been given an oriental makeover a decade before Fritz arrived, with the typical British flair for a theme run rampant – 'oriental' covered everything from chinoiserie to Islamic influence, and the café was a riot of coloured tiles, mother-of-pearl pilasters and intricate fretwork. There was another upmarket tea room at Marshall & Snelgrove, one of a small chain of highly fashionable department stores, with a flagship branch on London's Oxford Street and other stores mainly in Yorkshire, where its founder was from. Below part of the Harrogate branch was John Wood's grocery store, from which Queen Victoria's granddaughter, later the last Empress of Russia, ordered York hams, having gained a taste for them while on a cure. By the time Fritz knew the shop, it was run by John's widow, Mary.

Fritz was now doing well enough to send money back regularly to Switzerland, where Ida, despite writing of a 'disdain for marriage', was falling in love with an idealistic writer called Carl Wild. In the evenings, after her work was done, she'd stay up reading philosophy books so that she could help him, writing: 'I love him beyond all measure, and it is my wish to make his life easier.' But she was torn, admitting frankly that 'he is not suited to be a husband and we would both perish if we had to submit to living in tight conditions'. She, like Fritz, was very self-aware, writing: 'I am always in good spirits and strong-willed. Both of these characteristics have helped me overcome difficult times.'

Fritz, meanwhile, was lonely, despite having a series of girlfriends, including two at once in 1909. One, called Daisy, sent him postcards for his collection, which now numbered in the hundreds, yet still his letters caused Ida to burst out: 'I had to shed bitter tears when I read [your letter]: such pain is contained within those lines which, alas, I cannot alleviate.' Ida implored her brother: 'Fritz, you have the potential to become more than an average, everyday person. Live consciously so that you may find the way that will bring you full satisfaction and happiness.' She told him not to shy away from struggle, but also reminded him that in becoming hard on himself he should not become unsympathetic to others. Meanwhile, she investigated sourcing Swiss wine for him, presumably to sell on, as he was doing with chocolates, but to no avail – the freight charges were prohibitive, and the customs officials prone to opening the wine, drinking it and topping the bottles up with water.

Fritz was increasingly committed to Yorkshire. However, the family network that had sustained him on his journey from baker's apprentice to confectionery expert had long outlived its potential. Ida still refused to join him, saying: 'I know I need to stay here, that I am needed', tied both to Carl and to Karoline, who was now very ill and wanted to die. Fritz was left frustrated in his desire to progress, empty and alone. It was, therefore, fortuitous that, around 1914, he fell in love.

Top Carl Wild, c.1909

Opposite A postcard of the Royal Baths and Winter Gardens in Harrogate, 1910

Both Fritz and Ida were wary of marriage, fearful that it would not meet their high expectations. Yet marry they both did: Ida married Carl in 1914, and Fritz got engaged the following year. Ida was overjoyed, writing: 'I have the utmost confidence you will find complete happiness … and that the person chosen by your heart possesses all the properties of character and essence that are required for your happiness; and I do not doubt that you will strive to become a compassionate, dear husband. You have what it takes, dear Fritz.'

Claire Appleton, his fiancée, was 23, six years younger than him, and had five siblings. Her father Thomas was a watchmaker and jeweller who, 20 years before, had been a man of some substance, employing a man and a boy through the business and a maid at home. However, he was also an alcoholic, and, as Claire grew up, she and her family moved around Harrogate, leasing ever-smaller houses, dismissing their live-in servant and starting to take in boarders. By 1914, while her father still gave his profession as a watchmaker, he and his wife Annie were effectively boarding-house keepers.

Fritz and Claire Bützer punting
on the River Nidd, c.1916

Later, the story of how Fritz and Claire met became romanticised into a tale of love at first sight, occurring when Fritz, looking for lodgings, knocked on her door and Claire answered it. It may well be true, although it's more probable that he met her in the streets around their homes, for she lived on the next road over from his lodgings in Belmont Avenue, and he always had an eye for feminine beauty. Claire, who was also known as Bunny, was petite – even shorter than Fritz – with dark hair and expressive features. She worked above a florist on Station Road as a 'ladies' hair specialist', also offering massage, manicures and chiropody. Her siblings also worked servicing the needs of Harrogate's visitors and residents: her brother Sam was a chemist, and sister Mary was a milliner. Another sister, Kathleen, had married a blacksmith called Charles Elsworth and moved to Lincolnshire. Like Fritz, they were upper working class, grounded in the burgeoning service industry, but, unlike him, they had been Harrogate-based for many years. In marrying Claire, Fritz found himself a new family network – albeit one which regarded him with some suspicion: a foreigner, with a thick German-sounding accent, was not the easiest thing to be as the world headed toward war.

The day before the declaration of war, in August 1914, the government rushed through a new immigration act – the Aliens Registration Act. Had he been an enemy alien – a German or an Austrian – Fritz would very probably have been interned and certainly subject to rigorous restrictions. As it was, as he planned his marriage in 1915 he wrote that 'were it not for the newspapers we would forget we are in the middle of a big war'. He also declared: 'I am still Swiss, and therefore neutral.' But he was also feeling increasingly British, and as the war wore on he faced huge resentment as he carried on business as usual, when British subjects were called up regardless of personal circumstance. Worse was to come, for in May 1915, after the sinking of the *Lusitania*, anti-German feeling led to riots and, accented as he was, he must have felt an acute sense of danger. The rioters trashed the shops and homes of anyone they thought was German – mistakenly including foreigners of several other nationalities. The change in Fritz's tone in his letters to Ida showed his feelings –'the war is terrible, I wonder when people will come to their senses', and he asked her not to address her replies to 'Fritz – use Frederic instead, the former is too German'.

Meanwhile, in Switzerland, Carl was collecting signatures to petition the Swiss government to lead a peace conference. Characteristically passionate and single-minded, he went to Bern to present his petition in person to the President, where he was promptly arrested and sectioned to keep him out of the way. Ida wrote to Fritz that she could hear the canon booming out over the German border in Alsace. Fritz started to consider an application for British citizenship, for it was now evident that the war would not be over quickly: several facilities in Harrogate were converted to hospitals or convalescent homes for wounded soldiers. Shops were shuttered as conscription tightened, and the appetite for new hats waned. There were many refugees, in particular from Belgium.

The war affected Fritz's business plans. Despite the climate, he wrote: 'when the war is over I am thinking of going into business for myself. I see a good opportunity.' He was trying to raise money – he even considered asking the uncontrollable grandson of his and Ida's first foster family for a loan – but Swiss banks would not lend in such an uncertain climate. By 1916 food shortages were beginning to bite as the British government resisted introducing rationing, and the sugar that the confectionery trade relied on was in short supply. Ida, ever helpful, offered to send a few bags from her own small supply. Not all was gloom, though. In June that year he married Claire, moving to Glebe Road, from where he wrote: 'Claire and I are settled and very happy.' He expanded: 'We are very very happy: in my wife I have found a rare companion and through her my life has received an aim and a purpose. How I wish to bring her to you so that you can experience her grace and kindness for yourself.' Honeymooning in Switzerland was out: the looked-forward-to trip would have to wait for another six years.

In 1918 the war finally ended, although it took a year for the last of the soldiers to be repatriated from France. Many came back severely injured, mentally and physically, and for several years after the war the number of dispossessed increased dramatically: men who either couldn't function any more in a family environment, or who couldn't work and had no means of support beyond begging. While the Harrogate death toll was less than 5 per cent of its population, there would have been few families who did not know someone whose experiences had changed them for life. Anti-German sentiment still ran high.

MARY WOOD
FIRST CHAIRMAN OF BETTYS 1919-1925
Portrait by Victor Wild

Mary Wood, the first Chair of Bettys,
1919–1925. Painted by Victor Wild

Fritz's application for British naturalisation would be granted in 1921, in the name of Frederick Belmont. To get it, he had to have lived in the UK for five years, to be of 'good character' with an adequate command of English and to intend to live permanently in the UK. He wrote to Ida, claiming that he was still the 'same dear old Fritz' and 'in my heart I am still the same Bützer', although Claire, apparently, said otherwise. His naturalisation would be witnessed by Claire's cousin, solicitor George Wood, the son of Mary Wood, the owner of the prestigious grocery on James Street.

George and Mary were now family, part of Fritz's new Harrogate connections, and they, along with Claire and Mary's son-in-law Frederick Rose, were all intimately involved in his new venture. In a post-war England with sugar rationing still in force (until 1920) and the scars of war still smarting, Fritz and Claire had saved their money and sought backing from others. Fritz admitted that the 'country's industries were still in turmoil from the war', but he saw an opportunity to lead, rather than always follow. Opening what he called 'a high-class business' at such a time was, on the face of it, a risk, but he was a gambling man. He was confident that Harrogate would recover and that with premises cheap and labour easy to come by, as men returned from the front and women were ousted from the jobs they'd had during the war – now was the right moment. Throughout 1918 and early 1919 he had put the pieces together, and on 11 June 1919 the first official Board meeting of Bettys (Harrogate) Ltd took place. Fritz – Frederick – was 34, a respectable, almost-British citizen, an experienced confectionery chef, and a married man. He and Claire had no children yet, and they were a formidable partnership putting their energies into the business. In July 1919 their new café and tea room opened: Bettys was finally born.

Bright young things

1919–1929

What's on the menu?

When Bettys first opened in 1919 baking and confectionery making was all done on the third floor of the Harrogate café. In 1922 a separate bakery was opened, and the quantity that could be produced expanded. The bakery supplied both the Harrogate café and, as they opened, new branches in Bradford and, in the 1930s, Leeds and York. Fritz (now Frederick Belmont, except to his Swiss family), took advantage of the extra capacity to offer a catering service as well. This was not unusual – the most prestigious catering firm in London, Gunter's, had started as a confectioner in the late 18th century – and 1920s customers, whether rich or poor, expected to buy most of their goods via the delivery services offered by bakers, butchers and other food traders. From the very beginning of Bettys, the link between the goods available in the cafés and those that could be ordered was made explicit, with Frederick working hard to ensure that the Bettys name represented quality and consistency.

The menu shows how well Frederick had learnt to cater for Yorkshire tastes in his time as a consultant confectioner: long-established teatime classics such as Madeira cake (originally eaten with Madeira, rather than containing any), seed cake, queen cakes and pound cakes dated back to the 18th century, while the five types of scone, the layer cakes, cheese straws and various nut slices were of newer provenance. Party-givers wanting savoury food are catered for with the standard range of rather Edwardian cold meats: galantines, tongue and pies, along with York

ham, the recipe possibly based on Harrogate's prestige grocer John Wood's royally endorsed version (his widow, Mary Wood, was Chair of the Bettys Board until 1924). For parents with children at boarding school, the menu has 'tuck boxes', in this case Christmas-themed: the description emphasises that the puddings and cakes are of the 'finest quality'. Hygiene was in the news at the time, and the proud description that Bettys has a certificate of hygiene and that puddings are made under 'hygienic conditions' fed into a current concern.

The menu also plays to Frederick's strengths as a confectioner, although, as Bettys expanded, he now employed other chefs. A list of 'dinner sweets' contains ices and meringues – the items most in vogue on the 1920s dessert table just as much as they had been before the war. Finally, Frederick's pride in his chocolate skills were in evidence, as sugar came off the ration in 1920, and, for a brief period, high street shops innovated and produced sweets to rival anything emerging from mass-manufacturers. Harrogate was known for its toffees, which were reputed to alleviate the tang of the sulphurous waters, so valued still as a health cure, so of course they had to be on the menu too. Buying from Bettys also meant a handmade box. Both Frederick and Claire valued aesthetics, and the boxes were things of beauty: lined in silk, delicately illustrated and designed to be kept. It's not surprising that some of them survive still, and some are given to the Bettys & Taylors archive by the great-grandchildren of the original recipients.

CAKES, SAVOURIES, &c.

Dainty Afternoon Tea Fancies.
2¼d. each.   2/6 per dozen.
Filled with fresh cream.

Chocolate Fancies.
2d. each.   2/- per dozen.

Assorted Fancies, with various fillings and flavours. 2d. each.
2/- per dozen.

Plain Cakes, Buns, Tarts,
2/- per dozen.
Madeira Buns.
Sultana Buns.
Almond Slices.
Cocoanut Slices.
Hazelnut Slices.
Cherry Slices.
Eccles Cakes.
Almond Cream Tarts.
Queen Cakes, 2d. each. 2/6 lb.
Cocoanut and Rice Tarts, 1¼d.
Lemon Cheese Tarts, 1½d.
Jam Tarts, 1¼d.
Jam and Lemon Puffs, 1¼d.
Yorkshire Curd Tarts, 1½d.
Large Curd Tarts, 6d. and 1/-.

Vienna Rolls ... 1d. each.
Milk Rolls ... ... 1d. „
Crescent Rolls ... 1d. „
Dinner Rolls ... 1d. „
Sultana Scones ... 1d. „
Plain Scones ... ... 1d. „
Brown Scones ... 1d. „
Girdle Scones ... 1d. „
Scotch Pancakes ... 1d. „
Potato Cakes... ... 1d. „

Plain Cakes.
Madeira Cakes ... 1/6 & 2/-
Almond Sultana Cakes 2/-
Sultana Cakes ... 1/9
Cherry Cakes... ... 1/9
Rice Cakes 1/6
Seed Cakes 1/6
Cocoanut Cakes ... 1/6
Almond Pound Cakes 2/-
Genoa Cakes... ... 2/- & 3/-
Dundee Cakes ... 1/9 & 2/6
Chester Cakes ... 2/6
School Cakes ... 1/-

Sand Cakes ... ... 9d. & 1/6

Bridge Specialities.
Rolls, Scones, Girdle
Scones ... ... 6d. per doz.

Tea, as served in our
establishments 4/8 lb.

China Tea ... ... 4/8 lb.

Coffee, as served in our
establishments 3/6 lb.

Speciality :
Lemon Layer, 2/- per lb.
Moorland Slab, 2/6 per lb.
Ginger Slab, 2/- per lb.
Plum Slab, 3/- per lb.

Speciality Ginger Cakes,
10d. and 1/6

Tuck Boxes from 10/6.
A suggestion—
Xmas Cake,
Xmas Pudding,
Mince Pies,
Chocolates,
Tin of Petit Fours... 10/6

Our New Specialities :
Layer Cakes ... 1/6 and 2/3
Coffee.
Chocolate.
Raspberry.
Tangerine.

Glace Fruit Cake, The Cake of the Gourmet—consisting of Glace
Pineapple, Glace Ginger, Glace Cherry, 2/3.

Pineapple and Walnut Layer Cakes,
2/- and 3/- each.

Petit Fours (Dessert Biscuits). A large assortment of flavours and fillings.   Packed in tins, 3/6 and 7/-, or 3/- per lb.

Betty's Own Make—

Delicious Mincemeat, 1/- per lb.

Our **Xmas Puddings** are of outstanding quality. They are made underhygienic conditions and are of the finest quality.
1/6, 2/3, 2/9, 3/-, 5/6 and 6/9.

Xmas Cakes.
A rich plum mixture, made from the finest ingredients. Almond Iced. Beautifully decorated in various designs, or decorated to customers' instructions.
2/9 per lb.
3/- and 3/3 per lb. Almond Iced.

Genoese—fresh cream or Ice Cream filling. Beautifully decorated by our experts. Suitable for children's parties. 3/6 per lb. Any size made to order.

Cheese Straws, 6d. packets.
3/- per lb.

Savouries.
York Ham ... ... 5/- per lb.
Ox Tongue ... ... 5/- „
Galantine of Chicken 7/6 „
Galantine of Veal 4/- „
Galantine of Beef 2/8 „

Pork Pies, 1/-, 2/-, and 4/- each.

Veal and Ham Pies, 1/6, 2/6, and 5/- each.
Other sizes to order, 2/6 per lb.

Potted Beef Steak (in cartons), 6d., 1/- and 2/- each, or 4/- lb.

Hand-coloured Bettys menu featuring illustrations of the interior of the original Bettys Harrogate branch in Cambridge Crescent, c.1925

Orders by Post will receive our immediate attention.

Carriage Paid on goods to the value of 10/6 and upwards.

Cash on Delivery. Orders may be sent c.o.d., collection fee payable by the customer.

Accounts opened on approved references.

DINNER SWEETS.

All Sweets served in our Cafés may be obtained in the shop or made to order in the following sizes :—

1 pint size	... ...	**3/-**
2 pint size	... ...	**5/6**
3 pint size	... ...	**7/6**
4 pint size	... ...	**10/6**

The pint size will make from four to six portions, and the other sizes in proportion.

All Sweets will be sent out in returnable glass dishes, or in customers' own dishes, if desired.

Ice Moulds	... ...	**6/-** quart
Ice Cream in Bulk	...	**20/-** gallon

VARIETIES.

—

Vanilla Cream.
Banana Cream.
Pineapple Cream.
Peach Cream.
Strawberry Cream with Sauce.
Raspberry Cream with Sauce.
Caramel Cream with Sauce.
Chocolate Cream.
Charlotte Russe.
Meringue.
Chestnut Meringue.
Chocolate Meringue.

JELLIES WITH FRUIT.

Various flavours.

Cream Trifles ... **3/-, 5/-, 7/6** and **10/6.**

AWARDED THE CERTIFICATE OF THE INSTITUTE OF HYGIENE.

UNDER ROYAL PATRONAGE

Betty's Ltd
THE EXCLUSIVE CAFÉ.

HARROGATE & BRADFORD.

The original Bettys on Cambridge
Crescent in Harrogate, c.1920

Harrogate post-war was playing catch-up. The first two years after the war were a time of national grief, culminating in the burial of the Unknown Warrior in Westminster Abbey on Armistice Day 1920, the ceremony attended by tens of thousands of people seeking some form of closure for the loss of their loved ones. In Harrogate, as in so many towns and villages across the world, funds were raised for a memorial to the local dead – around 900 men, many of them from the Harrogate Terriers, a local Pals battalion (the Pals battalions were made up of men exclusively drawn from local recruiting drives: they guaranteed that soldiers would fight alongside their friends, but they also ensured that the death tolls were disproportionately large for the communities from which they were drawn). It would be unveiled by the most significant local landowner, the Earl of Harewood, in 1923 and still stands, an imposing stone obelisk, opposite Bettys in Harrogate, at the junction of Parliament Street and Cambridge Road.

Life went on, however, and, as the shops reopened and the wounded soldiers left, the visitors returned, flocking once more to the self-proclaimed 'London on the Moors'. The annual income of the baths and wells rose from £38,000 in 1919 to £59,000 in 1922, and hundreds of thousands of certificates were issued to those wishing to take the Harrogate waters. James Street continued to be the location for the most upmarket shops, and, although Marshall & Snelgrove had suffered during the war, it was now in partnership with Debenhams, and new openings were planned across Britain.

Bettys opened at 9 Cambridge Crescent, a set of 1860s buildings opposite the end of James Street where it meets Cambridge Road. The site had previously been occupied by the jewellers Ogdens, but they didn't reopen the branch after the war: devastated by the death of his youngest son and faced with economic uncertainty, James Ogden, the owner, opened in London instead. Frederick, however, saw only opportunity as the country recovered. He wrote to Ida that when his new business opened, as a 'first class confectionery and café', on 17 July 1919, it was 'sink or swim'. In his letter he gave himself the primary role, and, indeed, it was his idea and his vision driving it, but he couldn't have accomplished it without financial – and moral – backing. He was one of five shareholders, all of the others drawn from Claire's extended family.

Most important, from both a monetary and a political viewpoint, was Mary Wood, whose clout within Harrogate as the owner of Wood's grocery was significant and who, as Chair of Bettys, presided over the sometimes acrimonious Board meetings. She liked and admired Frederick, and having her as an ally was vital for him. She was an astute businesswoman, and he was a foreigner with many ideas but no real experience in running a business in Britain. She lent Frederick some of the money he needed to ensure he was a significant shareholder, and she guaranteed the £5,000 mortgage (the building, which the new company bought outright, cost £7,000 in total), but in return she brought her own family into the business: her son-in-law Frederick Rose, a fellow baker and confectioner, and owner of a business on York's Gillygate was a fellow Director, and her son George Wood, a solicitor (the witness to Frederick's naturalisation), was appointed Secretary. Also involved were Clarence (Clarrie) Rose, also a solicitor, who had won the Military Cross during the war, and Claire, both holding shares. Frederick Belmont, holding 25 per cent of the total shares, was given the title of Managing Director: in practice he and Claire would run the business on the ground, while giving regular reports to the Board.

Claire, meanwhile, had been suffering from the ear disease mastoiditis, picked up as a child and persistent ever since. Today it would be treated with antibiotics, but then it was a debilitating recurrent illness which necessitated her having repeated bouts of hospitalisation and convalescence. In 1920 she'd been very ill for six months: in an era before the NHS, her illness cost the couple a significant amount of money, and Frederick was also still sending regular sums back to Switzerland to help Ida. Bettys was a big gamble for him, and happily a very successful one. He wrote of Claire that 'I have my wife to thank for my possessions. She is not only my wife, but my colleague and my co-worker.' Her knowledge of the tastes of the middle- and upper-class

Top Frederick Rose and Mary Wood c.1915–1920

Opposite Bettys Harrogate, c.1920

potential customers of Bettys, gained through working as a ladies' hairdresser, combined with Frederick's artistic flair – and experience of confectioners' shops elsewhere – helped to inform the décor of their new venture.

The aspiring Bettys visitor would first enter the shop, its door flanked by two large glass windows displaying showpiece cakes and carefully arranged goods which could be bought to take home. Inside, cakes, chocolates and biscuits shared space with handmade silk-lined boxes in glass cases edged with precious woods. The shop space was long and narrow, so much use was made of mirrors and pale wallpaper. Skirting a pot plant and a plush velvet chair provided for less mobile customers (or those used to sitting while being served), the visitor would climb the

'... but this was a very inclusive form of exclusivity: all were welcome, with the aim that in entering they'd feel just that little bit more special than usual.'

stairs to the first floor, where the café was. There, the colour scheme was entirely modern: grey with pink panels and antique silver borders and silver electric candleholders. The porcelain was grey-blue to match the walls, with white insides, so that the food would take centre stage. Coffee and tea services were all of silver-nickel (an alloy of copper, nickel and sometimes zinc), almost certainly electroplated with sterling silver. EPNS (electroplated nickel silver) was the standard material for teawares and most silver homewares from the mid 19th century, and would have been familiar to many of Frederick's customers: this was a home-from-home, but with better cake. For those who came from lower down the social scale, the décor was aspirational, but not so upmarket as to be off-putting: it was a fine balance to achieve. There was, in addition to the shop and café, a second-floor smoking room and workshops (the bakery and confectionery) on the third floor. There was an orchestra which played daily.

Success was immediate: Bettys took £30 in the first day, £220 over the first week, and by 1920 was selling around £14,000 worth of goods a year. It fitted perfectly into the Harrogate scene, not as over-the-top opulent as Standings, but definitely not a rudimentary adjunct to the local bakers. Right from the start, adverts in local papers used the tag 'the exclusive café', but this was a very inclusive form of exclusivity: all were welcome, with the aim that in entering they'd feel just that little bit more special than usual. Bettys had a Continental flavour, not

Opposite, top The shop at Bettys Harrogate, c.1920

Opposite, bottom Interior of Bettys Harrogate, c.1920

obviously Swiss, but playing on Frederick's French-sounding name, and the menu was cleverly set up to include modestly priced English standards such as sardine or ham sandwiches, poached eggs and toast. The equally low-priced miniature pies (veal and ham, chicken or lobster) were labelled as pâtés, however, lending a debonair note to the menu. One of the leading cookery writers of the day, writing for the trade, gave a recipe which included veal, ham, hard-boiled eggs and parsley, commenting that 'there are patties and patties, and these … are of a superior quality'. The 'pâtisserie française' helped strengthen the impression of sophistication, although if all of that was too much, a healthy cup of Bovril could also be had – at 6d for a small helping, a penny more than a lobster patty. Bettys also offered ice cream, a luxury which for most was strictly an out-of-home purchase, often from street sellers. In 1919 most ice cream in Britain was still made using ice imported from abroad, which, when mixed with salt, would reach a temperature of well below minus 20° C. Over the course of the next decade, pioneers such as Walls and Lyons (the same company behind the tea shops and corner houses) would introduce electric freezers from America and start to ship their mass-produced ice cream nationally, but they were unusual, and the salt-ice method remained in use until the Second World War. Frederick kept a Progress Book, in which he pasted press coverage about Bettys as well as articles of interest, including one on the nutritional value of ice cream – he kept a careful eye on what was new or interesting. He was keen to adopt new machinery if it offered him an advantage, for example, in taking some of the physical labour out of repetitive processes or enabling his baking and confectionery team to concentrate on tasks requiring skill rather than simple force.

Even the Bettys name helped to convey a certain image. It was originally written with an apostrophe, dropped for design reasons in the Swinging Sixties. Neither Frederick nor Claire would give a definitive answer as to why they chose the name, given that Belmont's was the obvious option. There are several possible namesakes – from a popular rags-to-riches London musical, the theme of which may well have appealed to Frederick, given his own trajectory from indentured farmboy to managing director – to Betty Lupton, the Georgian 'Queen

ICE CREAM

is always in season, but it is a necessity at this time of the year. Supplied in bulk at 5/- per quart, in specially constructed Vacuum Bottles of up to 3 gallon capacity. No ice is required, and the Ice Cream keeps in perfect condition for 24 hours. A large variety of Iced Dinner Sweets from 3/6. Ice Bricks 6d., 1/-, 2/-, 3/6 and 5/-.

Betty's Ltd

HARROGATE.
Tel. 3272.

Betty's Corner, Commercial Street, Leeds,
Telephone 21724.

and 42 & 44, Darley Street, Bradford,
Telephone 211.

EAT SWEETS AND GROW THIN.

CHOCOLATE CURE FOR WEAK HEARTS.

Eat more chocolate and grow thin! That is the latest advice of the doctors. "Investigations conducted by a German heart specialist for 25 years," said a Harley-street specialist, "show that contrary to the popular belief, chocolate is the best for obesity. Experiments by the German specialist, Dr. Fredrick Bosser, also reveal that chocolate effects a permanent cure of weak hearts, arrythmenia, neuralgia, and 'nerves.'

"Chocolate is rich lime content, and sufferers should eat plenty of it, as that are rich in lime. Cocoa contains 5.7 per cent. of lime, almonds 8.81 per cent., walnuts 8.59 per cent.; cocoanut 4.82 per cent., and vanilla the remarkable figure of 27.4 per cent."

BUT
"YOU MUST EAT CONFECTIONS WHICH ARE MADE OF PURE INGREDIENTS & MADE BY A REPUTABLE FIRM."
Therefore eat BETTY'S CONFECTIONS always, because they are made under ideal conditions and of course are of undisputable quality.

WE SHALL BE PLEASED TO SEND YOU PARTICULARS OF OUR CONFECTIONS

Betty's Ltd

THE EXCLUSIVE CAFE.

OUR LATEST CONFECTIONS ARE WORTH A TRIAL. SOMETHING UNUSUAL.

Chocolate Manufacturers :: French and English Confectioners
CAMBRIDGE CRESCENT, HARROGATE.

of Harrogate Wells', in charge of dispensing the waters from 1778 to 1843. The most plausible story is that Bettys was named for Frederick Rose's daughter Winnifred Elizabeth ('Betty'), who had made an appearance with a tea tray at a Board meeting in early 1919. Betty was a common and classless British name, normally used as an abbreviation of Elizabeth. There were Bettys at the bottom of society and Lady Bettys at the top (including a Lady Betty in a 1917 silent film). It was also the name of a type of teapot and a sweet, originally American but now popular in Britain and a precursor of the crumble. With so many associations, it was a name with wide appeal: cosy, familiar but not at all downmarket.

It was also politically wise: the Board was united in 1919, but there were tensions. Claire later described Frederick Rose as a 'horrid, common little baker, married to Mary Wood's daughter who was no good either'. Although there were regular votes of 'thanks and continued confidence' in Frederick, he felt misunderstood, still struggling to fit in, writing to Ida that 'I am the only shareholder who knows anything about the business, and any organisational tasks rest squarely upon my shoulders.'

Top, left Clipping from the *Harrogate Advertiser*, June 1931

Top, right Clipping from the *Harrogate Advertiser*, September 1929

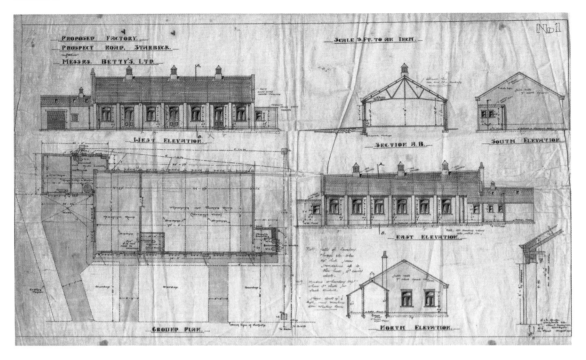

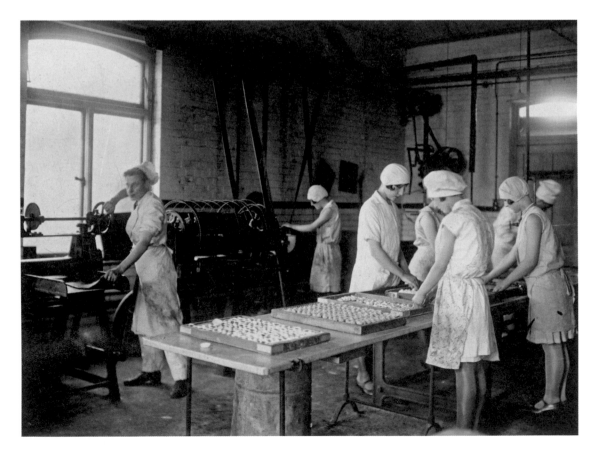

Given there were two other business owners on the Board, this seems unfair, but certainly reflects how much effort he put in and how devoted he was to Bettys.

Their efforts paid off: within a few months the company bought the adjacent building, and Bettys Café expanded across the upper floors, followed by the shop below. In 1922 the share capital of the company was increased to Frederick's benefit, for he was given the right to buy the new shares, becoming the major shareholder in the business he loved. At Frederick's urging, a former orchard was bought at Starbeck, on the outskirts of Harrogate, and a small factory was built to operate as a bakery, confectionery and chocolate-making and packing area. The technology was a classic 1920s mixture of steam power (an enormous coke-fuelled boiler provided both power and steam for heating) and elbow grease, as burly male bakers and pastry chefs cranked rolling machines by hand, before turning to power-driven mixing machines for their creams and fillings. Fan belts lined the walls, lethal to the unwary, but meaning that a variety of machines could be attached, making working at Bettys a cutting-edge experience. Meanwhile, the marble-topped tables and benches laden with cakes in wooden cake hoops, which would have been familiar to their counterparts a hundred years before, filled the middle of the room.

Opposite, top Architectural plans for Bettys' first purpose-built bakery in Harrogate, 1922

Opposite, bottom and above Bettys Bakery confectionery and pastry rooms, c.1926

Frederick Belmont driving his
Willys-Knight car in Switzerland, c.1922

The number of staff rose quickly from the original 20: men and women, the latter mainly employed in packing and finishing, and less skilled – and lower paid – than the men around them. Many were British, others were not, and Frederick employed a number of Swiss and Italian staff. A Bettys van soon started making deliveries between the bakery and the café, competing in the streets of Harrogate with horse-drawn carriages and fleets of bicycles as well as other motor cars.

Motoring was one of Frederick's passions, and, as the business flourished, in May 1922 he and Claire finally took off on the much-looked-forward-to trip to Switzerland to see Frederick's beloved sister Ida and her family. Frederick kept a diary for the first part of the trip, couched in his characteristically whimsical prose. They made the trip into a true holiday, stopping in London to visit Buckingham Palace where 'Claire wanted to know where the Queen hung her washing out, but [I] could not furnish the info'. Frederick had bought himself a glorious Willys-Knight cabriolet, all gleaming dark-brown paint and burnished silver (it proved distressingly hungry on fuel), and they drove cross-country from Dieppe via Beauvais, Compiègne and Reims. His pride in his status, his joy in life with a companion at his side, and the couple's interest in food were evident: 'went into a confectioner's and had chocolat [*sic*] and cakes, places are not all that bad, but nothing is so smart as Bettys'. The scars of war were evident as they went through France. Reims was 'in a sad state, ruins everywhere', but he was laid back, enjoying flirting with pretty girls as he enjoyed the outward trappings of wealth: 'I had to ask the way of a very beautiful girl, almond-eyed and all that sort of thing, very fine indeed, lost my heart entirely and incidentally lost my way, but found it again.' Tongue-in-cheek, he declared it was 'decidedly a drawback to take one's wife on holiday', and, while enjoying the fact that he could stay in good hotels and drink wine with every meal, he remained conscious of what he was spending, writing that 'we had a most enjoyable day until I counted … the money then I began to think for a while'.

As he entered Switzerland in his beautiful car, wife and business partner at his side, scattering coins for street children to pick up, Frederick must have reflected on how far he had come. His pride in what he'd accomplished in his adoptive country and his new

status as an Englishman sat together with an equal pride in his
Swiss roots and a desire to show Claire where he'd grown up,
but he felt torn. He was committed to becoming as English as
possible, even writing his diary in English, and his friends in
England now called him Dickie (Claire was still habitually called
Bunny). However, this meant he was now rusty in the dialect
he'd grown up with: 'had to ask for tea in Swiss but could not.
Felt an awful ass. Said so to Claire, she said "no more than you
look it".' He struggled to talk to Ida, and expressed himself like
a true English tourist when describing an excursion up the Rigi:
'the view from the summit is indeed indescribable. We walked
and climbed about a bit and met with a fellow who yodelled
most beautifully in a sort of falsetto warble. I was that pleased
with him that I gave him a shilling. A few hundred yards on I met
another, which I rewarded with sixpence, a third I passed in cold
exasperation. And after passing a fourth I gave him a shilling to
stop. There seems to be a good deal too much yodelling in
Switzerland.' However, his language skills came back, and
relations with Ida and Carl settled down. The diary stops abruptly
after 13 days in Switzerland: did the party visit old haunts, and it
all became too much? Or did he simply run out of steam?
Whatever happened, ties with Ida were renewed, and, especially
since their own longed-for family was failing to materialise, Ida
and Carl, along with their children Johanna (Hanni) and Verena
(Vreni) were cordially invited to visit England. Carl was still
writing utopian books and campaigning for a better world for very

Top, left Ida Wild (nee Bützer) with her
children Johanna (Hanni), Verena
(Vreni) and Victor. October 1923

Top, right Victor Wild with his sisters
Hanni and Vreni, c.1927

little money, and Ida's sewing skills had to support her growing family, so Frederick, naturally, offered to pay. A third child, Carl Viktor (always known just as Viktor, later anglicised to Victor), was born in 1923, and the family finally visited England in 1926 – Victor remembered ice cream in the Valley Gardens. As the years went on, Frederick continued to send money as well as more practical gifts: music and language lessons for the children, books and a subscription to the *Daily Mirror*.

Back in Yorkshire, Bettys was ready to expand. In June 1923 new shares were issued, not with Board rights, but promising excellent dividends, based on Bettys' profits to date. Most went to friends or neighbours of Mary Wood. There were changes too at Board level, when Albert Ashby was brought in as Secretary. All of this was in preparation for a new opening, at 61 North Parade in Bradford. A few months later, a much better site came up for lease – the same premises on Bradford's Darley Street previously occupied by Bonnet's, Frederick's first employer. Frederick later said that corner sites were key, and henceforth any new Bettys branch would occupy one. From an employee who could barely speak English to an employer at the heart of a well-regarded and expanding business, it was hardly surprising that in June 1924 both the Belmonts were recognised by the Board for all their 'energy and hard work during the year'. Claire was made joint Managing Director. North Parade stayed a Bettys shop for a while before being leased out.

With the Belmonts increasingly in charge, one of Claire's nephews, Neville Elsworth, joined the company. Frederick was now the benefactor, rather than the recipient, of family-based networking. He'd previously suggested bringing his stepmother Karoline's illegitimate son Ernst over to learn the trade, but nothing had come of it. However, another relative, Werner Muller, who was studying in Nottingham, joined the company in 1928. With an increasing reputation for elegant wedding receptions, the following year the company took on its first formal apprentice, and the local press suggested that 'there must be few who have not succumbed to the cheerful invitation of Betty's soft amber and rose lights and entered to sample those delightful cakes and chocolates so daintily served'. The interior decoration in Darley Street had touches of the late 18th-century Adam style about it, with pale walls and coloured relief patterns

Top Victor Wild aged three, 1926

Overleaf Interior of Bettys Bradford c.1920s

on the walls, and again made much use of mirrors to bring light to the darker corners and keep the space feeling fresh and modern. From 1928 Bettys also ran the Bradford Mayfair Rooms, a ballroom venue which could also be rented for large parties and suppers, but it was perhaps a step too far away from the confectionery and bakery and tea rooms around which the Bettys reputation was built, and the lease was sold on in 1930.

However, shenanigans were afoot at Board level. It's difficult to piece together exactly what happened, but the company minutes – along with later commentary – suggest that the years 1924–26 were crucial to the Belmonts and Bettys finally becoming an unassailable team. Frederick sent a letter to Ida in 1926 apologising for not having written, saying: 'I am back, and my only excuse is that I had to go through some difficult times.' June 1924 was Mary Wood's last Board meeting: in May 1925 she died, aged 76. Her shares were bought by Kaye Aspinall, a wine merchant (and 'big fat boozer', according to Claire, looking back on rather turbulent times), and William Buckley, the latter prejudiced against foreigners, and so left to Claire to deal with. Before they were brought onto the Board, however, Frederick Rose, Mary's son-in-law, mounted an unexpected attack. Given he already had a premises in York, he may have wanted to take over the Bettys name for his own business, and, at a meeting later declared void, he attempted to have his own nominee appointed to the Board and to oust Claire as joint MD. Frederick Belmont held out, stating that rather than resign, 'Mrs Belmont intended to acquire further shares'. Claire stood firmly by his side: 'Mrs Belmont then refused to resign.' Faced down, Frederick Rose gave in, progressively selling his shares over the next year and fading out of sight. George Wood also disappeared, family lore suggesting he was imprisoned for embezzlement, although no record of any incarceration or arrest can be found. By the end of 1926, fully in charge, Frederick Belmont was tightening working procedures for staff – who now were required to clock on and off – and streamlining and centralising production. The third-floor ovens at Cambridge Crescent, coke for which needed to be hauled up the stairs, finally went out of use. In 1929, when Aspinall tried a similar tactic to Rose's, he too failed: he died a few months later, and Buckley resigned as well. The next Director, John 'J. J.' Smith,

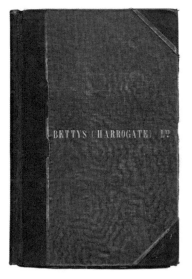

The first Bettys minute book, 1919-1936

Bettys liqueur chocolate box, c.1930s

was much more peaceable: very much a Belmont ally, he was eventually put in charge of the bakery, and with his appointment the future of Bettys as a Belmont-led family business seemed assured.

Claire was now 35 and Frederick 42. They both wanted children, and the letters of both to Ida (Claire was now a regular correspondent too) show an increasing interest in, and attachment to, Frederick's nieces and nephew. There was still a chance Claire might have a child, but in the 1920s 35 was regarded as very late to conceive, and she was still suffering with mastoiditis, which necessitated another set of operations and lengthy (and costly) convalescence in Antibes. When he married, Frederick had looked to Claire to give him a sense of purpose and belonging: Bettys now gave him the former, but he described himself with characteristic openness in a letter to Ida as 'healthy and strong, but a lonely human being'. He and Claire were growing apart. The economic situation put extra pressure on them: in 1926 the General Strike had seen martial law imposed, and in 1927 bad weather affected the tourist trade as the economy started to slump. At Bettys, turnover was down, so Frederick looked to innovate and to further build his reputation.

First up were chocolates, where Frederick proposed applying for a patent for a new process of producing liqueurs. Adverts were taken out in the press promoting 'full strength liqueur chocolates' without the sugar lining 'so distasteful to the connoisseur'. This was a real innovation, and a gamble, for the lack of lining shortened the shelf life – but Bettys chocolates sold well. As ever, the emphasis was on a quality, small-scale product, far removed from the output of mass-manufacturers, who were launching products faster than ever and increasingly pushing small chocolatiers out of business. (Flake launched in 1920, Cadbury's Fruit and Nut in 1921, Milky Bar in 1923 and Terry's Chocolate Apple in 1926 – the Orange version wouldn't launch until 1931.) Bettys held special show evenings in the lead-up to Christmas so that customers could see just how good the chocolates were – and how elegant their boxes. The company promised to post them to 'any part of the United Kingdom'. Now with the byline 'the exclusive café', Bettys adverts appeared across the local press, but, to alleviate any worries that the exclusive might not at the same time be accessible, Bettys now offered a special 'Yorkshire Tea' – not a blend of leaves, but a 'little surprise for their many patrons'. In both Bradford and Harrogate, for a mere 1s 3d, the discerning customer could have tea or coffee with cream; a sandwich (either egg and cress, York ham or potted beef); a toasted special Yorkshire teacake or a scone; and a cake – plain, fancy or cream. Lest this might seem too plebeian, the advert emphasised that the tea was 'daintily served in the luxurious surroundings which is exclusively Bettys'. Again, the fine balance between aspirational and affordable was struck – and a Yorkshire-branded tea had appeal both to proud locals and to tourists looking for some local colour.

Frederick's Swiss heritage wasn't neglected either, and in 1928 he produced a stupendous set of show windows for Bradford Shopping Week. One featured two chocolate donkeys, with a 'waggon drawn by gnomes' which weighed over 18kg. The other, even more delightfully quirky, had a Swiss mountain scene rendered in sugar, again with plenty of gnomes, this time in toadstool houses 'prettily lit'. It won a prize for the best novelty window display, but even better was to come, for Bettys won a whole host of prizes at that year's Universal Cookery and Food Exhibition at Olympia, including a special gold medal, sponsored by the British Confectioners' Association, for the same window. The Universal Cookery and Food Association, which organised the show, was Britain's leading professional culinary organisation, with a membership of several thousand drawn from across Britain (and beyond). It had been set up in

Top Bettys hand-crafted art deco iced birthday cake, c.1930s

Bottom Medals won by Bettys at the Universal Cookery and Food Exhibition at the London Olympia, c.1928

Bettys Bradford award-winning window
display, c.1927

Top A tray of Bettys fancies, c.1930s

Bottom An example of Bettys' acclaimed novelty cakes in the form of a fairytale-themed house made from a boot and complete with a witch and elves, 1927

1886 to promote the teaching of cookery as well as put on trade
exhibitions, spearheaded by the Swiss chef Charles Herman
Senn who, like Frederick, had found career success in the UK,
where he was a prolific cookery book writer as well as a leading
proponent of better training and standards in professional
cookery. Its governing council in 1928 included not only Senn
but also Auguste Escoffier, without doubt the most important
figure in cookery at that time, as well as Henri Cédard, the head
chef at Buckingham Palace, and Eustace Miles, a former
Olympic tennis player and pioneer of the vegetarian movement.

Bettys also impressed the judges in other confectionery
categories, winning silver for its Continental fancy goods and
birthday cake and bronze for its chocolate bonbons. Its wins
garnered good publicity back in Yorkshire, where the birthday
cake in particular was singled out as 'uncommon in design,
extremely pleasing'. Bettys had leapt gleefully and successfully
into novelty cakes – a rather recent innovation – and this one
was a tall cake with a crinoline-clad lady on top. Pictures from
the time show a wonderful set of similar cakes, along with others
which match the window display, featuring gnomes cavorting
round houses made in the shape of boots, Swiss chalets and – in
keeping with the fairytale theme – a nougatine spinning wheel,
with spun sugar wool.

As 1929 dawned sales were still not as healthy as might have
been desired, but the business was still very much in profit, and
those profits were slightly up. Negotiations were in hand for a
second corner site, this time in Leeds, projected to open in 1930.
However, the British economy was in trouble, with a post-war
slump exacerbated by traditional heavy industry failing to
modernise and losing sales in the face of competition from
overseas. In October the Wall Street stock market crashed,
plunging those countries reliant on US loans and trade, including
Britain, into full-on economic recession. The Great Depression
would severely affect Wales and the north-east of Britain, where
millions would lose their jobs, but almost everywhere would
suffer. A month after the crash, the price of a Bettys afternoon
tea was cut to 6d, ostensibly because so many people did not
take cream with their tea. The orchestra continued to play,
though, and it was guaranteed that 'our inimitable service, and
the cosiness and quality, would in no way be reduced'.

Afternoon tea in the Imperial Room

3 p.m., and there isn't a spare chair in the Imperial Room above Bettys Harrogate. You can't normally reserve a table at Bettys: the rich and famous queue up with day trippers, students, mums with buggies and locals, everyone eagerly awaiting their turn. Bookable afternoon tea, introduced in 2012, is an exception, and it's hugely popular. Already seated I can see twenty-somethings in full 1950s garb, a family with a young baby, older couples, and family groups. Around two thirds of the tea-takers are women. It's a mark of the almost unbreakable link between tea and women, which dates back almost 350 years.

Tea was introduced to Britain in the mid-17th century. It came from China and was initially only a wealthy person's drink. Green tea dominated the (small) market, usually drunk with sugar, and black tea only took over in the 1720s (now also with milk). Drinkers bought special Chinese ceramics: delicate pots and small bowls with saucers. Tea was marketed as a health brew, not dissimilar to the herbal concoctions used medicinally and which were prepared by women, for household medicine came under their remit. Tea quickly became associated with court life and leisure through Catherine of Braganza, Charles II's Portuguese queen, who drank it with her attendants. It was ideal as a way for ladies to show their wealth and gentility, for it was expensive, involved very delicate porcelain objects needing careful handling, and it was seen as healthy. Unlike the

Opposite Bettys Afternoon Tea, Imperial Room, Harrogate

other two new beverages introduced around the same time – coffee and chocolate – the leaves didn't need to be taken off to a kitchen for grinding and processing, so ladies could explicitly show their control over this most refined of products, keeping their tea leaves locked in a box to which only they had the key. Tea-drinking ladies are often shown in portraits of the time: women in control, at a time when women had very few rights indeed.

Tea quickly became feminised and remains so to this day (have you ever heard anyone suggest they 'play father' when they pour?). In the 18th century it was key to women's social rituals: taking tea with one's friends, a small snack in the afternoon became a key part of leisured life, especially in towns such as Bath and Harrogate. Dinner kept getting later, and the snack slowly morphed into something more substantial and, eventually, more public. By the late 19th century it had become a mini meal and was given a name – 'afternoon tea'. Tea was still

seen as essentially feminine, and the food which came with it was light and subtly flavoured. The menu today is very much in keeping with this, with a prawn-and-cucumber cocktail, smoked salmon and dill crème fraîche sandwiches, lemon scones and passionfruit and lemon macaroons, among other delectable goodies.

By the 1870s tea was being grown in India, controlled at that time by British administrators. Today I'm drinking a Rwandan Gisovu, a mark of how far tea-growing has spread across the world. It is deeply embedded in the British psyche. When tea rooms started to appear in the 1880s, they became havens for women of all classes to meet unchaperoned and free from unwanted male attention. As the women's suffrage movement took off, around the time Fritz Bützer was making his way from Switzerland to Yorkshire, some tea rooms became hubs for the movement, including the more violent side: it was from tea rooms in the West End of London that the window-smashing campaigns of 1909–12 were launched. Tea was sold in suffragette colours to fund the cause.

By 1919 women had won a limited extension of the vote, and, although when Bettys first opened most of its female workers still would not have been eligible to vote, its female shareholders certainly were. Tea remained associated with women, and part of the appeal of cafés such as Bettys was as a place where women could socialise together in public without censure – it was, after all, only 30 years since the Savoy became the first restaurant to encourage ladies to dine in the public rooms, not closeted in a private suite. The 1920s and 1930s saw afternoon teas become very popular, especially in tourist towns, where visitors, often on modest incomes, would have a stand of cake, or – in Devon and Cornwall – a cream tea and then save money by choosing a light supper rather than a big dinner out. It was now claimed that the whole thing had been 'invented' by the Duchess of Bedford in the 1840s, giving an alluringly upmarket glow to a quick break in the middle of the afternoon. At Bettys, customers could start with a sandwich or choose from a variety of buns and cakes or, if they wanted something more luxurious, opt for 'dainty afternoon tea fancies' filled with fresh cream. Teas, of many shapes and sizes, became associated with holidays and special occasions rather than necessarily being an everyday event.

After the Second World War, with rationing in force, and later, as increasing numbers of women worked, afternoon teas took a hit. Teacakes and toast replaced cream puffs on the Bettys menu. Bettys wasn't the only tea room to struggle as afternoon tea seemed both old-fashioned and unnecessary in the new post-war world, and the high street became increasingly based on national chains and mass-produced-

food outlets: after decades of trying to adapt, both the Lyons and ABC tea shop chains failed to reach their centenaries, closing all their branches in the 1970s and 1980s.

However, the 2008 financial crisis and subsequent recession, combined with a realisation that bigger wasn't necessarily better, brought with it a new era. With chain coffee shops opening up in every empty shop unit, independent cafés and craft businesses such as Bettys saw increasing numbers of people – particularly the young – sitting down to afternoon teas. Just as in the 1930s money-conscious tourists saw afternoon teas as a way to enjoy themselves without spending too much, and so too twenty-somethings with university debt and precarious jobs looked to teas as a lovely treat which wouldn't break the bank.

These new tea aficionados looked for small-scale production and artisan values, quality cakes and ethical provenance. Bettys, with its existing emphasis on in-house production, craft values and support for global environmental projects, therefore found itself, through long-standing principles, in the vanguard of the modern movement. The challenge for tea rooms was to reinvent afternoon tea, ensuring that it felt special and worthy of going out for, keeping its slightly retro appeal but elevating it into something which was also very modern and relevant.

Opposite, top Ladies enjoying afternoon tea at C. E. Taylors & Company tea-house in Valley Gardens, Harrogate, 1906

Financial depression

1929–1940

What's on the menu?

In the 1930s the Bettys branches in Harrogate and Bradford were joined by first Leeds and then York. This menu applied across all of them, making for a consistent customer experience and enabling Frederick Belmont to benefit from economies of scale. Bettys didn't offer a formal dinner, concentrating instead on luncheons, teas and suppers, and this menu reflects the range of people who ate at Bettys at the time.

There is now a decidedly English whiff to proceedings, and familiar brand names appear on the menu: Bovril and a biscuit for those in need of filling up (Bovril, derived from the beef tea of previous centuries, served as a health drink and was marketed as giving strength and vitality), along with Horlicks and Heinz. The Bettys in-house bakery was kept busy with all of the breads and cakes, with the list still hinting at Continental sophistication with its Vienna rolls and French petits fours. There were sandwiches for everyone – from the 5d basic version rising to a dizzying 1s 6d for the club. In the early 1930s Bettys also offered an entire four-course lunch for 2s 6d, so the 1s 6d sandwich must have been truly something. Cold roasts, pies and salads were all standard luncheon fare, and on the face of it fairly plain. However, the 1930s was an era of expanding horizons, when recipe books such as Countess Morphy's

Recipes of All Nations introduced those with money and broad taste to delicacies that ranged from American banana salads to steamed pigeon with Chinese herbs. Frederick's Japanese salad and pineapple and cheese salad are, therefore, entirely in keeping with the spirit of the time. So too are the tinned exotic fruits with cream, and the grapefruit. There was a brief craze for grapefruit in the 1930s, partly caused by the 'Hollywood diet' which promised to make you thin, so long as you were prepared to live mainly on coffee and grapefruit. The main savoury section was likewise very fashionable. When the Belmonts travelled first class on the *Queen Mary* in 1936, their luncheon menus also included spaghetti (*au gratin*), omelettes (Spanish and cheese), dressed crab, tongue and ham. The sweets on the Bettys menu included here were not the only sweet treats on offer. There was also an extensive cake selection, and Bettys still sold ices, both plain and fancy: the exotically named Cupid's Kiss involved vanilla and strawberry ice, chopped cherries, grapes, orange syrup and fresh cream for 1s 3d. There were also ice cream sodas, which had become phenomenally popular in the United States, mainly as a result of Prohibition, which meant bars had to seek alternative forms of revenue. The drinks then developed a cachet in the UK based on their perceived glamour.

SEE MENU FOR SPECIAL TEAS—1/-, 1/3, 1/6, 1/

MENU.

BEVERAGES, &c.

Tea, Indian or China, with Cream	6d.
Coffee, with Hot Milk or Cream	6d.
White Coffee or Black, with cream, per cup	4d.
Chocolate or Cocoa, with Milk and Cream	6d.
Café Glace	9d.
Fresh Fruit Orangeade	6d.
,, ,, Lemon Squash	9d.
,, ,, Lemonade	6d.
Lemon and Barley, per glass	6d.
Horlick's Malted Milk	6d.
,, ,, ,, with Egg	10d.
Bovril and Biscuit ... ... 6d. and	9d.
Glass of Milk	4d.
Tot of Cream	2d.

Bread, Scones, Teacakes, Etc.

French Roll, **1d.** Butter Pat	1d.
White or Brown Bread and Butter ...	3d.
Vienna or French Bun and Butter	3d.
Toasted or Buttered Scone	3d.
Toasted or Buttered Teacake	4d.
Split Toast and Butter	4d.
Toasted Muffin or Crumpet	4d.
Round of Buttered Toast...	3d.
Anchovy Toast	9d.
Cakes, Creams and Pastries	3d.
Jam, Lemon and Curd Tarts	2d.
Petits Fours	3d.
Chocolate Biscuits	3d.

SANDWICHES.

Egg and Cress ... ... Roll or Bread	5d.
Tomato, Crab ... ... ,, ,, ,,	5d.
Egg and Anchovy ... ,, ,, ,,	5d.
Beef, Potted ... ... ,, ,, ,,	5d.
Salmon ... ... ,, ,, ,,	6d.
Ham, Tongue, Sardine ,, ,, ,,	6d.
Lobster ... ... ,, ,, ,,	8d.
Chicken and Ham ... Roll 8d. Bread	10d.
Chicken ... ... Roll 10d. Bread	1/-
Hors d'Œuvres Sandwich	1/-
Club Sandwich	1/6

PÂTÉS—Hot or Cold.

Chicken and Ham, Lobster	6d.
Mushroom and Kidney	6d.
Sausage Rolls	3d.
Cheese and Biscuits	6d.

HOT LUNCHEON
Served Daily between
12-0 and 2-30 p.m.

GRILLS

Mixed Grill ... ...
Fillet Steak ... ...
English Chop ... ...
Lamb Cutlets (2) ... ...
York Ham and (1) **Egg**
Dover Sole ... ...
Fried or Grilled Halibut Steak ... ...
Fillet of Plaice ... ...
Chipped Potatoes ... ...

SAVOURIES.

Potted Beef Steak **7d.** and
Welsh Rarebit ... ...
do. (with poached egg)
Kidney & Bacon Bouchees (2
Lobster Toast ... ...
Heinz Baked Beans on toast
Herring Roes on Toast ...
Sardines on Toast ... ...
Sardines on Spaghetti ...
Fried Egg on Spaghetti ...
Fried Egg on Spaghetti on Toast ... ...
Scrambled or Poached Egg on Toast ... ...
Kidneys on Toast ... ...
Mushrooms on Toast... ...
Grilled Pork Sausage, Creamed Mushrooms
Hors d'Œuvres (various) 9d. &
York Ham Scramble... ...
Boiled Egg ... ...
Omelettes, Plain, Savoury and Sweet ...
,, Jam, Cheese, and Tomato
,, Kidney, Mushroom, & Ham

AWARDED THE CERTIFICATE OF THE INS

2/6—HOT or COLD.

SOUPS.

hroom, Julienne, Chicken and Rice,
Asparagus, Tomato ...   .   6d.

COLD.

in of Beef 1/6
k Ham or Ox Tongue 1/6
l Roast Chicken and York Ham   ...   2/6
l Roast Chicken 2/6
k Pie   ...   .   6d.
k and Kidney Pie (hot or cold)   ...   6d.

FISH, SALADS, Etc.

ch Salmon in Season   ...   .
h Lobster in Season   ...   .
ster Salad 2/-
ster Mayonnaise 2/6
 Salad 1/6
 Mayonnaise 2/-
 Salad 1/6
 Mayonnaise 1/6
nese Salad 1/6
apple and Cheese Salad 1/6
n, Mixed, Vegetable, Potato, Beetroot
Salad   ...   .   6d.
ch Salad   ...   .   9d.
m Dressing ...   .   3d.
onnaise   ...   .   4d.

SWEETS

e (per portion) or Cream Sweet   ...   6d.
e Fruit   ...   .   6d.
h Fruit Salad with Cream   ...   . 10d.
anas, with Cream   ...   . 10d.
h Whole Fruit (per portion) 4d. and 6d.
ed Pineapple, Peaches, Pears, or Fruit
Salad with Cream 1/-
en Figs or Golden Apricots, with
cream 1/-

OF HYGIENE

A typical example of a Bettys menu
across all branches in the late 1930s

Bettys Corner, Leeds, c.1930. The branch was located on the corner of Lands Lane and Commercial Street and described by the local press at the time as 'an establishment of irreproachable taste and refinement' and 'one of the most delightful shops in the city'

In 1929 the national chain of tea shops Lyons recorded its best profit to date: five years later it had virtually stopped expanding and its tea shops were in deficit. By 1931–32, unemployment in Britain stood at 22 per cent, most of it in the industrial north, where businesses folded and large-scale projects were brought to a halt through lack of money. In Clydebank, construction of the Cunard line's enormous new flagship the *Queen Mary* stopped for over two years; the workers were laid off, swelling the ranks of the jobless and starving. Bettys, however, expanded, not least because Frederick was already financially committed and had little choice. In 1929 the first extension (of many) to the bakery was built, so it needed as many outlets as possible for its now increased production capacity. Plans for expansion were already afoot before the financial crash, and in 1930 a new branch opened in Leeds.

Like Bradford, Bettys in Leeds occupied a prestigious corner site, taking over a series of shops on the corner of Lands Lane (numbers 8 and 9) and Commercial Street (2 and 4). In 1927 shoppers would have found a ladies' outfitter, a gramophone shop, a hairdresser and a costumier, all by 1930 made into one substantially larger unit, intended to house the shop. The upper floors were also purchased to make room for the café, offices and toilets. On the outside hung not just the familiar 'Betty's Ltd' but also another sign, which proudly proclaimed 'Betty's Corner', a faint echo of the upmarket (and huge) Lyons Corner Houses, which were that chain's prestige offering.

Frederick was determined that Leeds should be perfect, and both he and Claire worked flat out getting the new site ready for its opening on 10 November 1930. Claire wrote to Ida at the end of October that she was desperate to come to Switzerland for a holiday and to see the family, but that 'Bettys needed me so greatly that I could not think of holidays and now we are so busy with Leeds and are working almost day and night for the

responsibility is so great and the risk very much.' Tensions ran high: Frederick wanted the most modern of facilities, with a state-of-the-art kitchen equipped with electric heating and cooking apparatuses and situated on the top floor to avoid smells escaping into the café, as well as the usual exquisite décor throughout. It cost £8,500 – some £2,000 more than anticipated – but the local press was fulsome in its praise: 'Bettys needs no introduction for Yorkshire folk, for their places at Bradford and Harrogate are widely known.' Leeds was 'an establishment of irreproachable taste and refinement', with 'one of the most delightful shops in the city'. The Belmonts and Bettys were praised for helping to make 'a brighter Leeds'. Somewhat ironically in the light of this comment, on the opening night the fully electric premises were plunged into darkness when all the fuses went.

Inside, with the lights back on, the interiors echoed the trend toward art deco. The shop, on the ground floor, was fitted out with green marble and burnished French walnut, while the light from the enormous plate glass windows was reflected in stainless-steel surfaces and marble pillars. The windows were topped with angular patterns of coloured and frosted glass, and they and the doorway had the characteristic diagonal tops of the art deco movement. There were tulip-shaped uplighters and rose-tinted mirrors, reflecting cakes arranged at exciting angles in the windows, and chocolates and luxury boxes in the cabinets inside.

Top Press shot of the opening of Bettys Leeds from the Yorkshire Evening News, 10 November 1930. This opening-day image features Frederick Belmont, Mr C. Hitchen (President of Leeds Chamber of Trade) and Claire Belmont

Opposite The interior of the first floor café at Bettys Leeds c.1937–42

As in Harrogate, the café was on the first floor, decked out in old ivory and blue, complete with 'artistic wall brackets and light fittings', which contributed to 'the general impression of pleasant lightness'. On the second floor was a restaurant, intended for meals with hot food, which initially meant luncheons and high teas. The colour scheme was apple green and black, with blue-black tinted glass and lights concealed in 'embossed glass and silver'. Thick-pile carpets deadened the noise seeping through to the café below as well as giving 'a feeling of well-being'. There was also a basement with a 'men's own room' – intended as a smoking room and for business lunches – which had practical cane furniture, less likely to trap and hold smells. The *Yorkshire Evening Post* described the overall effect as 'tasteful in the extreme'.

Despite a few teething troubles, Frederick declared: 'Leeds is proving a great success. We have opened with great noise and in good style. It is really gratifying to have accomplished my

ambitions.' He noted in the company minutes that trading had been 'very satisfactory'. Claire disagreed, but by the next year the business was established, and profits rose. The shareholders proffered a formal vote of thanks to the directors for the 'able manner in which the business of the company had been carried on during a most difficult and trying period'.

Competition in Leeds was fierce, and there was a range of eating options for every budget. Bettys wasn't trying to compete with the high-end options – Powolny's on Bond Street offered real turtle soup, foie gras and a daily 'dîner dansant' – nor with the (predominantly male) business-oriented lunch joints such as Whitelock's First City Luncheon Bar. As with Harrogate, its clientele was mid-range, and in Leeds there was stiff competition from other restaurants for the luncheon crowd, as well as from other cafés including those of the departments stores at teatime and for morning coffee. Leeds, like Harrogate, had a Marshall & Snelgrove, as well as Schofield's, a home-grown department store on the Headrow. Bettys had to work hard to find a niche, expanding from high teas into grills and pre-theatre dinners at a

A Bettys hand-crafted 21st birthday cake typical of the 1930s

competitive 3s 6d and staying open until 8 p.m. Potential event-bookers could also take advantage of the services of a hostess, specifically employed to organise the many private events which could be held by booking out the restaurant. Weddings were a particular favourite, for Bettys could also supply the cake, advertised with the slogan 'we only make one quality – the best'. Customers were assured that 'everything sold in the café will be Betty's own make'. When the bakery was awarded a certificate by the Institute of Hygiene it was a further boost, and immediately found its way onto the menus. It worked. The *Leeds Mercury* was adamant that 'there is room for a first-class café in Leeds, and Betty's, as Leeds may judge for itself today, are making an enterprising effort to fill it'. Takings across the three branches now stood at a respectable £900 a week.

The Depression did not hit everyone equally, and the three Bettys sites proved to be well chosen. Nevertheless, the company decided that the Mayfair Rooms in Bradford weren't working and sold the lease on in 1930. The basement of the main Bradford Bettys was sublet to Timpson. The Bettys Board was now firmly in the Belmonts' hands: when the company secretary at the time objected to Frederick taking money out of the business to settle his personal debts, he was persuaded to acquiesce, and he was quietly replaced a few months later on the grounds that he wasn't devoting enough time to the business.

Staff loyalty mattered right across the board, and in June 1931 Frederick treated 120 of his staff to a Sunday outing to the Lake District. They occupied five charabancs (motor coaches), and started at 7.30 a.m., with breakfast two hours later. By lunchtime they'd reached Ambleside, where they managed a few hours in the sun before starting back. Supper was in the tiny village of Hellifield, where the staff gave a vote of thanks to the directors, and Frederick responded with a speech stating that the management 'appreciated the close harmony that exists between the management and the staff, and that each employee was individually responsible for the success of the firm, and that it was gratifying to know that in spite of difficult times the number of employees had reached 142'. Later he wrote in his diary that 'my affairs are not too good but might and could be worse! … we went for a staff trip, 120 of them … well, I am proud of them and of my firm'.

Overleaf Frederick and Claire Belmont, along with 120 Bettys staff, photographed outside the original Bettys Café in Harrogate, Cambridge Crescent, on Sunday 28 June 1931 before heading off on a staff excursion to Ambleside

The trip was remarkable enough to make the local papers,
complete with a picture of the whole group – plus buses –
outside Bettys in Harrogate. In Europe, the International
Labour Organisation was agitating for paid holidays to become
universal, but, although it achieved its ends elsewhere, the UK
steadfastly refused to ratify its proposals, and even on the eve of
the Second World War, many workers took their – limited –
holiday unpaid. Good staff were not easy to get, however, and

with Bettys priding itself on superb service, it could only be beneficial to be seen as an exemplary employer.

In Harrogate, the pattern of business was slowly changing. The spa trade was in what proved to be terminal decline: the Victoria Baths closed in 1930, the municipal orchestra was disbanded in 1931 and the late Georgian spa rooms would be demolished in 1939. The council tried to broaden its appeal to more of the middle classes, digging up part of the Stray for flowerbeds, tennis courts and other leisure amenities until stopped by public outcry over the loss of the open grassland. The Royal Baths were extended, the first flower show was held in 1934, and, for residents, acres of new housing spread out from the centre, part of a post-war promise to build more housing and replace slums. The vast majority of workers still returned home for their lunches, but the trend toward business lunches was growing. Also growing was the tourist trade – by 1937 around 15 million people took at least one week off away from home. Then there were the day and weekend trippers, who, like Frederick and his staff, needed meals on their days out. The boom in the motor-tourist trade was particularly marked, with 3 million motor vehicles on the road by 1939 (compared to 140,000 in 1914). Guidebooks aimed at the car owner, including the AA hotel guide, rated establishments, and suggested the best places to eat at popular destinations. In general, the standard was agreed to be pretty low, at least by Londoners bravely venturing out to the provinces. André Simon, an influential wine merchant and food writer, summed up the average British café-restaurant as having 'gaudy trappings, blinding illumination, noisome bands, everything', and wished that a little Continental sophistication could be brought to proceedings. Bettys, which oozed Continental sophistication, was everything he could have wished

Prospect Square in Harrogate capturing Bettys on Cambridge Crescent and the Taylors Café Imperial located on Parliament Street, 1936

Whatever will the boy ask for next, Mary!
In this morning's letter he writes:

"Dear Mater,—Please send me a sponge, toothpaste, pair of tennis shoes, a feeding trough for my white mice, a pocket knife with J.R. on. and four pounds of BETTY'S Assorted Cream Fudge. Your loving John.
P.S.—If Betty's Cream Fudge makes the parcel too heavy don't send the other things. XXX"

OF PARAMOUNT IMPORTANCE to the boy, because of the delicious moments of enjoyment whilst eating them. You would find the same enjoyment whilst trying them. Include a pound on your weekend shopping list.

Betty's Ltd

THE EXCLUSIVE CAFE,

CAMBRIDGE CRESCENT, HARROGATE.

MAKERS OF DELICIOUS SWEETMEATS IN A MODEL FACTORY.

Clipping from the Harrogate Advertiser, July–Sept 1929

for, and in 1932 Frederick paid for three billboard advertisements on the main roads into Harrogate and Leeds. Aimed squarely at motorists, they carried a picture of two figures in an open car with the caption 'Let's go to Betty's'. Illustrated adverts also appeared in the local press, with an elegant lady and her maid musing on the various ways to consume Bettys products – by post (for a son away at boarding school), as caterers (for a children's party) and for lunch (with a young daughter in tow). They were simple adverts, witty, instantly recognisable and to the point – especially compared to other competitor businesses, such as Taylors, whose adverts were

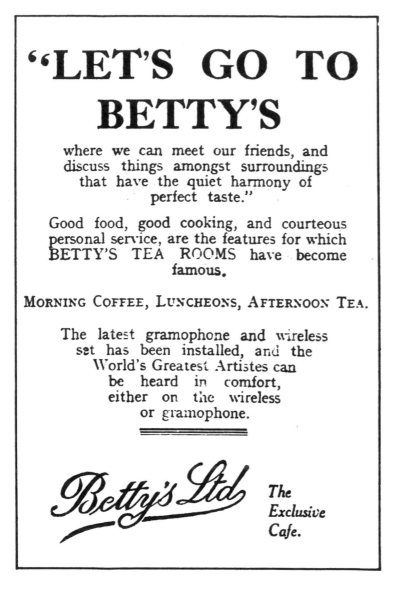

"LET'S GO TO BETTY'S

where we can meet our friends, and discuss things amongst surroundings that have the quiet harmony of perfect taste."

Good food, good cooking, and courteous personal service, are the features for which BETTY'S TEA ROOMS have become famous.

MORNING COFFEE, LUNCHEONS, AFTERNOON TEA.

The latest gramophone and wireless set has been installed, and the World's Greatest Artistes can be heard in comfort, either on the wireless or gramophone.

Betty's Ltd The Exclusive Cafe.

decidedly wordier and less well-designed. They also evoked the spirit of quirkiness that was so evident in the window displays and in Frederick's own personal writing.

Throughout the 1930s, Frederick remained alert to possible opportunities and ways to attract customers: a gramophone went into the Harrogate branch, and Bettys adverts appeared with a slightly bewildering range of messages as he experimented with ideas. Bettys had claimed to be 'under royal patronage' for nearly a decade (unsurprisingly, given the number of minor royals who enjoyed shopping and eating in Harrogate). In 1929 the 5th Earl of Harewood, he who had opened the Harrogate War Memorial, died and was succeeded by his son,

Harrogate Advertiser, July 1930

Top and bottom Bettys silk-covered chocolate box, also known as the 'Princess Mary Chocolate Box'. This is similar to a chocolate box Bettys made for Princess Mary, Countess of Harewood, c.1930s

who was married to Princess Mary (George V's daughter). They continued to play a large role in Leeds and Harrogate, including patronising local shops: Bettys made much of a chocolate box in 'Princess Mary's' blue edged with silver brocade, which they made specially for her in 1931. The luxurious chocolate boxes – hand-embroidered, tinselled and brocaded – continued to do well, and the range of confectionery of this type was expanded: in 1933 praline wafers were added, and in the run-up to Christmas the bakery was turning out everything from aniseed balls to fondant fancies.

Bettys also gained a spirit licence to start wholesaling Frederick's innovative liqueur-centred chocolates (rather against the desires of the local Temperance Society, which saw them as an 'insidious' gateway drug to 'something stronger'). Easter and Christmas were particularly important for chocolates, and

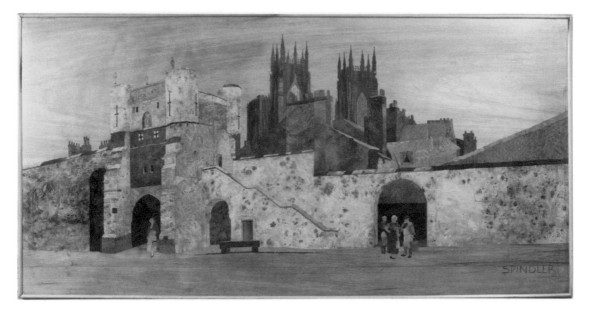

another approach tried was to emphasise quantity as well as quality – in 1933 one advert claimed that in the previous year Bettys had sold over 12,000 Easter eggs, ranging from 6d to £3 3s. Likewise, 8,625lb of plum cake was a cause for celebration in 1934. Another tactic was to promote price reductions – not anything as tacky as a special offer, but very sincerely, due to 'concentration of manufacture and the fall in price of raw materials'. The menus of the time offered a wide range of dishes, and special menus were also promoted, including a four-course lunch at 2s 6d (the same as Lyons charged). Generally, the prices were kept higher than those of Lyons, which aimed far more overtly at the working class – its ices, for example, were 3d, whereas at Bettys they started at 6d, rising to 1s 3d for more fancy treats. Bettys aimed at a much more middle-class audience, but the special deals and lower-priced items on the menu very carefully did not exclude an aspirational wider clientele.

In 1935 Fredrick wrote in his diary that 'everything I do I have to worry over, nothing comes my way easily. Leeds and Bradford are still a worry. Had a few rows with Bunny [Claire] she is such a silly girl and gives me quite a good deal of trouble. Financial position still very poor.' A mailshot aimed at increasing mail order sales had yielded dismal results, and, while Bettys won plaudits for its outside catering, Taylors had most of the major contracts in Harrogate via a contract with the town corporation. Taylors were a significant competitor, although it was generally outclassed by Bettys. Its Harrogate flagship was the Café Imperial, a corner site on Montpellier Gardens, but it also supplied the Winter Gardens, among other key sites, and

Spindler marquetry picture depicting Bootham Bar, York. This can be found hanging in Bettys Harrogate

Paul Spindler sketching in the streets of York, 1933

operated large cafés and its slightly smaller Kiosk cafés in several Yorkshire towns. Meanwhile, at Bettys, 16 years after opening, the décor at Cambridge Crescent was in need of a revamp. The town was about to get a gleaming new Odeon cinema in the streamlined modernist style, and the fussiness of the Edwardian era was now old hat.

A coat of white paint and some sun awnings helped, but Frederick had more ambitious plans. He'd previously bought several small pieces of exquisite marquetry work, very fashionable and time-consuming to make, from the studio of Charles Spindler and his son Paul in Alsace. Unlike many marquetry artists, the Spindlers specialised in landscapes, and the pieces Frederick had hanging in his den at home were of Alsace. This was his retreat, where he would sit for hours in his favourite leather chair, wreathed in cigar smoke, whisky in hand,

reading books on astronomy and history. Now, however, he commissioned a set of six entirely new scenes of Yorkshire. Paul Spindler travelled across to England, armed with a sketchbook, to make the preliminary designs: Bootham Bar in York, Fountains Abbey, Ripon, Burnt Yates, Bolton Abbey and Knaresborough. The new pieces were much larger than his existing set, and they would take time to make, at least six months each. However, he was determined to have them: they would be strikingly unusual but match perfectly with his ideal of Continental sophistication made for Yorkshire. They eventually arrived in 1939 – whereupon Frederick's lack of spatial planning proved an issue. There wasn't space for all six, so only two went on display, with the others stored pending a redesign, which was itself put on hold as Europe prepared for war.

1936 was a crucial year, both for Bettys and the Belmonts. Still short of money, the Board managed to negotiate the sale of the freeholds of all three branches to the Malton Investment Trust, who then leased them back to the company on 99-year leases. This not only raised £60,000 in immediate cash, but longer term was of fundamental value: no death duties were payable on rented properties, and the contracts had no rent revision clauses, meaning that Bettys were still paying annual rents at 1936 rates

Top Frederick and Claire Belmont on board the RMS *Queen Mary*, during its maiden voyage in May 1936

Bottom A sailor doll acquired by Frederick Belmont as a souvenir during the maiden voyage of the RMS *Queen Mary*, 1936

until the early 21st century, when they bought the properties back. Low rents would help keep Bettys in the black throughout many of the decades that followed: it was a masterstroke. Finally able to put aside some of his financial worries, Frederick achieved another long-held goal when he was elected a Freemason. It was a recognition of his status within the region and directly related to his work with underprivileged children in Leeds, putting on screenings of cartoons in local schools. Despite his accent, despite his background, he was now a stalwart of his adopted town, enthusiastically taking up the most genteel of British pursuits: golf and bridge. He also learnt to fly, and the following year would buy a (second-hand) Rolls-Royce. Truly, Frederick Belmont had arrived.

To celebrate his success, and perhaps to try and patch things up in their increasingly shaky marriage, Frederick and Claire Belmont booked a proper once-in-a-lifetime experience. They decided to sail first class (cabin class) on the maiden voyage of the *Queen Mary*, now resurrected from the docks of Clydebank and ready to sail to New York. The 2,100 tickets were snapped up immediately, such was the enormous publicity surrounding the launch, and crowds of thousands turned out to cheer as the ship left Southampton on 27 May 1936. There was a film crew on board, recording the historic voyage, but Frederick had bought his own cine camera before leaving, and his own seven-minute film is full of elegant ladies in hats, sporty women playing quoits and Claire and the couple's friends who had come to see them off posing on cars and on the ship itself. On board, the couple had access to an indoor swimming pool, a library, a lecture theatre, a music studio, a gymnasium and a Turkish baths.

The food was varied and plentiful, with American, British and French dishes jostling for space on the menus. At breakfast, choices included minced chicken creole, onion soup gratinée, buckwheat cakes with maple syrup, brioche, Yarmouth bloaters and Quaker Oats, while luncheon options were not dissimilar to those at Bettys, although the *Queen Mary's* menu also included Kraft cheese, escargots de Bourgogne, and creamed tripe and onions. Dinner was more serious, although again proved how on-trend Bettys was, with grapefruit as a starter. Thereafter, the menu included turtle soup, halibut with lobster sauce, braised

Top 'The Story of *RMS Queen Mary*'. A lavishly illustrated souvenir booklet published in the 1930s

Bottom Frederick Belmont on deck with his Cine-Kodak 16mm camera, 1936

duck and Grand Marnier pancakes. It was cleverly designed to sound splendid, but be easily achievable in a mass-catering context – for the first-class dining room could seat all 815 passengers at once if necessary. There was also a grill room, the Verandah Grill, which doubled as a night club, and served much simpler food, with an extensive cold buffet and a range of ices. The décor was magnificent, with elegant metal grilles on the doors, marquetry landscapes on the walls, etched glass panelling and woods, drawn from across the world, shaped and polished to form panelling on walls, ceilings and columns throughout the ship. Flowers were everywhere, tended by the four on-board gardeners (known as the 'flower stranglers'). Such was the level of desirability that when the ship docked in New York (accompanied by an aeroplane escort) after six days at sea, and opened its dining room to the paying public, they stole everything that wasn't bolted to the floor. Frederick commented ruefully that on the return journey there wasn't an ashtray to be had.

The trip had immediate repercussions for Bettys. Inspired by his trip and still looking for ways to make the bakery more profitable, Frederick decided to open yet another branch, this time in York, and explicitly inspired by the décor of the *Queen Mary*. Long-established as the service capital of Yorkshire, York was a town his Continental friends and family would have heard of, unlike Bradford and Leeds. Frederick claimed he'd spotted it from the air while flying and decided it would be a good spot, but he and Claire were cleverer than that, and a great deal more planning was involved.

There was now an established pattern to a Bettys opening: a corner site, a café and restaurant accessed through the shop and a number of floors. Bettys York had all of these, and more. It had previously been a furniture store, and, as in Leeds, required a lot of money investing in it to convert it to a café – around £30,000 (equal to around £2 million in 2019). Lord Middleton, officially opening it in 1937 suggested that it was the best site in the city, and the *York Star* commented: 'this attractive restaurant fills a very definite need in the city in supplying a really smart café, shop, restaurant and ballroom, where every entertaining facility is provided for'. As in Leeds, the basement was a smoking room with 'alluring odd corners and niches, which may be guaranteed to provide the privacy necessary for the discussion of business or social topics!', while the ground floor held the shop and café, with a restaurant on the floor above and a full ballroom on the floor above that. It was an extraordinary venture, fitting out a café-shop in the style of the most luxurious liner of its day, but Frederick was so determined that he even hired the same craftsmen who had made the *Queen Mary's* panelling. The interiors did not so much evoke the spirit of the ship as provide a carefully thought-out version of it on a smaller scale. Details included maple and walnut panelling edged with chrome, etched glass, decorative metalwork, crystal drop light fittings and tinted mirrors. A huge marquetry scene with flying ducks, installed in the restaurant, was extremely close to one of the pieces that featured on the wall of one of the private dining rooms on board the *Queen Mary*, while the overall feel was as close to being on board as was possible in the centre of York.

However, as usual Frederick had been inspired without entirely administering to the detail. Claire complained that she was picking up the pieces, and when the chef walked out on the second day after opening saying there wasn't enough space to work, they had to change the interior layout immediately. Frederick blamed the architects; Claire blamed her husband. The kitchens and toilets were re-sited, but the layout remained a problem until the 1960s.

Frederick and Claire Belmont greeting
the Lord Mayor of York as he arrives
at Bettys, St Helen's Square, York to
award them a liquor licence for the
premises, 1939

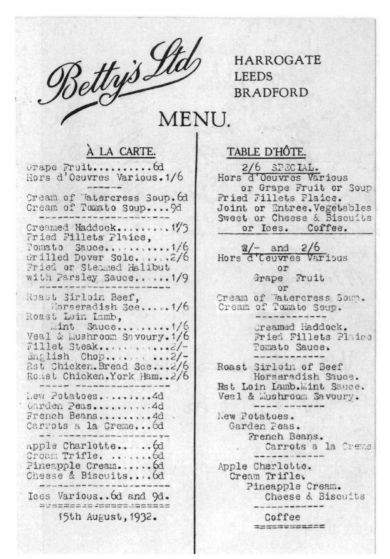

Betty's Ltd

HARROGATE
LEEDS
BRADFORD

MENU.

À LA CARTE.

Grape Fruit..........6d
Hors d'Oeuvres Various.1/6

Cream of Watercress Soup.6d
Cream of Tomato Soup....9d

Creamed Haddock........1/3
Fried Fillets Plaice,
Tomato Sauce..........1/6
Grilled Dover Sole......2/6
Fried or Steamed Halibut
with Parsley Sauce......1/9

Roast Sirloin Beef,
Horseradish Sce.....1/6
Roast Loin Lamb,
Mint Sauce..........1/6
Veal & Mushroom Savoury.1/6
Fillet Steak............2/-
English Chop...........2/-
Rst Chicken.Bread Sce...2/6
Roast Chicken.York Ham..2/6

New Potatoes..........4d
Garden Peas..........4d
French Beans........4d
Carrots a la Creme...6d

Apple Charlotte......6d
Cream Trifle. 6d
Pineapple Cream......6d
Cheese & Biscuits....6d

Ices Various..6d and 9d.
===================
15th August, 1932.

TABLE D'HÔTE.

2/6 SPECIAL.
Hors d'Oeuvres Various
or Grape Fruit or Soup
Fried Fillets Plaice.
Joint or Entree.Vegetables
Sweet or Cheese & Biscuits
or Ices. Coffee.

2/- and 2/6
Hors d'Oeuvres Various
or
Grape Fruit
or
Cream of Watercress Soup.
Cream of Tomato Soup.

Creamed Haddock.
Fried Fillets Plaice
Tomato Sauce.

Roast Sirloin of Beef
Horseradish Sauce.
Rst Loin Lamb.Mint Sauce.
Veal & Mushroom Savoury.

New Potatoes.
Garden Peas.
French Beans.
Carrots a la Creme

Apple Charlotte.
Cream Trifle.
Pineapple Cream.
Cheese & Biscuits

Coffee
===========

Another issue was that the main competition in York, Terry's, was directly opposite. Victor, Frederick's nephew, when working in York, ruefully commented that 'Terry's were our main rivals, the ladies with hats went to Terry's. They had better facilities than we had: marble toilets and all beautiful mahogany panelling. It was a beautiful dining room.' Terry's occupied a 1920s building with bronze-framed shopfront and windows and had a solid reputation in York, having occupied the site, first as a chocolate factory and latterly as a café, since 1818. It was an institution, and Bettys York struggled to attract clientele once the initial novelty had worn off. Frederick lamented that doing a three-course lunch for 1s 6d in *Queen Mary*-inspired décor was 'always a bad idea'.

With four premises operating, Bettys could at least now benefit more fully from the economies of scale Frederick was after. Even

A Bettys menu from August 1932. This was kept by Victor Wild as a memento from his visit to the UK, aged nine

before York opened, Bradford, Leeds and Harrogate had had universal menus. On 15 August 1932 the à la carte options for the restaurants included grapefruit, cream of tomato soup, grilled Dover sole, roast beef with horseradish sauce, roast chicken and York ham, garden peas, apple charlotte, pineapple cream and cheese and biscuits. It was very similar to the menus at their rival Taylors' Kiosk café in Ilkley but with more choice. On one occasion, Claire sat down with her sister-in-law Ida, plus Ida's children Vreni, Hanni and Victor, who were visiting from Switzerland without Carl: they wrote their names on the back of the menu, Claire writing hers as 'Auntie Claire'. It was obvious now that the Belmonts would not have children, and they no longer got on. Divorce, however, was still stigmatised in the 1930s, and Frederick felt a duty to show a good example to his staff. The couple were bound together by the business they had created and, although they argued constantly, they remained together, cohabiting while leading increasingly separate lives.

Frederick was 51, in the prime of life, but the future of Bettys needed to be considered, and that meant finding someone who could continue Frederick's hard work. Werner Muller, the distant relative who'd joined the firm from university in the 1920s, wasn't working out, and Claire's cousin Neville was proving nice but ineffectual. He acquiesced too easily to the Belmonts' demands – Claire even used him as a suitably uniformed chauffeur when the occasion seemed to demand it – and was seen to have 'no gumption'. However, Frederick – and Claire – were already involved in the lives of Ida's children, and as Claire and Frederick drifted apart, Ida remained as devoted as ever. Her own marriage, as she had foreseen, was proving problematic, for Carl continued to plunge his energies, and most of their money, into publishing his thoughts on making the world a better place. Although he'd come to England with the family in 1926, in 1932 he had refused to come, sparking a brutal letter from Frederick, who wrote bitterly: 'so you can't afford to go on holiday with your wife and children: instead, you feel obliged to throw away your entire money on some worthless infatuation. You state that you feel called upon to write and sacrifice yourself for the improvement of the human race. This is nothing but a colossal delusion on your part.' He said the things Ida could not: 'as a family man you are not entitled to sacrifice your income and your family on such an ungrateful field'. It did not work, and Ida

and the children came alone, a mark both of Ida's determination and the bond between her and her brother.

In 1934 Vreni had been invited to England, and sent to boarding school in Harrogate. She hated it, caught up as she was in the Belmonts feuding, and at a school intended to turn out well-bred wives rather than feisty women fit for (potentially) running a business. Two years later, it was Victor's turn: despite Vreni's experience, he was keen for adventure, and, while very close to his mother, felt largely ignored by his father, Carl. Later, Victor acknowledged how hard it must have been for Ida to send her youngest child away, for 'she thought I was marvellous. I thought I was marvellous as well, of course', but he acknowledged that she 'would have done anything for her brother'. At 13 Victor was aware that he was being tested for a potential future in England, and to him Frederick (still Uncle Fritz to him) and Bettys were synonymous. He admitted that Switzerland seemed like a backwater, 'whereas England ...'. He added: 'I always thought that there was a bit of magic about Bettys because where did they get all these sweets from, and these toys, and everything.'

'I always thought that there was a bit of magic about Bettys because where did they get all these sweets from, and these toys, and everything.'

Even when, on the 1932 trip, Bettys was revealed to be 'not a magic treasure trove, but a busy enterprise which took up a lot of my uncle's and my Aunt Claire's attention', the glamour – and sense of a more luxurious life – remained. Fritz was a benefactor, providing not just financial support but much-desired toys. When Victor was desperate for a model steam engine, it was Frederick who paid for it. Victor was so overjoyed that he took it to bed, although 'it was fuelled by methylated spirits, so my parents were a bit dubious about it'. He took it with him to Harrogate, flying into Leeds-Bradford airport with his uncle before being dropped off at Sedbergh boarding school three days early by mistake and spending the first night crying into his soup because Frederick said it was too far to go home and come back. Frederick wrote in his diary: 'I am sending him [Victor] to a public school with a view of taking him into the business. I wonder how everything will shape.'

Over the next three years Victor learnt English at high speed, although he found certain elements of the culture baffling, including the imperial measurement system, which he deemed (not unreasonably) to be 'maliciously derived'. He became a stereotypical English schoolboy, obsessed with food, for, as was usual at boarding school, it was dreadful – greying bacon and 'boiled baby' aka suet pudding. His letters to Claire and Frederick were full of schoolboy slang and requests for Bettys cake. (He shared this love of British slang with Frederick, whose description of Bunny after the opening of York was as a 'little brick' with 'any amount of pluck'.)

Opposite, top The Wild family. From left to right: Hanni, Vreni, Victor, Ida and Carl Wild, c.1933

Opposite, bottom Ida with Victor Wild dressed in traditional Swiss costume, c.1930

Victor was bad at cricket (like Frederick's, his eyesight was poor), but he excelled at art, winning prizes, and illustrating his letters with cartoons. He enjoyed school but remained conscious of the reason he was there – and interested in what was going on back in the business he was being groomed for. 'I've still some of the food left which you brought up on Sunday. The fame of the chocolat [*sic*] has spread all round the house and every evening after prep a hopeful crowd gathers at the study door, while I yield the chisel and the hammer. Why does it have these air bubbles in it? Has it been molten down? Is it the kind you use for covering cakes etc.? I would like to know all this for besides personal curiosity, I am constantly being asked these questions while people are devouring their spoil.'

He also started a small sideline selling Swiss hats to his classmates. Ida sent them from Switzerland with the warning: 'I want to counsel you not to … raise the price too much because that would be conduct unbecoming to a Swiss. Sure, you can make a small profit, but don't be too impertinent, agreed?' She also provided sausages. Meanwhile Victor was already being employed in the business – in the holidays in the bakery, where his greatest pleasure was building castles and race tracks in the huge trays full of starch in the starch room (used for moulding and drying delicate jellied sweets). He was also credited in print as their 'schoolboy artist' designing adverts for the press.

York was still struggling, although the Malton Investment Trust had taken it on in the same favourable way as the other premises, until in January 1939 the company managed to obtain a prized liquor licence, enabling it to sell alcohol. Frederick, who had been harbouring a desire to own his own pub, was overjoyed

Top, left and right School class photograph showing Victor Wild, front row, third from left. 1933

Opposite A self-portrait of Victor Wild distributing Bettys chocolate at Sedburgh Boarding School, Cumbria

and immediately added a cocktail bar on the ground floor and converted the basement into a bar. It was a significant coup. Europe seemed to be moving closer to war, and, in addition to Frederick's own drinking desires (whisky in the comfortable confines of home, or now his very own bar), diversification was a wise move: all of the directors well remembered the shut shops and food and drink restrictions of the previous war. If another was to come, and Bettys was to survive it, it would need as much help as possible.

France was already mobilising when Frederick, Claire and Victor decided to take a holiday in Switzerland in July 1939. Switzerland's neutrality meant that it was (in theory) safe from imminent invasion, and they went trekking with Ida in the mountains. In early August, however, the Belmonts decided it was too risky and flew home. Victor stayed, enrolling at the International School in St Gallen, those around him convinced that England would be bombed and Switzerland would be safer. However, when war was finally declared in October it proved an anti-climax: the Phoney War, during which very little happened apart from proclamations and, in the UK, the issuing of ration books, with rationing to start in the new year. Victor wrote: 'I hope that the war hasn't influenced business too much. Have you had to give up any vans?' He had made friends and was keen to stay in Switzerland and learn to cook before helping out in the business,

but at the same time he felt torn, as English now as Swiss, and missed the more prosperous lifestyle of Harrogate.

In January 1940, eight days after rationing came in, Frederick wrote to Victor begging him to return to the UK and to Sedbergh, not because of the exams he was due to take but because of the 'certain indescribable benefit which a boy acquires at an English public school. It is a stamp which helps him along wherever he goes.' He wanted Victor to be English in a way that, despite his car and golf and Freemasonry, he never was. He also felt 'that all my efforts and good intentions are wasted and your poor old uncle is just stranded and alone'. It was a heartfelt plea, ending: 'if you want to come back, do so at once. I am afraid that if you do not take advantage of your permit now you might not be able to come over again'. The Wilds held a family conference. Victor's decision was easy, and he set out to get the relevant visas for travel through France to England before the borders closed.

Ida wrote to Frederick, saying it had been wonderful to have all three children with her for six months. She went on: 'you are my brother and I give him to your charge in full confidence. You will have much trouble with him, but have confidence in him even if there are things which seem strange and incomprehensible, as long as he achieves good things in his own way'. She was well aware that Victor could be away now for a long time – and that at 16, he would have left school and possibly be into adulthood by the time she saw him again. She went on: 'I can understand, dear brother that the thought of entrusting your whole life's work to the hands of a stranger is painful for you. But you would have to be pitied even more if Victor did not show any interest and pleasure to continue your work in your own spirit: if he thought only of extracting as much money as he could. That would please neither you nor me, because in everything you have done, you have never lost sight of your ideals. If he lives up to this (and I believe he will), then you will have a worthy successor, and you might forgive him a few other faults, won't you?'

In April, as Hitler was invading and occupying Norway and Denmark, Victor got his visas. As Germany gathered its forces on its western border at the start of May, he travelled alone through a blacked-out France, troops hastening the other way, heading for Alsace and the supposedly impregnable Maginot Line. He reached England, registering, like Frederick 26 years

Frederick and Claire Belmont skiing at Pontresina, Switzerland, c.1930s

before, as a neutral alien. Just a few days later, on 10 May, German forces invaded the Netherlands, France and Belgium, neatly bypassing the Maginot Line. The French closed the borders. A month later the Germans occupied Paris, and a month after that the Battle of Britain was in full flow. Five years of war and 14 years of food restrictions would follow: Bettys had survived boom and bust, but now it faced bombs as well.

An essential public service

1940–1952

What's on the menu?

Rationing started in Britain in January 1940 and continued until 1954. While individuals had ration books, restaurants and catering businesses faced different regulations, a mixture of food and price restrictions. Wartime rationing was at times draconian, but shortages were worse after the war. This 1948 menu, from when Bettys in York was under the ownership of the North British Hotels Trust, is a rare survival – paper too was in short supply.

At first glance this menu seems varied and surprisingly opulent, but the aura of sophistication afforded by the French titles is misleading. There is a preponderance of vegetables, not just those explicitly listed, but also in the 'Cream Parmentier' (potato soup). Meanwhile the 'Savoury Macaroni' would have relied upon Marmite or pan scrapings rather than meat, and the fishcake would have been made from packet fish bits, whale or even snoek, a notorious post-war import which entirely failed to catch on as it was virtually inedible. Offal, which was unrestricted, appears in the kidney soup and doubtless in the steak pie as well, the pastry for which may well have been boosted with potato. Small amounts of meat and fish were allocated, hence the appearance of cod, lamb, plaice and chicken, but the menu is cagey on the amount and the form they take – almost certainly not large pieces, but smaller chunks in a sauce, or even minced to form patties. Sausages, meanwhile, were notorious for low levels of poor-quality meat, boosted with herbs and filler.

The sweets too can be read in a number of ways: for 'chocolate', read cocoa, and the sponge was inevitably recycled stale sponge from a previous sweet, soaked in sauce to moisten it and make it edible. The trifle was another cunning way to use bits and pieces left from previous menus, whether cake, biscuit or bread. Eggs were in very short supply, so the sauces would have been thickened with starch such as cornflour, and the custard was, inevitably, made from powder. Cream too was a somewhat hopeful title in 1948: mock cream recipes abounded, usually based on evaporated milk, gelatine and custard powder or milk thickened with cornflour with some flavouring added. However, there are hints that wartime shortages were lessening: those foods that were unrationed, but which had disappeared during the war as shipping space was prioritised for armaments were slowly coming back: hence the grapefruit, bringing a bit of pre-war glamour to a dreary luncheon. Likewise, the 'Coupe Jaffa'– probably a sorbet – is a hopeful nod toward the lifting of the ban on ice creams and a hint of holidays to come.

Prices were set by the government, and the 5s luncheon was standard across all catering outlets. Diners would also have been instructed on how to construct their meal from the available options; usually they could have one main and one side or starter or a sweet, or two sides only.

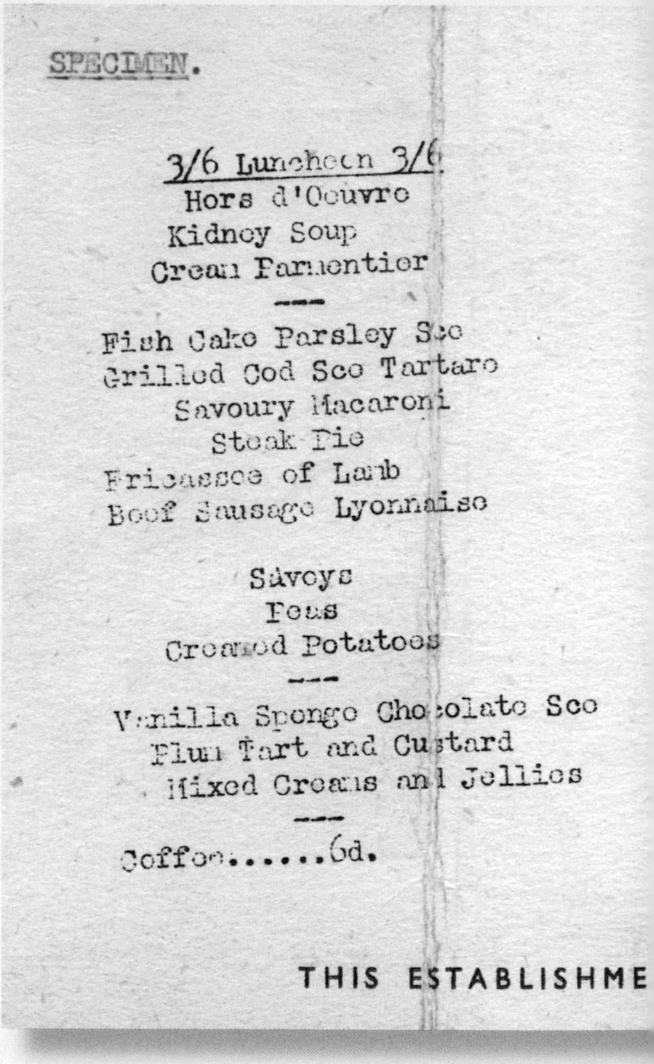

SPECIMEN.

3/6 Luncheon 3/6
Hors d'Oeuvre
Kidney Soup
Cream Parmentier

Fish Cake Parsley Sce
Grilled Cod Sce Tartare
Savoury Macaroni
Steak Pie
Fricassee of Lamb
Beef Sausage Lyonnaise

Savoys
Peas
Creamed Potatoes

Vanilla Sponge Chocolate Sce
Plum Tart and Custard
Mixed Creams and Jellies

Coffee......6d.

THIS ESTABLISHME

Bettys York menu,
February 1948

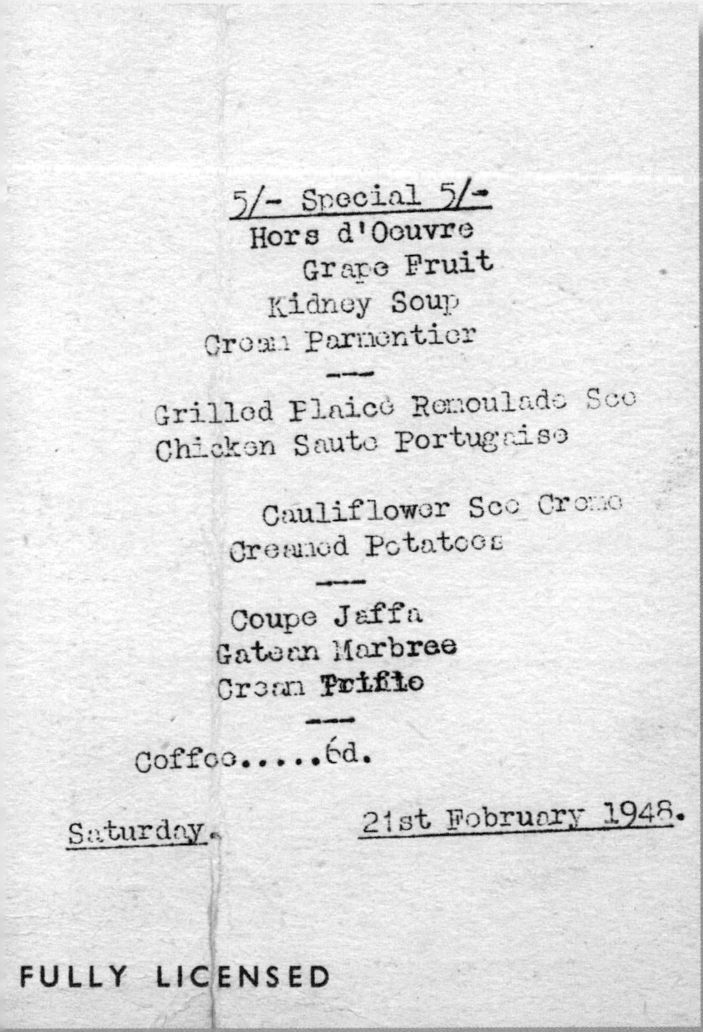

5/- Special 5/-
Hors d'Oeuvre
Grape Fruit
Kidney Soup
Cream Parmentier

Grilled Plaice Remoulade Sce
Chicken Saute Portugaise

Cauliflower Sce Creme
Creamed Potatoes

Coupe Jaffa
Gateau Marbree
Cream Trifle

Coffee.....6d.

Saturday.   21st February 1948.

FULLY LICENSED

N B T
NORTH BRITISH TRUST HOTELS

**BETTY'S RESTAURANT
YORK**

Telephone : 2323

As Victor Wild returned to school in Sedbergh, German forces swept through France, the Netherlands and Belgium. During the last week of May the British army was evacuated from the beaches of Dunkirk, and by mid June Hitler was enjoying the sights of Paris in person. Frederick and Claire Belmont, their nephew Victor and Bettys itself all now settled in for war. Frederick and Claire had already experienced a global war and knew all too well to expect personal and commercial food shortages, staffing issues and, of course, the potential for the sudden death of loved ones. Switzerland was neutral, as it had been during the First World War, but that neutrality was not guaranteed, and there was always a risk that Hitler would violate it. Switzerland was surrounded by Axis powers, and there too food would be in short supply, as imports were affected by the war raging around its borders. Every letter to and from Ida would be subject to censorship as it passed through occupied territory – if it got through at all. Victor later recalled the swastikas and censor marks on the post that he received, and communication with his family was sporadic, with many letters lost or destroyed en route.

Unlike in the 1914–18 conflict, the British government had recognised the need for rationing food well in advance: personal ration books were issued at the end of 1939, ready for rationing to start in January 1940. Every individual was allocated basic foods according to supply: meat (by price), bacon/ham, cheese, tea, fats (butter, margarine and lard), sugar, preserves (jams) and sweets/chocolate were all controlled, but supply was guaranteed. There was also a points system which enabled consumers a certain amount of choice and covered foods the supplies of which could not be entirely guaranteed, such as tinned fish. Eggs were both rationed and in short supply, supplemented by dried egg where possible.

Victor Wild in his prep school
uniform, 1936

A lot of foods were unrationed but scarce, including offal (which spoilt quickly), game, vegetables and fish. Bread also was unrationed, but it was regulated, with a high-extraction-rate national loaf taking the place of anything approaching white bread – the same went for flour. Certain foods, including bread and margarine, were eventually fortified with vitamins and calcium to increase their nutritional value. Over at Sedbergh Victor, like anyone staying in a hotel or catered institution for more than five days, had to hand in his personal ration book so that resources could be pooled for catering on a large scale. He retained only his personal butter ration, which had to be eked out over each week – the amount allowed was generally 2oz (about 50g). He wrote to Frederick and Claire asking, 'Two vital questions: 1. Could you send me a large tin of Ovaltine or Bourn-vita or some similar thing? 2. What are the possibilities of getting a two-pound jar of jam to last me for the whole of term?' The food was even worse than it had been, and the Bettys cakes and chocolates he was still receiving were all the more gratefully demolished by him and his friends.

Victor was 18 in 1941 and eager to leave school. As his friends reached conscription age, they disappeared off to train in the Forces, and there was a sense of waiting, of wasting time. Most boys joined the cadets. Victor, as an alien, was put to digging trenches instead, which given that the soil turned to granite after a few inches, was not the most useful of activities. He was torn

Rationing in the UK during the Second World War

between wanting to do his bit for his adoptive country and relief that he was prevented from joining up by his Swiss nationality. His mother Ida wrote, worrying that he wasn't getting enough fruit, saying she listened every night to the British radio news, and encouraging him to make the most of life, even in war – but not to forget what that life held: 'And now, jump my young colt, jump into life! Uncle blazed the trail for you, and now it is up to you!' More practically she also advised that 'it is imperative that you study French if you are supposed to read recipes because fine cooking comes from France and so understanding French is a must. At any rate, young men such as yourself should be fluent in at least 2 or 3 languages because some day war is going to be over and the world will be open to everyone.'

Without consulting him, Frederick decided that Victor should stay at school for an extra year, a chance for him to indulge in music and art, and because he really didn't know what to do with his nephew as the Blitz raged and the war seemed to go from bad to worse. Harrogate's only bombs fell in September 1940, when three bombs fell on and around the Hotel Majestic, thought erroneously to be the home to the Air Ministry. Bettys was untouched, and only one casualty was recorded. Bits of the bombs were later displayed in a shop window for the edification of the townspeople and its trickle of visitors, grimly determined still to have a holiday. There were various government officials too working out of hastily requisitioned hotels. Leeds and Bradford suffered more serious raids: 65 people died in March 1941 in Leeds, when raids damaged over 4,500 houses; Bradford town centre was badly affected, with Lingard's Department Store (apparently selling the 'best teacakes in Bradford') destroyed along with other buildings. However, Bettys stayed open, and the more cafés that closed, the better business got.

Eating out boomed during the Second World War. Bettys' profits and turnover went up, and dividends continued to be paid to shareholders throughout the war, while Frederick and Claire regularly awarded themselves (and their fellow Board member J. J. Smith) salary increases. Catering establishments were subject to a bewildering and very complicated set of regulations, which changed regularly – there were around 6,000 different bits of legislation in place by 1945. It led to a great deal of extra work, forms to be filled and inspectors to be shown around. Additionally, catering staff were not exempt from conscription, and as the war went on, able-bodied men up to the age of 51 were called up, as well as single and childfree widowed women. Bettys was not alone in being left with elderly or infirm men and women, along with younger female staff who had children to care for. There were a few long-standing older staff, whose experience was vital in keeping the bakery, in particular, functioning, but, even so, the image customers got was often one of slightly tottery ladies with more smiles and goodwill than stamina.

In the early years of the war Bettys nevertheless managed to produce menus which read as being almost at pre-war standards. Surviving menus are few – paper was scarce, and menus for special occasions were often taken as souvenirs – but one does exist for December 1940, for a meal put on for a group of officers. It started with 'hors d'oeuvres' (easy, the term covered a multitude of sins), then went on to tomato soup, fillet of sole with anchovy sauce, roast chicken with bread sauce, sprouts, creamed potatoes, sherry trifle, fruit tart with cream, cheese and biscuits and finally coffee. It was almost word for word the

Betty's Bar

perfect meal, as expressed by a war-weary public six years later in a national survey, and had barely a hint of rationing, except in the strict seasonality of the vegetables (and small portions). But this was early on, and by 1942 the Meals Orders were in effect, limiting the price of a meal to 5s. The price cap was intended to ensure that restaurants had to limit what they served, given that they still needed to make a profit from that 5s, but was accompanied with extra restrictions on how many courses could be served, as well as, eventually, outright bans on foods such as ice cream.

Bettys was helped greatly now by Frederick's purchase of the alcohol licence for York, and conversion of the basement into a bar in the evenings. From 1940 to 1945 the bar became known as the Dive and attracted a huge crowd. Britain was supported massively by the Commonwealth, and the airfields around York became increasingly full of Canadians, hastily trained and sent across to swell the ranks after the Battle of Britain in 1940 (during which the average life expectancy of a pilot was only four weeks). They were enthusiastic patrons of the Dive, which was so well-known that it was even immortalised in a cartoon in *Tatler*. Caught up in the war spirit, Frederick encouraged the

Opposite Menu for the Royal Army Ordnance Corps officers' dinner at Bettys York signed by the attendees. 19 December 1940

Top Bettys Bar at York branch. This image was taken for a leaflet announcing that the premises had returned to Bettys management in 1950

"Here's Betty's Bar"

airmen to etch their names with a diamond-tipped pencil on the vast mirror behind the bar: many of those who signed would never return from missions over Germany, and the mirror became quietly famous. Meanwhile, girls came to Bettys by bus from as far afield as Leeds to party the hours away and try to forget the ever-present risk of death. Across St Helen's Square, Terry's now had no queues, and, when they could spare the time, the Bettys staff took a mild pleasure in jeering at Terry's staff as their gentility now got in the way. York became the most profitable of the Bettys sites by far.

Another great help to Bettys during the war was the bakery. Bread was not rationed and was seen by the Ministry of Food as vital for morale as well as nutrition, and so bakeries such as Bettys got extra petrol rations for delivery. The Emergency Bread Scheme legislated that bakeries should support each other in case of bombing raids, and they had to be ready to leap into extra baking action to cater for any short-term local shortages. The weight of a loaf went down and the price went up, while over in the cake department sugar and fat rations were imposed, along with a ban on icing. Many small bakeries struggled to cope, especially once coal too went on the ration. Electricity, however, was unrestricted: Frederick's love of modern machinery, which he had kept updated, and the consequent high level of sophistication in the bakery meant it continued to thrive.

Top 'Here's Bettys Bar' cartoon by Edward Sylvester Hynes, which featured in *Tatler* on 8 November 1944

Opposite, top A sketch of the kitchen scene at Claridges, drawn by Victor Wild in 1942

Victor Wild in chef's whites, 1948

By 1942 staff shortages were really starting to bite as even women nominally exempt from conscription volunteered to do their bit. By mid 1943 90 per cent of single women and 80 per cent of married women were employed in war work. The obvious solution was to bring Victor, sound of mind and body but barred from joining up, into the fray. He was completely untrained, however, apart from a few summers spent in the bakery, and felt the lack acutely. Victor was keen to learn management skills, writing frustrated letters to Ida complaining that Frederick kept making decisions on his behalf. Frederick did, finally, address the question of training, but not into Victor's desired business skills. Instead he took Victor to London, where he attempted to persuade or bribe the chefs at the Ritz and Claridge's to take his nephew on as an apprentice. Marcel Percevault, the one-eyed chef of Claridge's, who had trained under Escoffier, agreed.

It was a prestigious and sought-after position – every year the top three pupils of the Westminster Technical Institute were

awarded a Claridge's apprenticeship – and joining the team with no further qualification than a love of chocolate and a probable succession to a small chain of northern cafés was definitely a challenge. The kitchens operated the usual high-end brigade system, orders shouted by an *aboyeur* (generally to catcalls from the staff) and cooks divided into specialist teams around which apprentices were supposed to circulate. Victor had to fight to move teams, though, falling back on surreptitious note-taking in spare moments. He was subject to the usual initiation rituals – told to stir a pan without letting it burn on the very hottest part of the coal-fuelled range until the sniggers from around him

Claridge's Hotel, c.1940s

made him realise it was simply water – and was shocked at how backward the equipment was compared to Bettys. The staff was drawn from across the world (except from enemy nations, whose natives had all been interned at the beginning of the war). He became friends with a Jewish Czech, a fellow apprentice, but there were also Poles, many French and a Chinaman as well as the sinister *plongeurs*, crouched with their washing up over wooden sinks in a dank basement. There they picked the scraps from the roasting tins and licked the sauces from the plates. Victor described it as like Dante's *Inferno*. He learnt culinary French, slang-laden and sweary, and which shocked Frederick's more genteel French friends when Frederick tried to show off Victor's language skills back in Harrogate ('but I didn't know', said Victor, looking back).

The food that Victor learnt to prepare was classical French – not particularly useful for Bettys. It was suspiciously plentiful, with money no object, and diners of sufficient status to pull every string going. The King of Greece was a permanent resident refugee, and the communist sauce chef would habitually spit in every dish announced as being *'pour le roi'*. Victor spent hours plucking and drawing game (sent from landed estates), chopping vegetables and cracking lobsters (all unrationed), as well as preparing more dubiously obtained chickens and ortolans (small French songbirds, traditionally eaten whole). People avoided him on the tube back to his lodgings when he was working in the fish department and stinking of salmon. The 5s restriction theoretically applied to Claridge's just as much as Bettys, but they got around it, charging extra for oysters, for dancing and a great deal for wine. Menus from other luxury hotels included novelties such as roast kid with Jerusalem artichoke, lobster and salad, goose with mushrooms and woodcock with wine sauce: excellent food, but with a telltale reliance on unrationed game and eked-out leftovers recycled into rissoles. No one was exempt from wartime inventiveness.

None of this was exactly useful to Victor, though, and he wrote to Frederick, more with hope than real conviction: 'the more I think about it the more I realised that there is a stupendous amount of other things to learn apart from cooking. There is quite a lot needed to bridge the gap between a worker in a hotel kitchen and a business-man. But I know that you will be giving

'I am worried about our business. We may be closed down, what a great tragedy ... everything seems to have gone my way and now this stupid war.'

the matter thought.' He was well aware that he needed to know much more than a multitude of ways with garnishes to help run a business back in Yorkshire.

Outside work, Victor was isolated. Frederick and Claire occasionally visited, staying in another hotel with suspiciously plentiful meat, but he had little in common with his fellow chefs, who looked rather askance at this tall, gangly youngster with his head in a book. Frederick described Victor as looking 'like a disarranged bundle of spaghetti – all arms and legs' and commented on his shyness. He was reading *The Science of Work*, studying systems for efficiency with an eye for improving Bettys when the time came to return to Yorkshire. He also rented a studio in South Molton Street, where he could paint and sleep in the four-hour afternoon breaks – Claridge's worked a split shift system. He went to lunchtime concerts, which were hugely popular: 'people were keyed up, and music meant a great deal'. He managed also to find somewhere to play the piano himself, describing it as 'a great emotional release'. He found London hard work, though, groping his way home in the blackout and locating his gate by touch, avoiding the prostitutes calling from doorways ('no response from me, but unease, unease') and hearing shrapnel rain down upon his roof from the still-frequent bombing raids. His sporadic attempts at romance all fell flat, although he did have a social life when fatigue and work allowed. One medical student friend roped him into helping perform pregnancy tests using live frogs (African frogs – injected

Opposite Letter dated 11 August 1943 to Bettys Harrogate from Lieutenant-Colonel J. Manson of Quartering Command No. 5 Area, relating to the possible requisition of its York premises

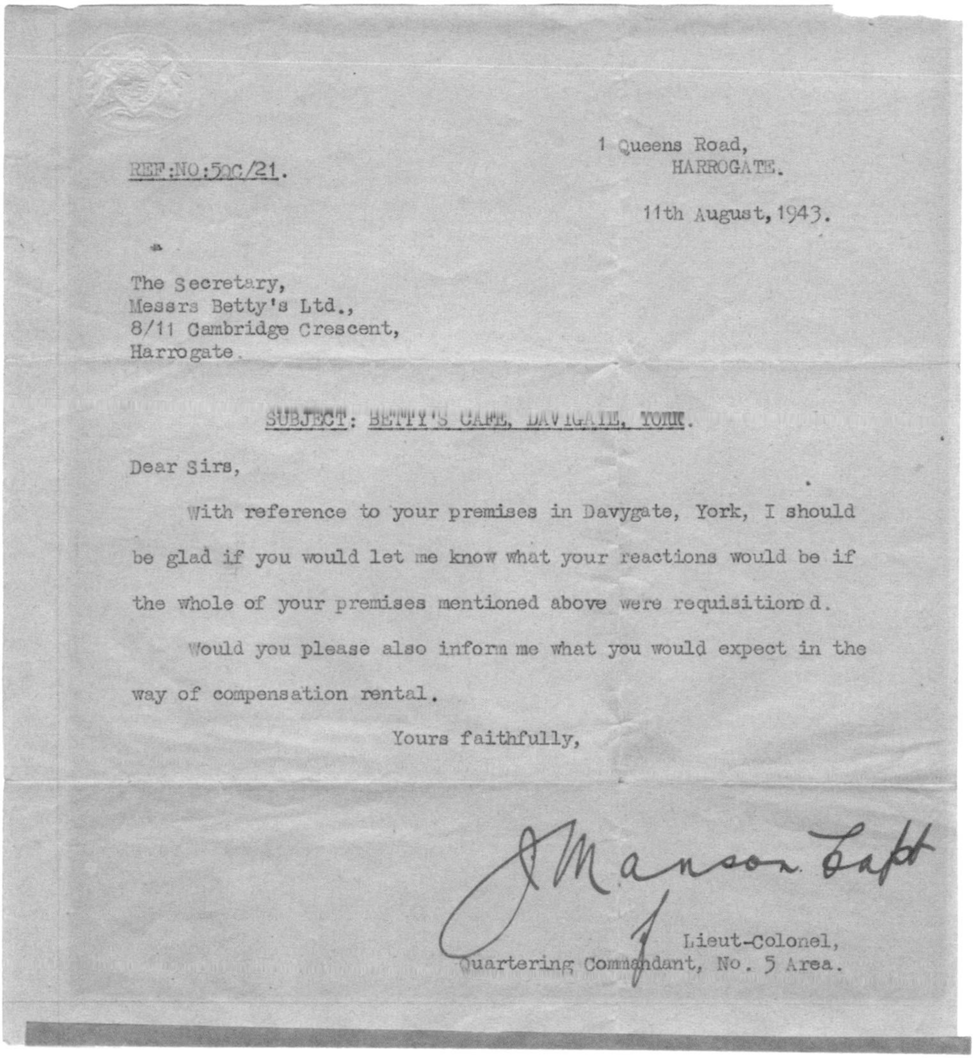

REF:NO:5QC/21.

1 Queens Road,
HARROGATE.

11th August, 1943.

The Secretary,
Messrs Betty's Ltd.,
8/11 Cambridge Crescent,
Harrogate.

SUBJECT: BETTY'S CAFE, DAVYGATE, YORK.

Dear Sirs,

With reference to your premises in Davygate, York, I should be glad if you would let me know what your reactions would be if the whole of your premises mentioned above were requisitioned.

Would you please also inform me what you would expect in the way of compensation rental.

Yours faithfully,

J Manson Capt

Lieut-Colonel,
Quartering Commandant, No. 5 Area.

with urine, they would ovulate if the woman who had provided the urine was pregnant). The method was incredibly reliable and led to a massive trade in frogs.

Back in Harrogate, Frederick wrote a rare diary entry: 'Lots of things have happened in the last five years. York is a great success. I obtained a full publican licence … It is like a fairy story. Our balance sheet shows profit for York £5,000, and £14,000 for the company. However, there is a war, the thing I never expected to be possible. How stupid and futile. I wonder how it will all finish … Victor had a good career at Sedbergh. I am very proud of him. It was worthwhile. He is now at Claridge's, London, in the kitchen. I am worried about our business. We may be closed down, what a great tragedy … everything seems to have gone my way and now this stupid war.'

Bettys staff (including cooks and waitresses) at Cambridge Crescent, Harrogate in front of a Bettys delivery van, 1949

In April 1942 it looked as if his fears would be realised. York was bombed in a raid intentionally aimed at killing civilians and damaging historic buildings: 92 people died, hundreds more were injured and the airfields and railway station were badly damaged as well as around one third of the housing stock. The medieval Guildhall, behind the Mansion House two doors down from Bettys, was gutted, and an incendiary bomb fell on Bettys itself. Fortunately, the fire watcher on duty that night, one of the Bettys van drivers, was quick enough to put out the fire, and the damage was only minor.

In 1943 Victor returned from London and plunged into the business, being sent wherever he was needed. Ida wrote to Frederick that 'the fact that you are sending him to your newest and most beautiful store in York really shows a lot of trust … maybe you have someone working in that store who could supervise and guide him a little in a fatherly or motherly fashion.' Victor did eventually find that guidance, not from Frederick or Claire but from the parents of a schoolfriend, Pat Evans, who lived just outside York. He stayed with them while he worked at the York Bettys, although as a neutral alien he had to get a special dispensation to be able to ride his bike from their house to the centre of York for work every day. Pat was sadly killed in action at the end of the war, but Victor remained close to Pat's parents for the rest of their lives.

Victor's presence gave Frederick something tangible to work for, at a time when he and Claire (especially Claire) were starting to slow down and look forward to a golf- and bridge-filled retirement. Victor struggled, though, to impose more efficient ways: the wartime atmosphere just wasn't conducive to new business methods. The York manager resigned in a huff, assuming Victor was there to spy on him. The various (female) supervisors were at loggerheads, not helped by one being great gossip buddies with Frederick and another being embroiled in both a 'financial and amorous' liaison with him. In August the army sent Frederick a notice seeking to requisition Bettys for the war effort. He wrote back by return, pointing out that 'we serve an average of 20,000 main meals, subsidiary meals, teas and hot beverages per week. In addition, we are retailers of bread and flour confectionery. The bars are also popular, and largely popular with Forces.' He went on: 'we maintain that we perform

an essential public service in York, and we sincerely hope that you will not find it necessary to commandeer the establishment'. Chastened, impressed or simply having taken advice from the large and enthusiastic Bettys clientele, the quartering commandant replied noting simply that in view of all of the above, the property would not be requisitioned after all.

Bettys remained under scrutiny, though, particularly in York, which by now employed bouncers to control the goings-on at the Dive. The stringent alcohol licensing laws were particularly difficult to navigate, and a row blew up at the end of 1944 after emergency work was carried out to improve the bar space. It was virtually impossible to manage the legalities around drinking while also navigating wartime restrictions on building materials and people, and Bettys found itself embroiled in a minor spat with the York magistrates' court. Predictably, the local temperance brigade was quickly on the case, claiming that the place was now little more than a 'glorified public house', but the authorities, well aware of the difficulties, simply remarked that 'in no other licensed house did [they] find trolleys of sandwiches and sausage rolls', and proposed to let sleeping dogs lie – 'or rather, drink'.

Meanwhile, food was in ever shorter supply and, unlike Claridge's, the Belmonts did not have a handy network of landed customers to send game as needed. Bettys steered very clear of the black market – penalties were severe and could have meant the end of what was, despite the problems, a very

Canadian airmen experiencing mechanical problems on their way to Bettys Bar successful wartime business. However, that did not mean not taking advantage of every possible opportunity. Victor was called into the bakery one morning to find that the coke-fuelled boiler was in full steam and the copper sugar-boiling pan was full – they were making fudge from a lorryload of honey, caught in a warehouse fire in London, and which Frederick had bought cheaply after getting the nod from a friend. The fudge went out to all the branches, causing queues as the sweet-starved public rushed to get their hands on it. In fact, there were perpetual queues at all the branches, four deep on the stairs at York, as well as occasional lines on the streets outside, sparked by rumours of cake. It was an era of constant struggle. Provisions were allotted based on meals served, which averaged around 300–400 lunches a day plus teas, but that still only meant fish once a week, and the meat ration tended to run out halfway through service. Spam and corned beef, part of the American lend-lease programme, helped a lot – even Simpson's in the Strand proudly advertised its creamed Spam casserole, so Bettys was in good company. A frozen 'fish mix' was a staple, made up of unrecognisable bits of fish offal and skin, but which, when

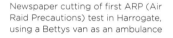

Newspaper cutting of first ARP (Air Raid Precautions) test in Harrogate, using a Bettys van as an ambulance

A FULL SCALE A.R.P. TEST, the first of its kind, took place in Harrogate on Sunday.

mixed with potato, powdered eggs and herbs, made passable fishcakes – the Bettys version of Claridge's Frenchified rissoles. Victor and the kitchen staff tried making omelettes and pancakes with dried egg (not brilliant), and there were 'a lot of things on toast'. These included, briefly, whale meat, one of many less than successful alternative meats that the government tried to encourage. Meanwhile, worn-out tablecloths and napkins were replaced with surplus sailcloth, and the Bettys-branded teaspoons were replaced with plainer versions as the services personnel kept nicking them for souvenirs (particularly popular in Egypt). Despite the silver teapots and the tasteful lighting, Bettys was tired: chipped crockery, patched carpets, worn and faded décor.

Eventually, the war ended. Restaurants did their best to put on a show: over at Terry's the Victory in Europe Day menu was cold pork pie or spiced ham, salad and ersatz ice cream. VE Day parties broke out across the country, and in York 'people were rolling round in the streets, singing and dancing'. For Victor, the evening was bittersweet: war was over, but the restrictions remained (and would get worse – bread even went on the ration in 1946). His schoolfriends were dead or scattered, and he hadn't seen his parents for five long years. Bettys needed rebuilding, but Frederick and Claire refused to properly train or involve him and seemed more focused on their luxurious life in Harrogate, impressing the Harrogate worthies, than on the hard work that lay ahead. 'That evening of the Victory in Europe celebration, I felt very lonely. I walked round the streets on my own … I could have joined a celebration, but was shy, felt out of it and not one of them.'

Ida, as ever, summed it up, calling it 'the tragedy of the Swiss abroad'. 'There,' she added, 'everything is big and expansive, here everything is small and tight, which creates contradictory longings.' She continued to advise Victor on his approach to the business too: 'at everything you do, examine how it can be done better or easier, and don't just think of making money but also of making life easier for the employees'. In Switzerland, rationing was lifted much earlier than in Britain, and, like many British families, the Belmonts weren't shy about asking relatives abroad to send food. Frederick wrote one of his increasingly rare letters to Ida, thanking her for bacon and cheese and longing for a 5kg piece of decent Emmenthal and wondering whether they should escape their families and see the Northern Lights together. In the

Valerie Belmont, adopted daughter of
Frederick and Claire Belmont

aftermath of the war, he wasn't the only person to reassess his
relationships and see the cracks. Ida herself wrote sadly to Victor
that she now realised the harm her husband Carl had wrought
on the family with his obsessive self-publishing and lack of
self-awareness: 'even his love letters were basically general
deliberations on universal questions and only marginally about us'.
She had finally taken control of the family finances and was now
focused on seeing her son again: commercial flights were once
more running, and she couldn't wait to feed him bratwurst and
apple tart. However, there were still travel restrictions, and it would
be the middle of 1946 before he finally made it to Switzerland.

Just before he left, there was a further unexpected twist. He woke
up one morning in his bed in Harrogate to find 'this small frilly-
dressed doll-like little girl sitting at my side, smiling at me. She had
a label attached to her arm "hello, I'm your new little sister".'
Valerie was two years old, the daughter of a member of staff at
a hotel in Bournemouth where the Belmonts had been on
holiday. Adopting her was an impetuous gesture, especially given

that Frederick was now 61 and Claire 55. As usual, the couple's feelings on the matter diverged: Frederick said he hoped it would give Claire something fulfilling to do; Claire said she had not been consulted. Ida summed it up in a letter to Victor: 'it is a very generous gesture of auntie and uncle to have adopted a little child. But one involuntarily wonders why they have not done this a long time ago rather than at an age when one finds all those troubles and tasks rather burdensome!'

Frederick had now been in Britain for 40 years, and running Bettys for 28 of them. Although he retained a thick Swiss accent, he was thoroughly anglicised, a devotee of bridge, golf and days at the races, along with prestige motor cars. To his friends he was Dickie Belmont, and his childhood poverty and determined struggle to succeed were now long behind him. In 1947 his employees clubbed together to commission a commemorative oil painting of him by John Berrie, a Yorkshire-based society portraitist, which they presented in a ceremony attended by the press as well as Bettys staff. One of his managers, Mary, who'd started as a waitress in 1919, lauded him as the 'best boss'. Meanwhile, he span for the press slightly exaggerated stories about his early days in England and lamented the post-war exigencies which meant his present-day confectionery was not quite of the standard of the 'mouth-watering delicacies he was able to produce before the war'. West Riding Council was considering offering catering training, and, despite continuing to emphasise Bettys Continental roots, Frederick added that he felt 'it was only lack of tuition that prevented English confectioners from being able to compete with Continental standards'. Over at the bakery, he still employed a number of Swiss bakers, but there were work permit restrictions on foreign nationals, so it was not surprising that he took an interest in a scheme that might help supplement Bettys' own, ongoing if occasional, apprenticeship scheme.

It was still hard going in post-war Britain, though, especially with Victor once more absent, and in 1947 Frederick seems to have suffered a sort of crisis. He went to visit Victor with the daughter of John Berrie, his portraitist, in tow, the subtext being that Victor should marry a polished English girl and return to Bettys. Victor demurred, leaving Frederick feeling adrift, desperately wanting a blood relative to succeed him and feeling unsure of Victor's commitment.

Portrait painting of Frederick Belmont by John Archibald Alexander Berrie presented to him by the staff of Bettys in 1947

York was particularly difficult to manage, and the newly appointed manager had just left. In 1947 the company sold Bettys in York, the most personal of their branches, to the North British Hotels Trust for £55,000. Fortunately for the continued profitability of the bakery, which needed to supply all of the branches to justify its existence, the NBHT ran the now ex-Bettys as if nothing had changed, still selling Bettys cakes and breads and with full permission to use the name. Unfortunately for the wider standing of Bettys, the NBHT's shop frequently sold stale cakes, and badly displayed and stored products, and did not uphold the reputation Bettys still had, despite the war, for good taste and 'good food attractively cooked and served'. Frederick wrote to Victor, begging him to return.

Despite his uncle's panic, Victor did not stay in Switzerland for long – just over a year – and the trip was entirely geared toward training for taking a bigger role at Bettys. He talked his way into jobs in restaurant and hotel kitchens, including the prestigious Zunfthaus zum Rüden in Zurich (he noted that there was a severe staff shortage, or he'd never have been taken on). However, his artistic flair meant that he got rapidly stuck with presenting the elaborate platters of mixed hors d'oeuvres then in vogue in Swiss fine dining. He decided he needed front-of-house experience, so moved to the Hotel Kronenhof in the ski resort of Pontresina to work as a waiter. He found the behind-the-scenes squalor and long hours, together with lack of care for staff, depressing and inefficient, and, although he learnt much about conditions on the ground (and got some skiing in), he still felt he lacked crucial management and business skills and that Frederick's approach to his presumed business successor was less than helpful. Part of the issue was one of communication. Frederick was autocratic, and Victor loath to make a fuss.

Victor had no doubt that his future lay with Bettys, and, despite the potential battles with Frederick and Claire which so obviously lay ahead, he was keen to be part of a business which had once thrived and could do so again. A strong persuasion lay in an open-top Triumph sports car, 'gleaming with chrome and bright red paint', for sale in a local garage, and which he knew could be within his grasp if only he could work hard and prove himself. The luxurious lifestyle of the Belmonts was a sharp contrast to the semi-poverty of his own family, and, despite the

questions raised by the sudden adoption of Valerie after over a
decade of Victor being prepared as Frederick's heir, he never
queried the wisdom of going back to Yorkshire. Being issued
call-up papers for Swiss national service was the final straw, and
he arrived back in Harrogate in June 1947.

Bettys now had a team of four at the top: Frederick and Claire,
J. J. Smith and now Victor, made company secretary in August
1947, and a director that November. J. J. died suddenly in 1949,
a real loss for the company: Claire's nephew Neville Elsworth
was brought on instead, but proved as sadly ineffectual as a
director as he was as a bakery manager. The team spent these
years consolidating, creating new shares through the formation
of subsidiary companies, and they also sublet part of the ground
floor in Leeds. Both Leeds and Bradford were in what Victor
called 'a state of emergency'; Bradford in particular was 'pretty
ramshackle … except for the café which had retained some
of its pre-war elegance … the business, and the town itself, was
sooty and dingy'. Attempts to motivate the managers of
individual premises with promises of shares fell flat – Bettys
simply lacked prestige versus the lure of running hotels, and
those who did join the company struggled to deal with Frederick
running it as a one-man show and Claire's habit of drifting into
the various branches to countermand decisions and collect 'slices
of ham, and deference from the staff'.

Victor Wild (second from right) and
fellow chefs at St Gallen, Switzerland,
1945

Kay Metcalfe in her Harrogate General
Hospital nurse's uniform, 1949

She occasionally took Valerie with her, to show her off, but she preferred to avoid the minutiae of bringing up a child and employed a series of nannies instead. When Victor first returned home, the incumbent was an ethereal 22-year-old called Kathleen (Kay) Metcalfe. She left after a few months to train to be a nurse, but Victor had already fallen in love. The Belmonts were enthusiastically introducing him to would-be wives, girls who were part of the county set and would go down well with their bridge-playing friends, and Ida too was keen to see him settle. Some hints must have reached her, for in her last letter to Victor in December 1948, she wrote: 'did you write your wish for the Christmas Christ-child? (Maybe a woman?) – but I don't want to ask too much'. She died the following January, Carl following just a few months later. It was the end of an era: Ida had been a pivotal influence on both Frederick and Victor, and, despite a hard upbringing and financial struggles caused by Carl's obsession with publishing, she had never lost her strong sense of right and wrong or her selflessness. Victor reflected that 'she did such a lot of things for a lot of people. You know she just cared for people and although she had a hard life herself she always took on more really. I wish I had inherited that characteristic.' Meanwhile letters of condolence poured in, describing Ida as 'your family's soul', 'one of the noblest, truest people that I have ever met' and recording that 'even as children we felt that this gracious being was someone magnificent'.

Victor flew back to Switzerland for his mother's funeral, but there were no further thoughts of staying there. He was now committed to England, where his burgeoning relationship provided an outlet from the stresses of keeping Bettys afloat, as well as helping him to deal with the grief of his parents' deaths: 'it was a young man's dream: a pretty girl, an open-top car, picnics and love, tours and excursions'. He became a naturalised British citizen in July 1949. Kay would sneak back into the nurses' college after hours, while Victor drove back to Harrogate revelling in time spent with someone who was outside the Belmonts' pressured world and who regarded Bettys as 'just a posh sort of café'. Then she fell pregnant. Claire was incensed; Frederick wept. In 1950 this was a scandal at the level of society they now aspired to – and what kind of example did it set for the Bettys staff? The couple were marched to the register office, the date hushed up, and the story went out that they'd married several months earlier. Victor, thrown into turmoil, had interviews with local art schools about becoming a teacher, but eventually he decided it was not for him. For the rest of his life he regretted not giving Kay the full white wedding he felt she deserved: Bettys, it emerged, was a demanding mistress.

With Victor now British, married and expecting, the Bettys succession seemed guaranteed. Frederick, long uneasy about the situation in York, now proposed to buy back the Bettys branch there, which he duly managed, for slightly less than the price for which he had previously sold it. The North British Hotels Trust had run it very badly, and matters weren't helped when Frederick appointed a manager who was less than conscientious but who had impressed Frederick with his suggestion of adding ham and pineapple to the menu – decidedly outré at the time. On the day

Victor Wild's mother, Ida Wild (née Bützer), c.1930s

Victor Wild holding his firstborn,
Elizabeth (Liz), 1950

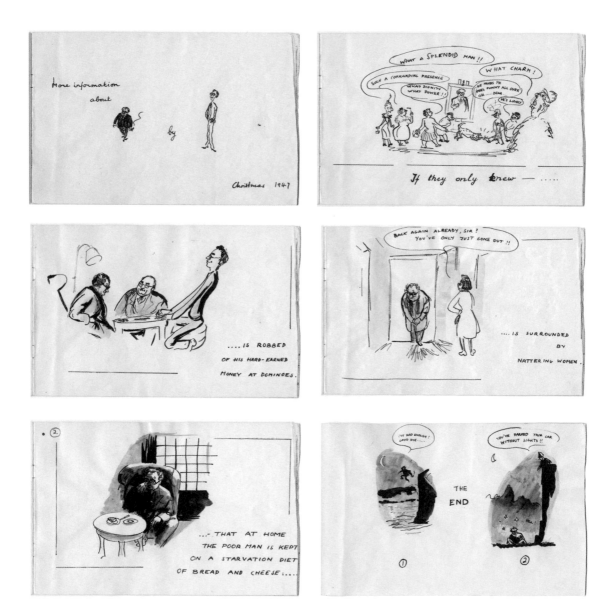

A series of sketches produced by
Victor Wild for Frederick Belmont,
Christmas 1947

Bettys took back possession of the premises, Kay went into labour: it was unheard of then for husbands to be present at a birth, and it had been made quite clear exactly where his priorities lay, so Victor went to York to take an inventory. Elizabeth Wild was born, and later the same day Bettys reclaimed its most prestigious site.

That same year the government price restrictions on restaurant meals were finally lifted, and canned and dried fruit, treacle, syrup and preserves came off the ration, along with soap, which Bettys had been making from exhausted chip fat for use in-house for the past decade. Recovery was erratic, though, and in 1951 the meat ration was slashed as the government argued with Argentina over tariffs on beef. By 1952 Kay was pregnant again, this time with a son: when Jonathan was born Frederick declared he looked just like Henry VIII and presented him with a cigar (he smoked it on his 21st birthday, and it cleared the room). The relationship between Victor and Frederick was never entirely easy, but it was close: Victor drew cartoons for Frederick's birthdays, mocking him gently, to his great delight, and they shared a sense of humour and interest in the wider world. But Victor also felt constantly under scrutiny, insecure, and he struggled with Frederick's desire for him to shine in every activity he participated in and resented his uncle's pushiness and inability to sit still.

1952 was the year tea came off the ration, shortly followed by sugar, cream, eggs and sweets. Finally it seemed that Bettys would be able to get back to doing what it did best: making quality products and selling them in an elegant environment. However, on 4 October, a characteristically busy Saturday, Victor was in York when he received a phone call from Harrogate. Frederick, who had the habit of spending most mornings in his office on the top floor of Cambridge Crescent, had had a fatal heart attack. Victor later said that Frederick's death affected him far more deeply than he would have thought possible, that it 'felt as though all joy had suddenly been switched off'. He was 29, and now (mainly) in charge.

Exterior of Bettys in Northallerton

Beautiful Bettys

Silver teapot display at Bettys York

There's a Bettys look book, a characteristically thoughtful document setting out the expected standards for cleanliness and the care of the interiors and exteriors of each branch. It starts with the simple explanation that 'each Bettys has its own unique identity. The interior design of each branch is inspired by the individual character of each building,' adding, 'it is said that "you haven't done Bettys until you have done them all".' Having done them all, I tend to agree.

Many Bettys customers would agree that Bettys has a sense of timeless elegance. Those I've talked to cite details such as the wood panelling in the basement rooms of York and Harrogate, the wrought-iron canopies of Harrogate, Ilkley and York, the stained glass at York and Ilkley and the marble tables and padded wicker chairs common to all the branches. Some customers have spent time admiring the Spindler marquetry or envied the luscious hanging baskets and window boxes, while others retain a general impression of quality and craftsmanship.

When Frederick Belmont opened the first Bettys in 1919 he wrote proudly to his sister Ida, describing in great detail the colour schemes for each floor and the way in which the woodwork, mirrors, lighting and glass all combined to create the impression of opulence and comfort. Frederick was not a brilliant spatial planner, and his cafés suffered variously from badly thought-out kitchen placement, not

enough space for staff or, at York, a toilet too easily accessed from the road, so that it became the place to pop into for all passers-by. But he was devoted to making Bettys a place to showcase the best of local artistry and craft.

When Frederick made the decision to buy a furniture shop and convert it into Bettys York, his ideas were particularly audacious. He later admitted that paying homage to the *Queen Mary* was perhaps a little ambitious, and the project was very costly, but he did succeed in recreating the feel of a luxury liner in the centre of a Yorkshire city, employing many of the same craftsmen as the cruise ship. He visited the site once a week to check on progress, and one apprentice joiner recorded: 'He was very kind always to leave a five-pound note. My share was 10s which was a lot of money when I was

Top The Bettys 'B' as designed by Lesley Wild

Opposite Stained glass entrance canopy at Bettys York

earning less than 20s a week.' When the upstairs room, which had been the restaurant, was reopened after years of being used only for storage, it was named the Belmont Room in honour of Frederick and the pride he had taken in the branch he regarded as the jewel in his crown.

By the 1950s, the various branches of Bettys had become tired and looked old-fashioned. A new age was dawning, and by the 1960s psychedelia and bright, bold colours, along with synthetic materials, were the fashion. Frederick's silver-gilt teapots and elegant cake stands were old hat. However, Victor maintained his uncle's habit of using local artisans to add artistic flair when he was refurbishing the branches. He brought his own sharp sense of aesthetics into the business, knowing what would feel modern while still retaining a sense of elegance. While the gold lions, bright linoleum floor tiles and stripped-back ironmongery in Bettys Bradford may on the surface have had nothing in common with what came before – or after – underneath lay the same desire to create a sense of beauty. Bettys customers did not have a cup of tea and a bun, they had a Bettys experience.

That sense of creating an experience became even more important as the next generation came into the business, and the fashions of the 1960s became as outdated as those of the 1930s. Jonathan and his wife Lesley created the design team, and, as the business grew, various departments became responsible for the way in which branches looked. The name of the team changed, as did the people, but the concept remained clear: that Bettys was about beauty, and that maintaining the look and feel of branches was about not just polishing the existing brass and watering the plants but also carefully and constantly enhancing the experience that every customer had.

By 2017 a set of small teams had been formed, covering property and interior design, visual merchandising, graphics and other related areas. Working closely together, their remit covered all of the various parts of Bettys with which a customer might interact. The interiors team looked after everything from 'door handles to hanging baskets, crockery, cutlery, paint colours'. This includes ordering the bespoke tableware that bore the Bettys logo, as well as the carpet that Lesley had helped design in the 1980s, inspired by the Fat Rascal ingredients and which was now in every branch. Most regulars won't notice the gradual changes which keep the branches looking fresh and which include a shift from a slightly beige off-white paint to a slightly grey off-white paint for the walls.

Toilets were particularly important. Back in the 1950s one of the key points of difference between Bettys and their long-time rivals, Terry's, was the latter's marble toilets. Most customers will nip to the loo during their time in the café, and lack of cleanliness, a paucity of loo roll or poor-quality baby-changing facilities will easily make the difference between a good experience and a bad one. The look book is very clear that loo-roll dispensers should not be overfilled lest the paper rip when pulled, and that everything should be scrupulously clean. This includes dusting the orchids. Artificial air fresheners are banned.

The Bettys windows now have their own dedicated team as well. From the beginnings of Bettys, window displays were crucial to bringing customers into both the shop and the café, and by the 1980s the yearly Easter extravaganzas and the ever-changing chocolate menagerie were established talking points. For the centenary, a dazzling white display has gone into every branch, suited to each individual window set-up and centred on a glorious sugarwork cottage orné, each one hand-made in the bakery.

The centenary is also being celebrated with more permanent additions, including new entrance mosaics for the Belmont Room in York and Ilkley. Made by a local ceramicist, the one at Ilkley is inspired by the light florals of the one already in the entrance at Harrogate. In York the mosaic fits the art deco theme, being burnished black marble with the Bettys B picked out in bronze. They set in stone the pride and confidence with which Bettys is celebrating the past, while looking forward to the future.

A brave new world
1952–1962

What's on the menu?

With rationing finally over, Britons were free to embrace the foods they most loved. However, the post-war appetite had shrunk, and even as eating out boomed, set menus slimmed down: fewer courses, smaller portions. Although many people still wanted predominantly British food, there was a real appetite for the foods of other countries, especially Continental countries. It was, to some extent, a reflection of post-war politics, as the bruised nations of Europe came together to emphasise shared experiences and tried to put in place policies to prevent another world war. The United States was also seen as glamorous, thanks in no small part to all those gum-chewing GIs during the war.

This 1960s menu from the Leeds Midway Room reflects Bettys' attempts to attract the restaurant crowd, drawn from both the middle and the upper working classes: cosmopolitan (but not too much) and looking for gentle new experiences. There's a heady mixture of sound British favourites – fried fish, omelettes, ham and egg, steak pie, grilled meats and classical-sounding French dishes – all those tournedos, plus slightly left-field Continental and American choices. The addition of the word 'Continental' in front of the mixed grill and the hors d'oeuvres could mean anything, but certainly adds intrigue. The raviolis Napolitaine reflects the growth of Italian restaurants outside London and nascent interest in Mediterranean cuisine, while the prawn cocktail (Britain's favourite starter by the 1960s) and chicken Maryland represent America. The Honolulu ham listed as a special was almost certainly gammon and pineapple, Hawaii having successfully cornered the market in tinned pineapple (any left over could cunningly be recycled into the pineapple Tia Maria).

Bettys' own roots are also on show still, in the assiette Suisse, and the Betty's Swiss trifle. In common with much apparently exotic food at the time, this latter was a case of a grandiose name disguising a more down-to-earth dish: it was a mixture of rum flavouring and sugar-syrup-soaked leftover sponge or biscuit, some fake, rather dubious tinned jam, cornflour-based custard and cream (not necessarily real). Still, it was presented with flair and sat within a decidedly exciting sweet menu. Ice cream was now back with a bang and served in sundae glasses topped with a wafer. There were two boozy at-table flambés, which were decidedly modish in 1961.

Despite the ongoing British love of a good piece of plain grilled meat, the menu also has a nod to the interest in vegetarianism in the 1960s, albeit in the form of a rather non-specific 'vegetarian dish'. It was very niche – there were still only 34 vegetarian restaurants in the country by the late 1960s (nearly half in London), and it was relatively rare to find a dish labelled in this way on a mainstream menu. Overall, the whole menu is lighter than pre-war versions, and more varied. The Midway Room was a move away from straight café provision, with a bold new graphic identity intended to show that Bettys was embracing modernity, and the food was intended to reflect that. The graphic for the specials insert hints at a later 1960s development: the loss of the Bettys apostrophe in 1965.

SPECIAL DISHES

a la carte

SOUP & HORS D'OEUVRES

Cream Soup	1
Fruit or Tomato Juice	1
Grapefruit Cocktail	1
Fresh Grapefruit	1
Continental Hors d'oeuvres	3
Raviolis Napolitaine	4
Prawn Cocktail	4
Smoked Salmon	6

FISH

Fried Haddock	4/-
Fried Fillet of Plaice	4/6
Grilled Halibut Steak	5/-
Fried Scampi	6/-

OMELETTES

Ham & Asparagus	4/6
Mushroom & Tomato	4/6
Spanish	4/6

SALADS

Green Salad	3/-
Large Hors d'oeuvres	5/-
Ham, Tongue or Chicken Leg	5/-
Beef or Pork	6/-
Wing of Chicken	7/6
Salmon or Prawn	7/6

GRILLS & CONTINENTAL DISHES

Grilled Lamb Chop	4
Grilled Pork Chop	5
Ham & Egg	5
Assiette Suisse	7
Grilled Fillet Steak	9
Mixed Grill	9
Chicken Maryland	10
Tournedos Maitre d'hotel	10
Tournedos Cheval	10
Tournedos Marchand de Vin	11
Tournedos Chasseur	11
Tartare Steak	11
Half Chicken American	15
Chateaubriand (for 2)	25

Neapolitan Ice	1
Betty's Swiss Trifle	1
Meringue Glace	1
Peach Melba	2
Coupe Jacques	3
Coupe Brasiliene	3
Crepes Suzette (Flambe)	6
Pineapple Tia Maria (Flambe)	6
Cheese & Biscuits	1
Tea - Indian or China	1
Coffee	
Swiss Coffee	1

IAL DISHES
1 Steak Pie   3/-
1 Chicken Leg   3/6
1 Wing of Chicken   5/6
inental Mixed Grill   6/-

TABLES
ped or Creamed Potatoes   9d
en Peas   1/-
ch Beans   1/-
led Tomatoes   1/6
led Mushrooms   2/-
ion of Asparagus   4/-
tarian Dish   5/-

A menu from Bettys Leeds Midway,
June 1961

When Victor arrived in Harrogate, having driven post-haste up from York, he was plunged into business immediately. Frederick was dead, stretched out on the floor of his office, and the café below was rammed. The process of registering the death and the immediate administration now started. Claire had been notified, but Frederick had been closeted with one of his long-standing Swiss female coffee companions, Wanda Reynolds, at the time. In Claire's view they were decidedly more than friends, and she was so enraged that she now steadfastly refused to have anything to do with dealing with his death. The undertakers arrived and promptly said they could not take the body out via the service stairs at the back of the building and that the coffin would need to go out of the front. Taking a coffin down three flights of stairs through a café crowded with clientele would have been disastrous. Victor did what Frederick would doubtless have done and waited out the long afternoon until the shop and café closed.

However, this was only the beginning. Frederick had been the major shareholder, and his death was unexpected, albeit not altogether unsurprising with hindsight, given his weight, lack of exercise and heavy smoking. He had made no provision for death duties, then applied between spouses. Bettys' own assets were held by the company, but all of Frederick's personal wealth was subject to tax, and the Belmonts simply did not have the ready money to pay the Treasury. At the first Board meeting after Frederick's death: 'Mrs Belmont said it had been a heavy blow to everyone concerned with Bettys. As the main-spring of the company, his death would have far-reaching results, but she said that everyone should be determined to keep alive the tradition established by him, and that the business should continue in the same spirit as before.'

Frederick Belmont in his study, 1946

Bettys was a finely balanced business now: the mixture of cafés, shops and some wholesale provided the sales necessary to sustain the bakery, and having a dedicated Bettys bakery was, in turn, vital to control costs and maintain the quality upon which the company had built its reputation. There was very little wiggle room, although mortgages were taken out on the sites the company owned, both to start saving the tax money and to finance bakery improvements which were already in hand. An external legal advisor called Bill Dixon was brought in to try to work out some way by which Bettys could pay the death duties without destroying a business which was only just emerging from the hardships of the war. Fortunately, the Treasury was well used to such scenarios, and willing to allow time for negotiation and payment. Other much-needed renovations were immediately put on hold while Victor took stock of what Bettys was, who was in charge, and what more could be done.

It was a rapidly changing world, caught between the drabness of war – tea and coffee were still rationed in 1952 – and the colourful

The exterior of Bettys York

'... everyone should be determined to keep alive the tradition established by him, and that the business should continue in the same spirit as before.'

1960s whirl of mini-skirts and the summer of love. By 1957 the then Prime Minister, Harold Macmillan, was confidently proclaiming that Britain had 'never had it so good', adding: 'Go around the country, go to the industrial towns, go to the farms and you will see a state of prosperity such as we have never had in my lifetime – nor indeed in the history of this country.' Nevertheless, the high street was caught in flux, with many of the stores which had been damaged by bombs closing for good.

The traditional tearoom model was particularly hit: the ABC had shrunk by two thirds, and Lyons too was closing branches. Lyons pumped money into its three London Corner Houses, especially the one on Oxford Street, which notoriously never made any money but did provide a site for experimentation, as it was a huge space, easily subdivided into smaller concessions. Their names were mainly self-explanatory and included Haversnack in 1952, along with Snack Corner, Bacon and Egg, Grill and Cheese, The Trolley (roast meats), Chicken Fayre and, in 1955, the first American-style burger and fast-food restaurant, Wimpy. Wimpy was the most successful by far – serving over 40,000 customers a week and eventually spawning a global chain.

The public was moving away from set-price three- or four-course lunches and toward quicker meals, led, in towns, by the needs of workers with short lunch breaks. More meals were being eaten outside the home by the working classes, who now found they had more disposable income as living standards rose

and salaries grew. Where once the average household spent one third of its income on food, now more money was available for leisure – or mortgages – and home and car ownership slowly crept up to over 40 per cent. The first motorway in Britain, the M1, opened in 1958, and the BBC gained its first TV rival when Independent Television (now ITV) launched in 1955. Horizons were broadening, especially with regard to food, and Italian, Chinese and Indian restaurants were starting to expand outside London and ports with resident ethnic communities.

Meanwhile, on the cookery shelves, books reflecting cuisine from around the world shared space with a rash of books written by old-style country-house cooks, harking back to the days before the Second World War when meals were lavish and servants more plentiful. Notions of old English generosity jostled with (as ever) French sophistication, but onto the scene now came Elizabeth David and Patience Gray, waxing lyrical about Mediterranean food, and Constance Spry encouraging cooks to commune with their gardens. This was also the age of the ebullient Fanny Cradock, who blazed a TV trail from 1955 exhorting housewives to cook with all restraint abandoned. She

An early Wimpy Bar, Barnsley, South Yorkshire, 1960

The iconic Lyons Corner House, 1931

played to full houses at the Albert Hall, where she cooked in heavy make-up and an evening gown (made in a slightly more wipe-clean format than most of her fans necessarily realised). Her shows were broadcast in full colour from 1968, showcasing her infamous delight in food colouring and food that was, unlike during the war years, emphatically not brown.

In Yorkshire, the economic boom helped to boost all of the
Bettys towns: Bradford's textile industry was in terminal decline,
but the city now had manufacturers turning out tractors and
televisions instead. Leeds was also shedding its traditional
industries, to be replaced with the service sector, and city centre
rents rose astronomically. York still had tourism, the races and
chocolate, and was a hub for the surrounding countryside. Even
in Harrogate, business was doing well, and the much-feared
impact of the new NHS had, in fact, turned out to be a good
thing, as NHS doctors prescribed water cures for their patients,
now state-subsidised. The once-private hospitals enjoyed a brief
boom thanks to state-sponsored healthcare: there were 130,000
treatments in 1955, of which only 20 per cent were private.
However, the nature of the clientele changed, and debate over
the future of the town raged (NHS treatments would be stopped
in 1968, effectively ending Harrogate's days as a spa town).
Tourism was one answer, playing on Harrogate's existing

Miss Vera Morgan hand-decorating
wedding cakes at Bettys, Cambridge
Crescent, Harrogate, 1960

reputation for elegance and rejuvenation, and in 1953 the former Royal Pump Room opened as a museum. The same year saw the first 'flower academy', and by 1956 the Harrogate Flower Show was well on its way to becoming the biggest flower show in the UK. The Northern Horticultural Society had opened a garden on the moors above the town, at Harlow Carr, in 1950. There was also the burgeoning conference trade, which continued to be a source of local income, and in 1959 a purpose-built exhibition hall and car park were constructed in place of the old rose garden behind the Royal Hall.

Bettys was, like most of the towns in which it was present, in need of renovation. The premises were all very tired still, and the staff overall lacked the expertise that had existed pre-war. Some people did return – or tried to. The ex-manager of Bettys Bradford, who had been called up in the 1940s, reappeared, but had to be gently rejected as he was now an alcoholic. There were a few long-standing employees, including stalwarts such as Jessie Radcliffe, who had started at Bettys in 1926 and stayed for over 60 years. She headed up the confectionery room in the bakery, making brandy snaps, toffees and truffles – all the craft items which needed personal attention – and was married to the storeman. There was also Vera Morgan, the cake-decorating specialist, who worked out of the top floor of Cambridge Crescent, fulfilling the wedding cake orders which now started to come back in. She trained up a junior, Shirley Fell, and after Vera's retirement Shirley and Jessie Radcliffe of the main bakery formed the Bettys cake-decorating team until the 1980s. When they were busy, orders had to be turned away. Shirley later recalled that one of the highlights of working at Cambridge Crescent was the view out onto the square below, where on one particularly windy day she and Vera Morgan watched a small dog float momentarily above the ground.

The (female) supervisors of the branches were also long-term staff, far outlasting the (male) managers put in above their heads, who had a habit of leaving for more glamorous jobs in hotels, or falling out with Claire, or who simply weren't suitable. All called 'Miss', regardless of marital status, the supervisors kept the branches running smoothly in the face of financial turmoil, managerial upset and family tensions at the top. The exception was Miss Bradford, in Leeds, one of Claire's relatives who 'rather did what she felt like doing'. She couldn't be removed while Claire was still around, and since both Claire and Victor appointed themselves directors for life in 1956, she looked set to be there as long as she wanted. Claire's nephew Neville too was still an issue, and his inability to work as part of a team or to communicate impacted on the bakery, especially in relation to passing skills on. Victor had bemoaned his own lack of training, but company training did not improve when he took over. Bettys still couldn't recruit enough staff to allow those who were there to spend time learning in any other way than piecemeal and on the job. Catering was badly paid and unglamorous. Bettys front-of-house uniforms hadn't changed for decades, and the 'nippy' style black-and-white uniform with starched white collars and cuffs and bibbed apron and hat was out of step with new fashion. Additionally, despite government legislation requiring companies to pay their waiting staff (instead of them relying on tips), they were badly paid – Bettys waitresses were on 25 shillings a week.

Luckily, the competition was not in a much better state. In Harrogate, described as 'desolate' by the *Good Food Guide* in 1955, both the Café Imperial and the Taylors' Kiosks were very shabby, and the council contracts which had sustained the company during the 1920s were no more. Both premises were largely inhabited by elderly gentlemen, and the smoke room at the Imperial had become a quasi-club for its regulars, who spent as little money as possible, mainly ordering soup, and had their post directed there when they were on holiday. It closed early, even during the flower shows, when Bettys had queues around the corner. Charles Taylor, who had co-founded the company with his brother Llewellyn in the 1880s, had died in 1942, and it was now run by their sons, Bernard and Douglas. Both had fought in the First World War, and Bernard was by now a hedonist alcoholic, while Douglas's existing learning difficulties had been compounded by shell shock. Like Bettys, Taylors was de facto run by another nephew, Jim Raleigh, but it had badly lost its way and was now retreating to its roots as a tea and coffee blenders. Standings too had gone downhill, which left Bettys' main rival as Hammond Mann's, a confectioners with a café, of superb quality but amateurishly run. In York, the principal competition for Bettys was still Terry's, which recovered well and quickly regained its position as the city's pre-eminent

Bettys waitresses in the Belmont Room
at Bettys York, c.1950s

café-restaurant. Within the local market especially, it won hands down. Unless Bettys could find the money to refurbish, Frederick's flagship now looked set to fail.

In 1955 a plan was finally drawn up which would enable Bettys to pay off the £40,000 death duty bill while remaining viable. The company was sold in full to another business and bought back the next day, minus its accrued undistributed profits (there were legal limitations on what could be distributed at the time). The price difference left Claire with cash, enabling her to pay the Treasury. It was an incredibly complicated deal, which occupied Victor, Bill Dixon and the Bettys legal team for years – Bill would later be made a director in recognition of his invaluable role.

Unfortunately, in the wealth of administration related to this in the spring of 1955, the legal team failed to arrange the renewal of the lease in Bradford. By November Bettys was embroiled in what would be a six-year court case against its landlord, first winning and then losing twice at successive stages. The case hinged upon whether the landlord giving notice of its intention to refurbish the property halfway through the first hearing counted as enough notice to warrant Bettys, as the tenant, being evicted. It was an important enough point of law that the case set precedent, and, although it eventually went all the way to the House of Lords, most of the legal costs were borne by the other side.

Looking back, Victor wasn't convinced that the time and hassle were entirely warranted, but at the time he was desperate to prove himself, and losing a branch so early on in his career at Bettys was unthinkable. Taking the case all the way, even after they'd lost the second hearing, also bought the company valuable time, first to secure a lease and then to make ready an alternative premises, just across the road at 43–45 Darley Street. Victor also enjoyed both the intellectual stimulation of the case and

The first floor restaurant at Bettys, 43–45 Darley Street, Bradford, 1958

the chance to peer into one of the most hallowed of British institutions. He recorded gleefully that 'one felt one was moving in very exalted corridors', being able to go anywhere in the Lords' building (except the Lords' loo) and said he'd thoroughly enjoyed it. Part of the joy lay in the distraction it provided from the continuous angst of running Bettys.

By 1956, with the court case rumbling on but death duties now paid, Victor was finally able to turn his attention to the branches. Bettys had achieved a certain cachet despite its difficulties, and in 1956 when the AA rosette system first came in, and the AA released its first annual handbook of hotels, all four Bettys branches were listed. There were very few eating places in the handbook, for this was before rosettes were awarded for restaurants, so clearly Bettys was deemed to be the kind of service AA members needed to know about – along with the garages, petrol stations and mechanics which also made an appearance. However, it was a long time since the branches had looked their best. Harrogate was given a basic refurbishment but otherwise mainly left alone, Frederick's remaining four prized Spindler pieces now stored indefinitely. The new carpets were a bespoke Bettys pattern which later became known as 'splodge', being a classically 1960s

Coffee bar area on the ground floor of
Bettys Bradford, 1958–1965

abstract pattern of blue-grey daubs. It was designed by Victor with the specific brief of not showing food spills.

Bradford was a more serious undertaking, following the move across the street. The site had previously been Fullers Café and Bradford Ladies' Club, and the move was a chance for Victor to flex his artistic muscles. He could also implement all of the spatial planning thoughts he had had through long years of working in Frederick's badly planned branches (where waitresses seemed at times to spend more time running up and down stairs to the kitchen than actually serving their clientele). As a result, it was splendid. It stuck to the usual formula, with a ground-floor shop and café, exuberantly decked out with coloured vinyl floor tiles, ultra-modern laminate chairs and Chinese-influenced wallpaper featuring giant golden lions on a black background. The local paper described it as 'striking'. The first floor held the restaurant, 'treated [in a] more subdued manner', with somewhat more traditional furniture surrounded by modern, light wood panelling and minimalist chandeliers. It could be converted into a function room if necessary, meaning Bettys could now cater for two (or even three) weddings at a time, for this was in addition to the second-floor ballroom. The ballroom had a 'slightly Spanish' feel, with built-in bar, 'gay curtains, maple dance floor and elegant chairs'. Overall, the café would seat 120, with Victor hoping to serve 300 lunches a day. There was now a customer lift, with a view onto a mural which ran the height of the building and depicted fashions of the 1850s. It was all defiantly modern, very much a rejection of the Edwardian-meets-art-deco feel of the previous premises, but then there was no appetite for that now: in an age when the Russians were about to launch the silvery *Sputnik* into orbit, all those pastel-coloured uplighters and tinted mirrors seemed old-fashioned.

While Bradford was being readied for opening, in 1958 Victor turned to Leeds. It was another problematic site. It was a prime location – one of the best in town – but spend per head was low, and, as demand for city centre space soared in the mid 1950s, the profits generated from selling set lunches plus cakes and bread didn't match up to rising rents. Mid-range cafés like Bettys were being priced out of central locations, and it was now that Frederick's purchase of the freeholds really made a difference. Still, no branch could afford to be unprofitable.

The interior of Bettys Leeds,
c.1960s

With interest in foods from southern Europe apparently growing, Victor decided to open a delicatessen counter. It was a very forward-looking move: the Mediterranean food revolution was hardly noticeable outside Soho, and even the arch-promotor of olives and Italian cheeses, Elizabeth David, admitted later that it was virtually impossible to get the ingredients at the time. In spite – or perhaps because – of this, the counter, under a Polish émigré called Mr Symackz, was very successful, quickly branching out from Bettys-made sausage rolls and meat pies and into cooked meats. In 1960 Bettys opened a deli counter in York, and also reclaimed one of the shops under the café over at Cambridge Crescent to open a separate delicatessen in Harrogate (it remained open until 1976). Leeds was the town chosen for a venture into suburbia, as Victor pondered whether city centres would become too expensive for any stores selling anything other than luxury goods. He bought the freehold for 71 Street Lane and opened a stand-alone coffee shop, with no Bettys branding (but selling Bettys goods exclusively).

Emerging again from Soho, the British coffee shop craze was all about Italian chic, and in Leeds the first thing any customer saw in The Coffee Shop was the gleaming Gaggia espresso maker on

The Coffee Shop, Street Lane, Leeds,
15 April 1955

the back counter. The front of the Street Lane shop was angled plate glass, stacked with Bettys loaves but affording a full view of the interior, complete with bar stools and chequered chairs. It was a cake shop by day and a gloriously cool coffee bar by night. The night-time venture tapped into a new clientele for caterers, a discernible youth culture, made up of teenagers (the school leaving age was now 16) and young twenty-somethings with money to spend. The customers weren't always of legal drinking age, and pubs in any case were often very down-at-heel, while restaurants were too expensive. Milk bars had catered to the start of this market before the Second World War, but, with coffee shops, youth culture exploded. By 1960 there were around 2,000 in the UK.

Finally, Victor turned to York. The Dive had lost its clientele with the departure of the Canadians, and Victor was eager to cast off its highly dubious reputation. The basement was now converted into an upscale restaurant called the Oak Room, with a menu ranging from turtle soup to lamb korma, served and cooked by Italian staff in a room with plush carpets and immaculate white tablecloths. It took £12,000 to convert the room and upgrade the general décor, which also included the cost of expanding into the building next door, and yet another attempt to reorganise the kitchens and other facilities to enable more efficient service (and move the ladies' loo from the front entrance, where passers-by could nip in and use the facilities).

It worked: the Oak Room was immediately successful, and Mario Poggi, the restaurant manager, was dispatched to Italy to recruit more staff. By 1961 it had made it into the *Good Food Guide* (first published in 1951), which described it as 'underground but well-ventilated … it provides what York has long been needing – a careful menu of international cooking, not large, but skilfully prepared'. The guide remarked that: 'even the curries have their proper accompaniments', although the writer noted that the bottled tartare sauce with the scampi was a bit alarming. Some dishes were prepared at the table, including the veal escalope à la crème ('the star of the show'), and by 1960 the menu included several sweets to be flambéed in front of the customer. (Marguerite Patten, one of most influential food writers of the time, remarked of 1960s cuisine that 'we flambéed meat, we flambéed fruit salad – it was one of the great show-off

dishes'.) In 1962 the fritto misto was singled out for praise in the
guide, which also noted that 'Betty's café has existed for a long
time', and that the Oak Room 'is serving food much above the
usual York level (which is low)'.

Meanwhile, the ground floor was expanded (part of it had been
sublet to a florist, who had now left), still keeping the cocktail
bar, but with more space for the shop-café (now also an
occasional off-licence). On the first floor a new Belmont Room,
named for Frederick, was opened in the building next door, with
a huge mural of Swiss mountains painted by Victor. It was set
up as a self-service restaurant, another concept which was
breaking new ground in the 1950s. Lyons had put in self-service

Opposite The interior of Bettys, St Helen's Square, York, showing coffee bar and shop, c.1960s

Top The Oak Room, Bettys York, with Italian waiters, 1960–65

during the war, and never really converted back, and, over in grocery retail, the first self-service Sainsbury's had opened in Croydon in 1950. It was not universally popular. As one shopper put it: 'I think it is very cold and there is not much conversation goes on, and it's not so cheery as what the old shops were.' At Bettys the experiment was more successful, and people happily queued for fish and chips and steak pies supplied by the bakery. Victor tried expanding the more successful elements from York, such as the delis, elsewhere, and he opened the Midway Room in Leeds in October 1960 as a slightly toned-down version of the Oak Room. Unfortunately, the internal arrangement of the branch was less than ideal, with problematic kitchen access, and it only lasted for a few years.

By 1960 the business was doing well, reborn as a fashionable but comfortable café-restaurant with quality home-made products. At home too life had settled into a routine: the Wilds now had three children (Antony was born in 1955). Auntie Bunny had insisted that the family relocate from the bungalow that had been their first home. Now they lived on Kent Road, doors away from Claire, in a house which she had insisted on buying for them, for the address was prestigious enough to impress her friends and close enough that she could easily drop in several times a week. It was rather too close, especially given that relations between them remained fraught. Claire and Frederick's adopted daughter Valerie, now a teenager, was caught in the middle.

The final straw came when Valerie and Claire's elderly live-in housekeeper Agnes had a falling out, at which point Valerie went to live with Victor and Kay. However, they struggled to balance her needs with those of their own small children, especially when Claire was always on hand to countermand a rule or buy her lavish gifts in lieu of offering affection. Jonathan remembered her as being like a 'cooler older sister'. Claire then insisted that Valerie be sent to a Swiss finishing school, after which, following stints training to be a beautician and working at ICI, she joined Bettys as a supervisor. Despite Claire's desire for control, Valerie wanted to make her own choices in life, and to Claire's dismay this included falling in love. Rodney Light was doing maintenance work at Kent Road, and he and Valerie were instantly attracted. They started going out, and when Valerie fell pregnant, they got married, remaining happily together until Valerie's sudden death at the age of 54.

Victor found all of this increasingly frustrating, but he shied away from conflict, and, as with the business, he found ways to work around Claire rather than confronting her. He worked long hours, more often away from home than present, and when he was at Kent Road, he kept himself busy – 'frenetic', as Jonathan later put it. Victor admitted that 'I built walls for all I was worth'; he terraced the large, steep garden at Kent Road, constantly remodelling it, as well as building a fish pond with a viewing mirror and a small swimming pool. The children enthusiastically joined in, and together they built treehouses and dug trenches, the three of them 'following him around as willing servants'. He also had a large first-floor studio and spent hours painting as well as playing the piano.

Outside these activities, Victor sometimes seemed isolated, his Swissness and unconventionality marking him out at the occasional parents' event he attended at the children's schools.

Menu for the Oak Room, Bettys York, 1960

BETTYS
OAK ROOM
RESTAURANT

OPEN 12 - 2.30p.m. & 6 - 10.30p.m.

SOUP & HORS D'OEUVRES
Cream or Clear Soup with Croutons	1/6
Real Turtle Soup with Sherry	3/6
Fresh Grapefruit Maraschino	1/6
Iced Melon & Ginger Sugar	2/6
Hors d'oeuvres Varies	4/6
Prawn Cocktail with Brown Bread & Butter	4/6
Ravioli in Tomato Sauce	5/-
Smoked Scotch Salmon with Brown Bread & Butter	6/

FISH
Fried Fillet of Plaice with Tartare Sauce	5/-
Rainbow Trout Meuniere & Parsley Butter	6/-
Fried Scampi with Lemon Tartare Sauce & Buttered Patna Rice	10/6
Scampi Mornay with Buttered Patna Rice	11/6
Fresh Scotch Salmon Steak Meuniere & Parsley Butter	11/6
Large Dover Sole Colbert	11/6
Large Dover Sole au Vin Blanc	12/6

SALADS
Fresh Scotch Salmon	10/-
One half of Spring Chicken	9/6
Ham	8/-
Prawn	8/6
Fresh Lobster according to size	

POULTRY
One half of Roast Spring Chicken with Bacon, Sausage & Stuffing	9/6
Chicken Maryland with Sweet Corn, Fried Banana & Tomato	9/6
Roast Duckling with Apple Sauce, Sage & Onion Stuffing	12/6
Coq au Vin Rouge	14/-

OMELETTES
Chicken & Asparagus - 4/9   Mushroom & Tomato - 4/6   Prawn - 5/-

GRILLS
Lamb Cutlets with Mushroom, Tomato & Mint Sauce	7/6
Pork Chop with Pineapple ring & Savoury Stuffing	7/6
Ham with Egg & Grilled Tomato	7/6
Rump Steak with Tomato, Mushroom & Fried Onion	10/-
English Fillet Steak with Mushroom, Tomato & Fried Onion	11/6
Mixed Grill - Lamb Chop, Gammon, Steak, Sausage, Egg, Mushroom, Onion & Tomato	11/6
Tournedos Chasseur 12/6 Steak Diana	12/6

CURRIES
Anda Ka Salan - Eggs	7/6
Koormah - Lamb	7/6
Bagda Chingree - Prawns	9/6
Maddrassi Ka Moorgi - Quarter of Spring Chicken	9/6

(Curry Dishes served with Buttered Patna Rice, Popadums, Asparagus, Rajah Pickles, Banana & Mango Chutney)

VEGETABLES
Roast Potatoes 1/6	New Potatoes 1/6	Chipped Potatoes 1/-	Whole Carrots 1/-
Celery Hearts 2/-	Green Salad 2/-	Garden Peas 1/-	French Beans 1/6
	Grilled Mushrooms 2/-		

SWEETS
Peach Melba 3/-   Banana Split 3/-   Vanilla or Strawberry Ice 1/6   Pear Melba 3/-
Betty's Sherry Trifle 3/-   Pineapple Melba 3/-   Crepe Suzette (Flambé) 9/-
Coffee or Chocolate Ice 1/6   Fresh Fruit Salad with Ice Cream 3/6
Banana, Pineapple, or Apple Fritter with Fresh Dairy Cream & Hot Jam Sauce 3/6

CHEESE BOARD & BISCUITS 2/6
POT OF COFFEE WITH FRESH DAIRY CREAM 1/3
WINE BY CARAFE 5/-

St HELEN'S SQUARE
YORK

Jonathan remembered that he didn't seem as much of a businessman as some of the other fathers (and he was embarrassingly bad at cricket). He eschewed the social climbing of Claire, with her bridge and golf and concern over what people thought, quietly believing in humanism when the Harrogate great and good were ostentatiously Church of England, and never quite caring about the opinions of others as much as Claire wanted him to. He was still an artist at heart, joining the Choral Society and the local Dramatic Society, quickly rising to be a primary organiser of their events, as driven in his leisure pursuits as he was at work. But he also tried hard not to bring work home, and, while inevitably discussions circulated over the dinner table, he was determined not to pressurise his children into feeling that they had to be part of Bettys or that their choices should be limited by the background of being part of a family business.

Kay, at this stage, was also not officially involved, other than playing a muted role as the boss's wife. She was an impeccable hostess, elegantly and expensively dressed, masterminding New Year's parties in the biggest room of the house, which had a proper dance floor and chandeliers. The food was all from Bettys, mainly made by a Mr Cass. He'd started in Bettys under his full name, Kasimir Brasinskas, as an Oak Room chef but was now the catering equivalent of Miss Morgan the cake decorator, and essentially a highly skilled one-man band, capable of turning out a whole salmon with pastry and cucumber scales, and even, one year, a stuffed boar's head. Jonathan, clearing the glasses the morning after, drank flat Moët champagne (years later, he would add Moët to the Bettys menu in homage to the past).

Parties were a potentially lucrative market for Bettys, hence the improvements at Bradford, designed to secure Bettys' reputation

Victor and Kay Wild with their daughter Elizabeth in the sun porch at their Harrogate home, 1965

Photograph taken by the *Yorkshire Evening Post* of Italian waiters and Bettys Manageress, Miss May Carter. This was the waiters' first visit to England to learn the language and gain experience of working in the country. 21 July 1960

as the best place to hold a catered event. However, with the Street Lane coffee shop open and the delicatessens doing well, it made more sense for the bakery to concentrate on products that could be easily made and supplied to as many outlets as possible. Now Victor started supplementing the in-house range with bought-in goods, including pies and Easter eggs, which were bought from the Continent, as the bakery's own attempts at mass production had been unsuccessful. In 1960 another stand-alone branch was opened at Allerton Road in Bradford. Again, this was a small café, and, like Street Lane, it did not have the Bettys branding (both stores operated under a subsidiary called Belmont & Co). From outside, all seemed to be going very well. However, all six branches operated very independently. All of Victor's grand plans for American-style efficiency, with integrated systems and a full training plan for new apprentices, had so far been lost in the reality of running a business in the midst of legal wrangles and with a fellow director who was both uninterested and obstructive. In 1962 a chance conversation, overheard by the Harrogate branch manager May Carter in the street in Harrogate, offered a new set of opportunities for distraction: their great, if faded, rival Taylors was about to go on sale. Victor, never averse to a challenge, picked up the phone.

Bettys and Taylors

1962–1975

What's on the menu?

By 1967 Bettys was nearly 50 years old. Very little of its Swiss roots was evident on the menu. Beady-eyed customers after a snack to go with their morning coffee or afternoon tea would, perhaps, spot the 'Swiss cakes' (general pastry goods with a Continental bent) or the apple strudel and elsewhere the (rather un-Swiss) 'Swiss trifle' still featured on other menus of the time. The menu overall is decidedly British, though, with tea cakes and scones, rarebits and sardine sandwiches. Despite Victor's scathing view of the York competition serving 'things on toast' in the 1950s, this menu is centred on exactly that, including the quintessentially British spaghetti on toast. (When the Italian chain the Spaghetti House had started in 1955, its slogan was 'spaghetti! Not on toast.') Even the hot dishes are utterly mainstream, with an emphasis on fried meat and all with chips.

It was a difficult era: even the iconic Lyons Corner Houses had just closed, despite increasingly desperate attempts to revive them with different concessions within the main buildings, and Bettys did well by offering exactly what its customers wanted. The aesthetics of the menu were Victor's; while he employed local artists to illustrate the covers of some of the menus (especially in the Oak Room), he retained control of the overall feel, and regularly tweaked the look throughout the 1960s and 1970s. In this case, the look of the menu fits the food, which, in turn, reflects the image that Bettys now had: classy but traditional, a safe pair of hands. This was a Bettys where one could sup an elegant Ceylon tea, but also slurp a hefty cup of Bovril, a drink that had developed from beef tea, the health beverage of choice for Victorians and Edwardians.

Upstairs at York, the self-service Belmont room offered a very similar menu, with the addition of battered fish and chips, a Cornish pasty and pizza. The offering was fairly uniform and worked well across the branches, even when the menu design was changed to a more funky, brightly coloured version in the early 1970s, the food remained very similar. One of the 1970s menus offered a 'weight watchers' special (cottage cheese), a half-hearted nod to the latest fashion to influence British food, and space was left for weekly specials. In the main, though, despite the growth of package holidays and the rise of Indian, Chinese and Italian restaurants, British food tastes remained conservative: the pineapple with pork was as exotic as most people wanted to get. That said, the Oak Room continued to operate throughout the era, offering curries and Italian dishes alongside a more generally Continental cuisine. Meanwhile, in Harrogate and Leeds the Continental delicatessens also remained a fixture, admittedly selling steak pies along with the salami, sauerkraut, Eastern European and French cheeses.

TEA MENU

BEVERAGES

Ceylon Tea . . .	1/6
China Tea . .	1/6
Russian-style Tea .	1/6
Coffee , , .	1/9
Black Coffee with Cream	1/9
Chocolate or Horlicks .	2/-
Bovril . . .	1/3
Milk – hot or cold .	1/3
Schweppes Fruit Drinks	1/3

TEACAKES, ETC.

Toasted or Buttered Teacakes	10d.
Toasted or Buttered Scone	10d.
Buttered Toast . .	9d.
Buttered Bread . .	9d.
Gateau . .	2/3
Swiss Cakes 10d. 1/- 1/3 &	1/6
Jam – per person . .	9d.

TOAST

Beans, Sardines, Tomatoes or Spaghetti . .	3/3
Poached Egg on Toast .	2/9
Grilled Mushrooms .	4/-
Buck Rarebit .	5/3
Welsh Rarebit .	4/9
Creamed Mushrooms .	3/6
Mushroom Vol-au-Vent	3/3

SANDWICHES

Tomato . . .	2/6
Egg & Cress, Mixed Salad, Ham, Cheese or Sardines	2/9
Chicken . . .	3/9

Y.6/67

GRILLS & POULTRY

Rump Steak with Tomato, Mushrooms and Onions . .	12/-
Gammon with Egg and Tomato .	9/-
Lamb Cutlets, Mushrooms, Tomato and Mint Sauce	9/-
Pork Fillet, Pineapple & Stuffing .	9/-
Pork Sausages, Bacon, Egg and Tomato . . .	8/-
Pork Sausages and Tomato . .	5/6
Fried Egg with Tomato . .	3/6
Half of Roast Chicken with Bacon, Sausage and Stuffing . . .	11/-

FISH

Fillet of Plaice with Tartare Sauce	8/6
Fillet of Haddock with Lemon .	8/-

OMELETTES

Mushroom, Ham, Cheese, Fine Herbs or Chicken	7/-

CHIPPED POTATOES
ARE INCLUDED WITH THE ABOVE DISHES

Green Peas 1/-

New Potatoes 1/3

* * * * * * * * * *

TEA   MENU

COLD BUFFET

Salmon Salad . .	11/6
Prawn Salad . .	11/6
Ham Salad . . .	8/-
Egg Mayonnaise . .	7/-
Hors de Oeuvre . 5/- & 7/-

ICES

Ice Cream Meringue .	2/3
Pineapple Centre .	2/9
Chocolate Nut Sundae .	2/9
Peach or Pineapple Melba	2/9
Banana Split .	2/9
Knickerbocker Glory .	4/-
Vanilla Ice with:	
Fresh Fruit Salad .	3/6
Crushed Pineapple .	2/3
Fruit Jelly .	2/3
Chocolate Sauce .	2/3
Coffee & Walnut Sauce	2/3

PLAIN ICES

Vanilla, Strawberry, Coffee, Chocolate . .	1/3
Assorted Ice Cream Bricks	1/9
Assorted Ice Cream Sodas	2/3

BETTY'S SPECIALITIES

Sherry Cream Trifle .	2/6
Vanilla & Pineapple Slice Melba . .	3/3
Apple Strudel & Dairy Cream	3/3
Fresh Dairy Cream .	9d.

A Tea Menu from Bettys York,
June 1967

C. E. Taylor & Company's Café Imperial
(later Bettys Harrogate), 1 Parliament
Street, Harrogate, c.1920s

In July 1962 Victor Wild bought the entire Taylors business, then called C. E. Taylor & Company, for the asking price of £180,000. He was paying mainly for its property portfolio; the business itself had been run virtually into the ground, retaining only the tail end of any customer loyalty in the towns where it had branches. The two cousins who had taken it over in the 1940s had invested neither time nor energy into it as trading conditions improved, and, when Bernard Taylor died in 1956, Douglas was left in nominal charge. Incapable of running a business as Douglas was, as a result of shell shock and mental incapacity, it was only because of Bernard's nephew by marriage, Jim Raleigh, that Taylors limped on as long as it did.

As part of the sale, Douglas agreed to stay on for a while to provide some continuity for staff, but he was never a great asset. Jim, on the other hand, who was Chairman at the time, was a crucial figure. He was 60 and looking forward to retiring on the proceeds of the sale, but Victor managed to persuade him to

Left Charles Edward Taylor, co-founder of C. E. Taylor & Company

Right Llewellyn Henry Taylor, co-founder of C. E. Taylor & Company

stay and act as an interim caretaker for the coffee and tea wholesale business, of which no one at Bettys had any experience. It was not Bettys' core business: the company had very suddenly acquired a whole new set of buildings, staff and customers, and, despite the potential opportunities around coffee and tea, that part of Taylors that was neither a bakery nor a café was hardly a high priority.

The most prestigious of the new cafés was in Harrogate, the Café Imperial at 1 Parliament Street, an impressive mock-Scottish baronial castle dating from 1901. It had been purpose-built as a catering outlet, starting life, like Bettys, as a confectioners and café, offering musical interludes over afternoon tea. By the 1920s, now under Taylors management, it had undergone a complete refurbishment, with a café offering light meals on the ground floor, a tea and luncheon room on the floor above, and various function rooms on the floor above that. In the basement was the male-oriented smoking room. It would perhaps have made sense for Bettys to move in, but the whole set-up was dismally lit, badly decorated (in 'fire-engine red') and falling apart by the time Victor took it over. Downstairs, by a huge window facing the road, was the main safe, the justification being that if it was always on view, this would put off would-be thieves.

The lack of profits probably did the same, for it had made a trading loss of £618 in the six months leading up to the sale. The Bettys staff had had a glimpse into the inner workings of their once-rival earlier in the year, when a fire had broken out at Cambridge Crescent the day before the top floor was due to host a wedding. Victor had been at the cinema at the time, and had to be found, as no one else had the keys to the branch. He was mortified, but at least saved Bettys with only minimal damage. The cakes had to be hastily, redecorated though, and water damage rendered the room intended for the wedding unusable, so the party decamped to the Imperial, which was empty. It was a better location than Cambridge Crescent but needed a lot of money spent on it if it was to match the elegance of its new owner. For now, therefore, it remained the Café Imperial, with Mr Cass, the main force behind event catering, brought over to manage it. Profits did go up, but, as Victor remarked, 'it wasn't a Bettys, and not even Cass could turn it into one'.

C. E. Taylor & Company's Kiosk Café,
16 Parliament Street, Harrogate, c.1920

'... a good blender was "as much an artist as a good painter".'

Taylors had other cafés too, despite having sold off branches in Keighley and Wakefield as part of an earlier attempt to boost the business. There were Taylors' Kiosks in Harrogate and Ilkley, as well as a single, non-Yorkshire outpost in Lytham St Annes. These were all ground-floor shops selling tea and coffee, ground and/ or blended to the customer's requirements, with first-floor cafés offering a slender menu of light meals and cakes. Ilkley also had another Café Imperial, also operating at a loss. Then there were two bakeries, one in Ilkley and another (which came as something of a surprise to Victor) on Oxford Street in Harrogate.

In addition, there was the main Taylors blending and packaging factory, and the head office, which since the 1930s had been squashed into various rooms and an ever-expanding wooden shed in the backyard of 12 Blenheim Terrace in Leeds. Once a relatively substantial Georgian townhouse, this was extremely badly set up as an industrial unit, especially as machinery – and vehicles – got bigger in the 1960s. There was no access for cars to the back of the house, so twice a week the front window of what had been the drawing room had to be removed, and a temporary conveyor belt installed, in order to dispatch the packed boxes into the waiting delivery vans. The building was listed, so it was hard to make any alterations.

The business had originally thrived on supplying small-scale grocers and caterers with proprietary blends of tea, each tweaked slightly to suit the local water. Both Llewellyn and Charles Taylor, the two original founding brothers, had started out as buyers and blenders with Ashby's Tea Merchants in London, before returning to Yorkshire to set up their own business, with Charles firm in his belief that a good blender was 'as much an artist as a good painter'. Now, like their cafés, Taylors' tea and coffee business was struggling to compete: grocers were increasingly being eclipsed by self-service supermarkets, and pre-packaged brands such as PG Tips (owned by Brooke Bond), Typhoo and Tetley

Above First Prize medals for coffee roasting awarded to C. E. Taylor & Company at the Grocery Exhibition, London, 1896

Opposite, top left Taylors Kiosk coffee tins, c.1905

Opposite, top right Taylors Pagoda Tea caddy, c.1970s

Opposite, bottom Offices of C. E. Taylor & Company 11 & 12 Blenheim Terrace, Leeds, c.1950s

were spending a great deal of money and effort to ensure that supermarkets stocked them and that customers, regardless of where they lived, recognised their names as guarantees of quality.

With the addition of the Taylors sites, Bettys was now a significant property owner. However, it was clear that not all of the branches could happily coexist. Harrogate, in particular, could not support three cafés and two bakeries owned by the same parent company, and the Harrogate Kiosk was the first Taylors site to close its doors. The Taylors bakery in Harrogate was sold to Marks & Spencer, which wanted to expand, although in Ilkley the bakery continued to operate until 1969. The Lytham St Annes Kiosk didn't fit with the Yorkshire focus of Bettys and was sold when the managers retired a few years later.

In Ilkley, it was the Taylors Café Imperial that closed permanently, while the Kiosk, which was more spacious, with more potential for expansion, was shut for a two-year full refurbishment, to be reborn in 1964 as the first new Bettys since 1937. It was resolutely fashionable, with the latest logo, designed by Victor, proudly proclaiming 'Bettys' in a gold sunburst-style fanfare above the door. The apostrophe had been slowly disappearing for several years now, gone from the main branding by 1960, but surviving on menus for rather longer. By the end of

The exterior of Bettys Ilkley, c.1980s

the 1960s it was definitively gone, the rationale being that the logo looked cleaner without it, and that standard written grammar did not apply to company logos.

Although Victor used outside artists on occasion, he was the force behind the Bettys visual identity, designing the menus himself as well as changing the logo repeatedly throughout the early 1960s until he reached one which worked. He was also heavily involved with the refurbishments, determined not to repeat Frederick's bad spatial planning, and enjoyed working with architects and builders on the interiors of each branch. With the children growing up, Kay now also started to become more actively involved in the business. She was a shareholder, although not on the Board, and not officially recognised with a job title and salary, but she became drawn into the daily business of Bettys through the need to prepare the Kiosk sites for sale. Victor noted that: 'what Taylors were really good at was keeping things in attics. They wouldn't throw anything away … it was pretty dusty, smelly, and not very clean.' Kay, who thrived on organisation and detail, went through the accumulation of decades' worth of fixtures and fittings, sorting what could be sold, used or discarded. Jonathan and Antony, when they weren't at school, went with her, amusing themselves by pretending to be mannequins in the empty shop window, posing with dishes of tea and scaring the passers-by.

The mid 1960s is often characterised as an era of sex, drugs and Beatlemania. The 1967 'summer of love', focused around a specific gathering of hippies and students in San Francisco, has come to stand for a whole range of counterculture movements, which included anti-nuclear marches, rising interest in self-sufficiency

Victor Wild in his office on the top floor of 1 Parliament Street, Harrogate, c.1970s

and a love of psychedelia as embodied in both recreational drugs and music. However, in Britain it was also an era of consensus politics, when society quietly but profoundly started to shift. In came the birth control pill and the legalisation of abortion and of homosexuality. Out went the death penalty – the last execution took place in 1964. In 1968 the women workers at the Ford factory in Dagenham walked out, paving the way for the Equal Pay Act in 1970. Meanwhile skirts rose above the knee for women for the first time, and innovations in synthetic fibres meant that fabrics were available in ever greater variety.

The motor car was now king, with more cars than ever on the – expanding – road system. The age of steam was also over, the last mainline passenger train to be hauled by a steam locomotive running in 1968 – a year after the last horse used for shunting on the railway was put out to pasture. Thomas Cook started running package holidays: the first flew from Manchester to Palma with 80 people on a 13-day trip. Air traffic doubled, and by the end of the 1970s there were over 40 million air passengers a year.

Meanwhile, British food was also changing. In 1961 the Chorleywood bread process was invented, enabling bread to be produced in under four hours. It decreased costs for large manufacturers who could invest in the required machinery, and was embraced by supermarkets as well as consumers, who happily bought convenient ready-sliced loaves. By 1970 it accounted for around 75 per cent of the bread made in Britain. Bread consumption itself dropped, as living standards rose, from 1.3kg on average per person per week to just over 1kg in 1970.

Foods from abroad started to make more of an impact, especially on the middle and working classes, as foreign travel increased, and as communities were founded based on immigrant workers. In Bradford, thousands of Punjabis came to work at the surviving woollen mills, themselves now in sharp decline. Migrants from what would become Bangladesh, as well as Chinese coming via Hong Kong, arrived seeking work and then established restaurants, initially for their own communities but which quickly became part of the British culinary landscape. There were around 4,000 Chinese and 2,000 Indian restaurants in Britain by 1970, with over half the population regularly eating at 'foreign' restaurants. The ABC chain of tea rooms had disappeared in

Coffee pot styling one of three Bettys logos introduced in the early 1960s

the 1950s, and Lyons was visibly in trouble, but new mass-market caterers were coming in: the first Pizza Express opened in 1965, the second in 1967; Berni Inns offered grilled dishes in pub-like surroundings; and on the roads 44 Little Chefs echoed the American diner. Wimpy, meanwhile, now had 1,000 outlets in over 23 countries.

Despite all of this, the majority of people remained conservative in their food choices, preferring spaghetti on toast or a Welsh rarebit to anything too far beyond their comfort zone. Bettys added pizza to the Belmont Room menu and continued to offer an eclectic international menu in the Oak Room, which the *Good Food Guide* praised again in 1968: 'when on form, this can be one of the best places to eat in the city'. The saltimbocca, curries and escalope à la crème were singled out as particularly noteworthy. In the cafés, the menus were solidly British, with just a hint of Continental excitement. Macaroni cheese and bacon rubbed shoulders with various rarebits, fish and chips and tongue or ham salads, and there were all sorts of things with chips, including braised kidneys and the classic gammon and egg. The restaurant menus included roasts as well as meat casseroles and used the skills of the Italian staff from the Oak Room to produce specials such as curried lamb with Patna rice, banana and tomato chutney or braised liver Italian style with tomato risotto. Meanwhile, Bettys bakery, which was flourishing with all the extra trade from the new sites, provided everything from scones and teacakes to chocolate biscuits and dairy cream cakes.

By 1965 Taylors was as improved as it was going to be for the time being, and Victor, who still felt unable to tackle the wider structural issues within the company while Claire was still a director, started looking for another set of challenges. The company bought a new site, on Stonegate in York, opening it as a Kiosk, without either Bettys or Taylors branding. Like the other Kiosks, it had a ground-floor shop and an upstairs café, which expanded up to the second floor at weekends, and was aimed predominantly at workers looking for a quick lunch. It also became popular with students from the newly founded University of York, which opened in 1963. The top-floor back room, staffed by only one waitress, was nicknamed 'lovers' corner' by the managers because of the unerring ability of

students to find somewhere quiet to canoodle on a hungover Saturday morning. The reputation of Bettys within Yorkshire was now very strong, among both the public and the business community. When the Ripon-based King sisters decided to sell their bakery as a going concern, their agent approached Bettys. Bettys already had two bakeries, that at Starbeck and the Taylors site at Ilkley, so on the face of it buying another was unwise. But Victor still wasn't convinced that the future lay in Bettys cafés, or, at least, not only in them. The potential for wholesale, based on Bettys' existing reputation for high-quality cakes and breads, was too much to resist. Kings was making good profits, far in excess of those of the bakery, still labouring on under the ineffectual Neville, so even if Bettys did nothing other than maintain them, they were a good opportunity. Victor paid the asking price of around £40,000, saying: 'I thought why not, and there I felt I could put somebody else in charge without offending Auntie Bunny.' In went a mainly female team, including a new bakery manager and a shopfloor manager, whose husband promptly fell off the roof while inspecting it (he also later blew the front off, looking for a gas leak by the light of his cigarette lighter). The majority of existing staff were retained, however, and initially very little changed, including the name. Victor was keen to innovate with the Bettys product range, but it was hard to do so under the Bettys name in case it went wrong (and because of resistance in the main Starbeck

46 Stonegate in York before it became Taylors Kiosk, with a sign pointing the way to the air raid shelter at the rear of the premises, c.1940s

bakery). An important part of the Kings role now became testing new baked goods on the North Yorkshire public.

Over at Taylors too it was time for change. Jim Raleigh was still keen to retire, and so a new general manager, Eddie Hardy, was employed as a partial replacement. Under him, Taylors bought its first teabag-making machine. Tea bags were less than 3 per cent of the total tea market at the time, but in a country addicted to its tea, this was still a substantial amount of sales, and Eddie saw potential for growth. Supermarkets didn't care about tea blended to order, so Taylors badly needed a new direction. The new machine made a tea bag every two or three seconds, but they did sell, and before long there were several machines, 'all clicking away as they (slowly) produced bags'. The tea bags were hand-packed into cake boxes. The main market was still loose leaf tea, though, weighed out in the shops and individually wrapped in a waxed paper outer wrapper, neatly tucked in at the ends and surrounded by a decorative band with the branding on. Although instant coffee was available, popularised by US forces in Britain during the war, coffee was overwhelmingly bought fresh, and at weekends the Kiosks had queues down the street. Nescafé Gold Blend was launched in 1965, using a new process supported with heavy marketing, and instant coffee sales grew exponentially. In response Taylors launched an instant coffee called Pagoda Coffee, but its core market was in roasted beans, freshly ground to order. Overall, the company was now turning over £1 million for the first time.

Business was patchy, though. In Harrogate, as noted, NHS water treatments ended in 1968, with only the Turkish baths surviving as a relic of the town's spa past. Fortunately, the conference guests and tourists kept coming. In York, Terry's had finally recovered its glory and now featured alongside Bettys in the *Good Food Guide*, which noted that Terry's was 'the kind of lunch place most cities need'. The Oak Room, meanwhile, was criticised for 'pretentiousness and poor curries', and it dropped out of the *Guide* the following year. Most of those who frequented both restaurants commented on Terry's vastly superior gleaming marble loos.

Competition in York was fierce, not least from Victor's own staff. Bettys now owned staff housing in Bootham, as a mixture of xenophobia and complaints about the Italians' late-night parties

and lasciviousness had made it hard for them to find accommodation. But as the numbers swelled, they had a habit of leaving to set up their own restaurants. This was nothing new, for one of Frederick's Swiss bakers, Silvio Lanfranchio, started the Silvio's confectionery chain in the 1930s, much to Claire's intense anger. Now, though, the longstanding Oak Room manager Mario Poggi retired through ill health, and the Oak Room lost its way. Nevertheless, in an attempt to boost quantity, if not quality, York was refurbished in 1971 with extra capacity added upstairs and down – 8,000 tonnes of earth were excavated by hand – and the entrance was moved to its current location on Davygate.

By then the two coffee shops in Leeds and Bradford were no more. It wasn't just a Bettys problem. All over Britain, the coffee shops so popular in the 1950s were closing as their customer base grew up, and new clientele moved in: the mods and rockers, moped and motorbike gangs, who piled in after the pubs closed and enjoyed pitched battles outside. It was hard to make a profit just on lunchtime coffee and snacks, and Victor's forecast that shopping would move to the suburbs was proving unfounded. Allerton Road closed in 1969, and Street Lane was leased to its managers in 1971. They continued to run it for another decade, stocking Bettys bakery goods, but as an independent concern.

Yorkshire Evening Press article covering the extension of the Oak Room Restaurant at Bettys York, 1971

While the layout of the cafés was being improved by Victor, the fittings and tableware owed more to Kay. Since the Taylors clear-outs, she'd been increasingly active in the business, the face of the family when Victor was occupied with buyouts and closures and fixing errant machinery, and she was more familiar with the staff than her husband was. She remembered birthdays and anniversaries and was aware of any personal problems. Like Claire before her, she found herself occupying the traditional woman's role of dealing with décor and finishing touches, making sure flowers were fresh and uniforms neatly pressed. Like Claire also, she moved beyond this. With Scandinavian interior design becoming fashionable, along with a colour palate of browns, beige and orange, she presided over a rethink of the tableware

Bettys Harrogate staff wearing uniform typical of the late 1970s on the occasion of Bettys Diamond Jubilee. 1979

and staff uniforms. Bettys were still using the original silver-plate teapots from the 1920s, now seen as out of date and certainly not in keeping with a stripped-back modern aesthetic. Out they went, to be replaced with stainless steel, easier to clean and care for and, as the silver had been in its time, a slightly aspirational version of what their customers had at home. Meanwhile, the black-and-white uniforms, tweaked for changing fashion (and underpinnings) but not properly overhauled for nearly half a century, were also relegated. In the Café Imperial the Lunch Room waitresses wore bright-yellow overalls and served set lunches. Over at Bettys the new uniform consisted of a zip-up brown nylon knee-length pinafore, with cream blouse, sensible brown shoes and waist apron with a point at the centre bottom.

After nearly 20 years running a company that he was not entirely in command of, things were changing for Victor. Claire was now bedridden, years of smoking having caused respiratory failure. Neville was about to retire, and the other directors were Victor's appointees. The children were leaving home: Liz was training to be a teacher, Antony was about to start at Bristol University, while Jonathan was now at Oxford, that most British of institutions, reading history. He had a serious girlfriend, Lesley Allison, who he had met in Harrogate while he was working a holiday job at WHSmith and she was at boarding school, bored and buying books. It turned out that her father Geoffrey had been Victor's 'fag' at Sedbergh. Jonathan claimed it was love at first sight; she said he had a few other girlfriends on the go and was initially less keen.

They were going out by the time she left school for art college, and, when Jonathan invited her down to Oxford for a weekend, she went. 'I arrived to find him in a blind panic. His first words were "Thank goodness you're here – can you make potato salad?"' After preparing salad for 300 people at a college hog roast, she said: 'I'd shown my hand – I was his willing helper, and I could cook.' She moved to Oxford, studying law, anthropology and English with the University of London as a distance learner, cooking meals on a tight budget in their student digs.

Victor had been very clear that his children need not feel beholden to the business, yet although he gained more control of Bettys as they grew up and away he also started to step back. In 1970 he

Top Lesley Wild as a student, c.1960s

Opposite Lesley and Jonathan Wild (dressed to sit his final exams) as students outside their bedsit at 16 Walton Street, Oxford

appointed Simon Simpson as a catering and retail director. By now
he was referring to the business in private as PRODISCO (property
in disguise company) and was spending increasing amounts of
time at home. However, he could not sit still and bought a small
bakery and café in Bedale in 1970 with the intention of turning
it into a new Bettys. Having tried suburbs, he now felt that the
future of Bettys lay in small market towns – but Bedale was too
small, and the site became a Kings instead. He was still keen to
expand, though, not least to maintain capacity at the bakery, and
Bettys Northallerton eventually opened in 1972, two doors away
from the present site. It was not ideal – too hot in summer and
very open plan, which was noisy and left the kitchen exposed.
However, it did well, with a menu that now moved slightly more
toward Yorkshire, including Brontë fruit cake and Yorkshire curd
tart (Frederick had included the latter on his menus in 1938,
and they'd been reintroduced by Victor in 1968). Brontë cake
was a new Bettys special, made by Kings, and named for the
Brontë sisters. The 1970s saw the gradual reawakening of
interest in British regional food: Jane Grigson, author of the
Observer Guide to British Cookery, was one among many writers who
started to urge the revaluation of British cuisine before it
completely died out.

The Midway Room at Bettys Leeds, c.1970

In 1971 British coinage was decimalised, and the menus all had
to be reprinted, tills upgraded and systems overhauled.
The first major credit card, Access, was launched, and cashpoints
started to spread. The rise of the supermarkets was now
unstoppable, and they all wanted own-brand products in order
to undercut the market leaders. Taylors got their tea bags into
Supasave – hardly a major player, but demand rocketed. They
brought in computers, better bag-making machines and a
cellophane wrapping machine. In 1972, however, the University
of Leeds threatened to serve a compulsory purchase order on
the Blenheim Terrace building, meaning that they had to move
out. The obvious solution was Starbeck, where the remains of
the old orchard still surrounded the bakery, and a new factory
could be built with room to expand. Taylors therefore moved to
Harrogate, where Victor spent much of his time devising
technical solutions to machine issues, using acres of black plastic
and gaffer tape. Then, aged 81, Claire Belmont died.

At last, Victor was free of Claire's interference, but after years of
working around her, adding to the business rather than touching
its core, he now had a sprawling set of businesses which did not
all work, and found it hard to adjust. The mid 1970s were tough.
Between 1973 and 1976 Britain experienced massive inflation
combined with falling output, a banking crisis and a stock market
collapse, along with industrial unrest on an unprecedented scale,
culminating in the three-day working week, when commercial
users of electricity were restricted to operating for only three days
a week. (Bettys resolutely stayed open six days a week, for 'it
wasn't our ethos to close in difficulties', with candles on the tables,
and with staff relieved that most of the cooking facilities were
gas). Now, at least, he could make drastic changes to cope with
the downturn. Bettys in Leeds closed in 1974 after 44 years
because 'we couldn't make it pay'. It was now too big, and city
centre rents were too high. While Bettys owned the 99-year lease,
paid at 1936 rent levels as a result of Frederick's canny financing
deals, it made no commercial sense to occupy a site that could
make a great deal more money, with much less hassle, if rented
out. The company was continually being offered 'enormous sums'
for the lease. Closure was also a typically non-combative way for
Victor to get rid of Miss Bradford, Claire's relative and the
branch manager. The same year Bettys also left Bradford, now

in terminal decline as a manufacturing centre, selling the lease to another restaurateur, who, in turn, went bust a few years later.

Inflation was now running at 25 per cent, and Victor found himself reprinting all the menus every few weeks as prices rose sharply and continuously. Bettys was a significant local employer, with over 400 employees, but the majority of its £1.3 million turnover – over 80 per cent – came from the confectionery and wholesale business, and so Victor decided to turn his attention more toward that. In 1974 Betty's Cafés Ltd changed its name to Prospect Foods Ltd. This much more generic name was Victor's idea: he hoped it would enable the company to broaden out beyond cafés and baked goods and into more general wholesale catering. Taylors, now investing more seriously in new technology, was demonstrating that there were profits to be made in supplying quality products to even small supermarket chains. Bettys (and Kings) were not using the industrial Chorleywood bread process and therefore had the potential to build on an existing reputation as a traditional bakers. They already supplied several grocers and department stores, as well as all the Bettys shops, and had started producing frozen tarts for the trade as well, using a new industrial fruit pie machine (later scrapped when wholesale was stopped). Victor also bought a sausage roll machine, but it was never used, and instead became a dumping ground for pots and pans and trays, the rolls being made by hand as they always had been. Now, with freezer sales increasing, Victor looked seriously at developing a range of frozen foods, something not widely available. Harrods had its own range, and Birds Eye had launched fish fingers, but this would be entire meals. The project got as far as a name – Bettyfayre – and outline product designs, before it was scrapped as being just too much of a stretch. Other, more established, aspects of the business were scrapped too, notably the chocolates, made in-house since 1919.

Bettys – Prospect Foods – was increasingly disparate. The cafés (or at least the well-established ones in York and Harrogate) were a Yorkshire institution. While the cafés were still major customers for the bakeries, wholesale was a separate area, and one which Victor remained convinced might be the future, with or without the Bettys name attached. Meanwhile, Taylors was separate again, joined to Bettys really only through being located on the same site as the main bakery. Victor was now 52, the same age Frederick had been when he'd sold the freeholds and gone on

GROUND FLOOR RESTAURANT

BEVERAGES

Tea, Indian or China	14p
Russian Tea, per glass	13p
Coffee per cup	13p
per pot per person	19p
per cup with fresh crea?	15p
Hot Chocolate	12p
Horlicks	12p
Milk per glass	10p
Schweppes Fruit Drinks	13p
Schweppes Orange Squash	12p

Plain Ices:

Vanilla or Strawberry	15p
Vanilla Ice with Fruit Jelly	28p
Ice Cream Meringue	
(Two Meringue Shells, Vanilla Ice and Cream)	28p
Peach or Pineapple Melba	
(Vanilla Ice, Peaches or Pineapple, Melba Sauce and Cream)	33p
Chocolate Nut Sundae	
(Vanilla Ice, Chocolate Sauce, Chopped Nuts and Cream)	33p
Raspberry Sundae	
(Vanilla and Strawberry Ice, Raspberries and Cream)	35p
Fresh Dairy Cream	9p

Toasts & Teacakes

Buttered Teacake	13p
Toasted Teacake	13p
Buttered Scone	9p
Toasted Scone	10p
Buttered Toast	9p
Bread and Butter	8p
Jam	8p
Fresh Cream Trifle	28p
Gateaux and Cakes	10p to 25p

Sandwiches

(in brown or white Bread)

Roast Beef	38p
Chicken	38p
Ham	35p
Cream Cheese with Pineappl.	28p
Egg and Cress	28p
Mixed Salad	28p

Grills & Omelettes

Cold Boiled Ham, Tomato & Chips	70p
Ham, Mushroom or Cheese Omelette & Chips	60p
Fried Egg, Tomato & Chips	40p
Two thick Pork Sausages, & Chips	60p
Mushroom Vol-au-Vent & Chips	55p
Welsh Rarebit	45p
Portion of Chips	12p

Fish

the holiday of a lifetime before opening his most elegant branch in York. He was jaded, and the future looked uncertain.

However, down in Oxfordshire, discussions were afoot. Jonathan, now teaching history, was disenchanted with battling for teenage attention and wondering if he could do more good working at Bettys. Lesley was still training as a lawyer – and could easily continue back in Yorkshire. The biggest question was whether Victor, so used now to doing things his way, would welcome having to think about succession planning: did he genuinely want Bettys to continue as a family-run business?

Bettys Harrogate menu, 1975

Postcard of a typical Swiss Alpine
scene sent to Fritz Bützer
(Frederick Belmont) in 1904

A trip to Switzerland

In 1922 Frederick Belmont and his wife and business partner Claire took a trip back to Frederick's native Switzerland. His diary of the trip, written in characteristically tongue-in cheek prose, is full of anecdotes about his car and the pretty girls he admired, but his emotion also comes through.

Bettys is a Yorkshire institution, but it is also a Swiss business, and proud of it. Frederick, Victor, Jonathan and Lesley and their families all have deep personal links with Switzerland, and physical trips to the places associated with key moments of the company's history have come to form part of staff training. Regular visits to where it all started not only inspire but keep the company grounded in its heritage.

In 1922 Frederick fell back in love with the Swiss scenery: 'beautiful place, indeed'. They climbed the Rigi, 'which in respect of view is unrivalled in the world'. But Claire wasn't much of a climber, and back in England Frederick's lifestyle, of golf, whisky and cigars, wasn't conducive to fitness. By the time he made his penultimate trip, in August 1939, he was frequently out of breath and nervous at heights. His nephew and eventual heritor of Bettys, Victor, on the other hand, adored the mountains. He would name his bungalow 'Saentis' after his favourite peak, and throughout his life he took frequent trips back to go walking, often with Len Evans, who had taken Victor under his wing after Len's son Pat, one of Victor's best friends, was killed during the Second World War.

The 1939 trip was the last time that Frederick, Claire and Victor would holiday together. Victor spent much of the Second World War longing 'for the time when I could go back and see my family', and there were no Swiss trips for six long years. His return visit was deeply emotional. His mother Ida 'made a pot of English tea and just looked at me … the most astonishing thing that ever happened. She nearly fell over herself with delight.' Despite the privations of war, he found Switzerland almost unbearably beautiful after the drabness of post-war Britain. He and his sister Vreni set out to explore areas they'd never had a chance to see growing up, when money was so scarce.

Victor worked in St Gallen, where he found himself stuck with arranging large, ornate platters of hors d'oeuvres, spending his days on the Saentis. Next he headed for Zurich, working in the Zunfthaus zum Rüden, one of the most upmarket restaurants in the city and battling with his roommate over whether they would sleep with the window open or not. Finally, he spent the winter skiing season in Pontresina, a village in the Engadine, about eight kilometres from St Moritz. The Kronenhof Hotel where he worked was the grandest in the resort, but he and his fellow waiters slept in a dormitory under the central dome. The beds were arranged around the beams at strange angles and were all too short for him. He helped out in the office as he was fluent in English, watching his precious time off disappear in return for a glass or two of

wine, commenting that they did not exactly help
his language skills. However, as the peak season
calmed down he managed to go skiing again,
which he loved.

As Victor and his siblings grew up, they stayed
close. By the 1950s he and Hanni both had
families of their own, although Vreni never
married. Victor and Kay welcomed Victor's
Swiss family to Harrogate every year or so and
made the return visit with their own children as
well. Every year a Christmas parcel would arrive
for the Wilds from Switzerland, filled with treats
including a large decorated Berner biber – a
Bernese speciality similar to lebkuchen, with
honey, spice and a leavening agent to give it a

characteristic chewy, yet light, texture. It remained an abiding Christmas memory for the Wild siblings.

Both Frederick and Victor had learnt vital skills in Switzerland, and they both recruited Swiss staff for the bakery. As Victor's son Jonathan and his wife Lesley joined the business in the 1970s, the Swiss link deepened. Lesley, as a Yorkshire-born outsider to the family, saw strengths in their Swissness that they had not been able to recognise themselves. The attention to detail, the strong sense of belonging and the discipline and precision for which the nation is renowned were all part of the ethos that Swiss roots had brought to the company. She urged them to put their Swissness at centre stage in Bettys, starting with the staff.

In 1988 two of the senior bakery staff spent a week at Richemont College in Lucerne. Founded in 1945, the college was one of Switzerland's foremost catering colleges, and this was one of a series of trips which would be sponsored by Bettys. The newsletter commented that 'staff who are selected to attend these courses bring back new ideas, recipes and inspirations and above all enable us to retain our Swiss connections'.

By 2003 the Swiss connections had been deepened even further. Jonathan and Lesley had come to regard Pontresina as their *Heimatort*, a very Swiss concept of a sort of ancestral homeland. They'd been visiting Jonathan's cousins in Switzerland since they'd first become a couple, initially popping in en route to Greece. As poverty-stricken students, they'd been sleeping in their car as they travelled through Europe, and Lesley eagerly seized upon the opportunity to wash her hair. Now they were devoted mountain trekkers, as well as taking inspiration home from the cafés and confectioneries which had been the model for Bettys back in 1919. Lesley had become firm friends with Jonathan's cousin Nelli, forging close links between all the members of that generation of the family. Now Lesley arranged a fact-finding mission for some of the staff, taking in Zurich, Kandersteg, Sion and Bern. They also visited Wangen-an-der-Aare, scene of the mill fire which had killed Frederick's father and sister. It would be the first of many such trips, and later excursions also included Pontresina.

The links weren't all one way, either. Through working with Swiss suppliers, especially for wine and chocolate, and regularly visiting certain key sites, Lesley and Jonathan forged relationships which went beyond simple commercial dealings. In 2017 Liz Wild presented a plaque to the mill at Wangen-an-der-Aare to commemorate the 1890 fire. Meanwhile, suppliers and hosts came to Yorkshire too. One bakery, which had invented the Engadine torte upon which the Bettys version was based, was so inspired by the Bettys miniature Engadine that they, in turn, reinvented it for their own shop.

Back in Starbeck, the Bettys Craft Bakery, itself modelled on Swiss Engadine architecture, sports a huge cowbell in its foyer that was proudly carried back by Lesley from a fact-finding visit to Lucerne. The site is landscaped to hint at the steep terraces of the Swiss mountains, and the huge teapot clock on the Taylors factory is a knowing nod to the watchmaking industry for which Switzerland remains famed. But precision and what Jonathan calls a sense of Swiss 'properness' is a double-edged sword. Frederick left Switzerland because he felt stifled and unable to develop. Bettys is proud of being Swiss, but the family is equally proud of its Yorkshire side, which tempers all that discipline with a maverick and creative bent as well.

The new wave

1975–1986

What's on the menu?

Within five years of first Jonathan and then Lesley joining the company, the Bettys menu had shifted firmly toward both a more regional and a more modern British feel. There was a real renaissance in British cuisine from the 1980s onward, including a renewed interest in the country's culinary heritage, although dishes directly drawn from the past rarely appeared on menus. However, the Bettys cinnamon toast was developed from a 17th-century recipe and appears here in a new section, 'Toasts'. Gone is the spaghetti topping of the 1960s, though: now the toasts are given a slightly nostalgic makeover, with plainer toppings, all sweet, which allow the bread itself to shine.

The bakery is generally much more in evidence now, with the choice of bread for sandwiches explicitly including granary, a nod to the health food movement. There are many more meat-free and light choices, and not everything comes with chips. French croissants sit happily with English scones, omelette with *fines herbes* rubs shoulders with mushroom-and-bacon omelette, and Bettys' Continental roots are gently highlighted with the café complet. Meanwhile, the daily specials section, along with emphasis on the fresh pineapple and seasonal fruit, marks a move away from the reliance on tinned goods and preserves which had characterised so much of the food of the preceding decades.

The Brontë fruit cake, which was introduced after the purchase of Kings and opening of Ilkley, is still on other menus of the time, and the Yorkshire nature of Bettys is now in the ascendant, with the rarebits proclaimed a speciality, made with Yorkshire ale, and the county lending its name to a number of other dishes. The Yorkshire curd tart, which had first appeared in the 1920s and was brought back in the 1960s, was by this time an established Bettys favourite (and remains so to this day). Although it was not yet on this menu, the Fat Rascal, another Bettys speciality, was in development, based on an idea of Jonathan's. The special rich fruit cakes were Lesley's contribution, based on family recipes or developed in the kitchen at home. Serving the fruit cake with cheese, a classic Yorkshire combination, was another of Jonathan and Lesley's introductions, along with hot mokka and café Vienna (much copied elsewhere). Taylors isn't mentioned by name, the two parts of the company remaining very separate in the way they were presented to the public, but the greater integration of the tea and coffee business with the café and bakery element is nevertheless evident in the extended list of teas. Bettys also started to offer a separate tea and coffee menu, emphasising that they bought and blended their own coffees and teas.

They also now sold wine, sourced from a small family vineyard in Alsace, for the draconian restrictions of the licensing laws with which Frederick and Victor had struggled had now been relaxed. Alsatian wines were something of a novelty in the UK at the time, but there was an existing link for Bettys, for the Spindler studio was still based there and still producing marquetry: one of the unifying decorative features of the Bettys cafés as they underwent significant refurbishment in the 1980s was the rehanging of the existing Spindler collection and the addition of more pieces.

Tea

served with Milk or Lemon
Teapot for One

The Tea Room Blend	58p
Darjeeling Indian	65p
Fine Assam	65p
Earl Grey	65p
Special Scented Blend with Exotic Flowers	65p
Lapsang Souchong	65p
Formosa Oolong	65p
China Rose Petal	65p
African Mint	65p

Coffee

served with Hot Milk or Cream

The Café Blend
Cup 49p   Pot for One 75p

Café Glacé 85p
with ice cream and whipped cream
Hot Mokka *or* Iced Mokka 85p
coffee and chocolate with cream
Café Vienna 85p
with whipped cream and cinnamon

Morning Coffee Selection

Special Coffee of the Day
Cup 49p   Pot for One 75p

Café Complet

Pot of coffee for one with
breakfast rolls or croissants,
butter and preserves 1.45

Hot Drinks

Hot Chocolate with Cream	90p
Hot Milk with Honey and Nutmeg	70p

ALL PRICES ARE INCLUSIVE
OF 15% VAT
SERVICE NOT INCLUDED

Toasts

Lemon Curd, Honey or Preserves	1
Granary Toast	4
Cinnamon Toast	4
Toasted Teacake	4
Spiced Yorkshire Teacake	4

Toasted Scones

Sultana, Cheese, Lemon, Walnu
or Wholemeal Date 42p each

Cream Tea

Scones with Whipped Cream
and Strawberry Preserve
Teapot for One 1.85

Sandwiches

in Granary, White or Brown Brea

Roast Ham or Chicken	1.
Egg & Cress 95p Cucumber	8
Peanut Butter & Hazelnuts	9
Cottage Cheese & Pineapple	9
Hot Bacon	1.

Open Sandwiches

Prawn and Egg Mayonnaise	2.
Prawn, Celery & Walnut	2.

****

Cheese and Herb Pâté	1.

Yorkshire Cheese Lunch

Blue & White Wensleydale Chees
with Apple Chutney, Celery and
Granary Bread   2.

Salads

82p per portion or
choose any three for 2.35

Cottage Cheese Waldorf
Cauliflower & Bacon
Tomato & Kidney Bean
Pasta   Mixed Green

or any three with Roast Ham
Chicken, *or* Quiche 3.35

Menu at Bettys Northallerton,
September 1984

Hot Dishes

shrooms on Toast	1.95
ached Eggs on Toast	1.60
icken & Ham	
ol-au-Vents	2.30
ep Fried Granary Mushrooms	
ith Tartare Sauce	2.65

Rarebits

he Speciality of the House.
ade with Yorkshire Ale, served
ith Apple or Tomato Chutney

iginal Welsh Rarebit	2.65
rkshire Rarebit with Ham	3.00
rebit with Bacon Rashers	3.25

Omelettes

eese & Ham	2.45
shroom & Bacon	2.45
awn	2.60
nes Herbes	2.45

Grills & Fish

rk Sausages & Bacon	
ith Apple Chutney	2.65
mmon and Eggs	3.10
ied Fillet of Plaice	
ith Chipped Potatoes	3.20

Late Breakfast

con & Eggs with Toast	2.65

Side Dishes

y One Salad	82p
ipped Potatoes	55p
rb and Garlic Bread	44p
shrooms Cooked in Butter	1.15
anary Bread and Butter	34p

Specials

Homemade soup & other dishes
are prepared each day.
Please enquire

Cakes

from our own Bakery
selection from the Trolley

Fancies from	35p
Supremes & Tortes from	90p–1.20
Cream Cakes from	55p–80p
Yorkshire Curd Tart & Cream	95p

****

Selection of Biscuits	36p

Special Rich Fruit Cakes

A taste of Lemon & Almond,
Honey & Fig, and Ginger & Walnut.
Served with *either* whipped
cream *or* Wensleydale Cheese
1.10

Ices

Vanilla and Strawberry Ice	98p
Ice Cream with Brandy Snap,	
and Chocolate Sauce	1.40
Raspberry Meringue Melba	1.50
Chocolate Nut Sundae	1.50
Chocolate Meringue Swan	1.55

Fruit

Fresh Pineapple with	
Maraschino Liqueur	1.35
Fruit in Season from	95p

Minerals

Ice Cream Milk Shakes	80p
Chilled Milk	40p
Orange Juice	52p
Coca Cola	55p
Sparkling Perrier Water	55p
Carlsberg Lager	60p

Wine

a selection of wines from Alsace
imported direct
By the glass or bottle
See Wine List

NA 984

In 1975, when Jonathan moved back up to Yorkshire with Lesley, neither he nor Victor were entirely convinced that it was the right move. Victor later admitted to him, 'I wasn't all that keen really, I was perfectly comfortable without you breathing down my neck,' a feeling that he also made clear at the time. But Jonathan was disillusioned with teaching: he was teaching a subject he loved but conscious that 200 miles away was a family business with no one apparently interested in taking it over. He reasoned that 'if I don't find out if it's an option for the future, it may not be there in the future'.

Jonathan wasn't sure that commerce was for him, though. Brought up by an unconventional father, encouraged to read widely and to engage with social and political issues in the heady atmosphere of the 1960s, he wanted to change the world. If he went into Bettys, it would be as a 'shock to the system', to rejuvenate what he saw as an increasingly tired business, and to make cultural changes more in line with his worldview. Idealistic, imaginative but also driven, he compared himself to Carl, the grandfather he'd never known but who, like him, had a vision of a better world. Victor thought this was unfair to Jonathan, for Carl was also blind to the hardships he imposed upon his family and unrealistic about how to achieve the changes he spent so much of his time writing about.

Characteristically and helpfully, Victor drew a set of pictures for his son, showing how businesses could actively contribute to the world as well: through not shirking their taxes, through being a good employer and through being thoroughly embedded in the local community. In August 1975, therefore, at the end of the school year, Jonathan agreed that he would start work, with two thirds of his time to be spent working through all the areas of the business, while in the remainder he would shadow his still slightly reluctant father. Kay was overjoyed and offered to buy them a home (they preferred to buy their own smaller house

Jonathan and Lesley Wild on their wedding day, 6 September 1975

instead). However, Jonathan and Lesley did get married, realising that 'it was the right thing to do'. The students at Jonathan's comprehensive school had taken a great interest in their unmarried teacher, referring to Lesley and 'sir's mistress'.

The newly-weds had a snatched honeymoon, for Jonathan was now officially a management trainee and did not dare ask for a holiday so soon after starting. Like Victor, he started at the bottom, working alongside counter staff and delivery men, bakers, confectioners, tea blenders and coffee buyers. Unlike Victor, he didn't find himself immediately trying to manage an unmanageable set of circumstances at a problematic branch with a war on. Nevertheless, the experiences he had, and frustrations he came up against, were uncannily like those his father had complained about so vociferously 30 years before: lack of training, lack of structure and lack of a clear vision for the future.

Lesley, now Lesley Wild, was involved from the start. She was training to be a lawyer but, like Claire Belmont and (to a lesser extent) Kay Wild before her, she was never going to be just the boss's wife. Claire had been a director early on, rising to be Chair of the Board and then lifetime director; Kay was a shareholder, and would join the Board as a non-executive director in 1979. Lesley, in 1975, had no thoughts of joining Bettys, but she was Jonathan's trusted confidante and sounding board, and she shared his views on what the company could be – and what it was not. Her art college background meant that she had a keen interest in aesthetics, along with the knowledge and skills to contribute in a very real sense, and she combined this with a lawyer's eye for detail and recognition that what happened behind the scenes was as important as what the customers saw in the cafés and on the supermarket shelves. Jonathan, meanwhile, brought a deep commitment to the family business, along with a desire to change the world, the spark that had led him into teaching still present but now about to be channelled in a new direction.

Under Victor there had been constant innovation and reinvention, in line with changing social needs and fashion, and the business was now on a solid footing, well-established and with a good reputation in Yorkshire. The two parts of the company remained separate. Taylors, contributing around 15 per cent of the overall turnover, was now purely a tea and coffee business and, although

Jonathan Wild behind the counter at
Bettys Harrogate, c.1975

Supasave was about to go bust, negotiations with Morrisons had begun: Chairman Ken Morrison was a fan of Taylors' Pagoda tea, their own-brand blend, and wanted something of matching quality to sell under the Morrisons name. This would bring much-needed stability and maybe even a chance to re-evaluate the wider business. Over at Bettys, the cafés now catered less for society ladies being seen to have tea and more for busy workers, men and women, as well as students, retirees, conference-goers, holidaymakers and locals in the small and medium-sized towns which had become the focus of the Bettys model. However, the shop-cafés which were the public face of Bettys were inconsistent and had once more become rather shabby. Lesley, who knew Bettys having grown up outside York, had been very much a Terry's girl, but now both she and Jonathan brought fresh eyes to Victor's mini empire.

The food was central to their concerns. Lesley's upbringing was centred around fresh ingredients from her father's farm, which was a mixed smallholding, or sourced by him locally with great care. Her mother, who had studied catering, was a superb cook and had taken care to teach her daughter to appreciate and to cook very good food. Family holidays to France, where her father took delight in throwing their newly acquired and huge American car around mountain passes (he was a rally driver in his spare time), had introduced her to the produce of the south of France, including gloriously stinky cheese. She, in turn, was introducing Jonathan to new ingredients and flavours (the first time they visited a cheese shop in Switzerland he panicked and asked if they had Baby Bel – they didn't).

Now they found that the family food business did not reflect the quality of even the basic meals they had at home. There were step-by-step menu books, illustrated by Victor, showing how each dish should be made, with supporting images of the equipment and presentation. These were immensely useful, but the various branches sourced their ingredients individually, using small grocers and butchers – great for the locality but terrible for fixing consistent prices across the branches and for guaranteeing quality (or supply). Many of the fresh items had, partly as a consequence, been replaced with easier, mass-catering fixes: canned fruit, long-life cream, custard powder and ready-made jelly. The staff at the main bakery, for so long left alone by Victor in

Lesley Wild as a young girl at her father's farm

his desire to avoid conflict with Claire's nephew Neville, the head of the bakery for nearly all Victor's time in charge, had become deeply entrenched, resistant to anything that made their lives more complicated – even down to cutting up a strawberry rather than opening a tin. They did not bake on a Saturday, for there were no deliveries after a late-night Friday slot, so the food in the branches – and in the wholesale market – became increasingly stale as each Saturday, the busiest day of the week, wore on. None of the branches opened on a Sunday.

Then there were the buildings themselves. Seen with outside eyes, they were dated: the last big refurbishments had been in the early 1960s, except for York in 1971, and fashions had changed. The Formica tables, stainless-steel teapots and rarebit holders, the nylon uniforms and the 'splodge' carpet hardly screamed modern elegance. There was also little evidence now of Bettys' Swiss roots, and, with the exception of York's *Queen Mary*-inspired décor, nothing tangible to suggest its long heritage.

Jonathan was convinced that Bettys should return to its beginnings as a special place to take tea, butting up now against Victor's dislike of anything he termed 'showy'. It was partly (and inevitably) a generational clash, for Bettys did have a good reputation; indeed, it had become a veritable institution in Harrogate. James Wight, better known as the author James Herriot, wrote that for 30 years his leisure routine had consisted of driving into Harrogate with his wife for 'lunch at Bettys or Standings, shopping in the afternoon, tea at Bettys, then the cinema … and finally a late meal'. (Jonathan remembered that he would order a pot of coffee for one – 'oh, and bring two cups please!') Standings, already a shadow of its former self, would close in 1981, leaving Bettys the only one of Harrogate's most sought-after inter-war cafés still going. (Terry's in York closed the same year, converted into offices for the bank next door.)

National surveys showed that British food culture was still deeply conservative, and that despite the growing interest in healthy eating and Mediterranean food presented on terracotta plates, the ideal meal for the majority was still prawn cocktail or a soup (minestrone rather than tomato), steak and chips and ice cream. In 1977 the national reputation of Bettys as it stood was confirmed when the company was commissioned to provide one of the Queen's silver jubilee cakes. Cake decorator Shirley Fell, bakery stalwart Jessie Radcliffe, and Victor drove the cake down to Buckingham Palace, stopping off at Watford Gap services so that the ladies could change into 'real posh frocks – I wore a hat', as Shirley put it. After constructing the cake *in situ*, with Shirley casually pointing out to the royal staff that 'we do a nice line in christening cakes too' (the first of the Queen's grandchildren had just been born), they spent two nights in London, where they toured the set of *Upstairs, Downstairs* and had a 'wonderful' time.

The year after Jonathan started, Bettys in Harrogate moved across the road. The Cambridge Crescent building had serious structural problems and needed a great deal spending on it, necessitating a lengthy closure. The Café Imperial was still underperforming, so it made sense for Bettys to take over the more prestigious corner site and lease Cambridge Crescent to a bank which had the cash to fix the structural issues. The Continental deli next door to the café closed down as well. There were real fears that Bettys would lose custom, for the Imperial site had a terrible reputation. Kay stopped talking to one of her friends who declared that if Bettys moved to 'that dump' she

Top The cake created by Bettys to celebrate the Queen's Silver Jubilee in 1977. Bettys, along with other chosen suppliers, were asked to make a cake to mark the occasion to be displayed at Buckingham Palace

Opposite, top Spindler marquetry depicting Burnt Yates, Nidderdale, Yorkshire

Opposite, bottom 'Spindler at Bettys' leaflet detailing the artworks in the Harrogate and Ilkley branches, c.1970s

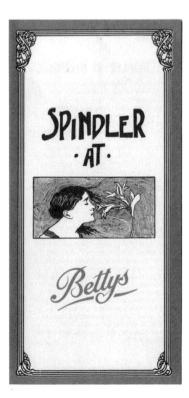

would never darken its doors again. However, move it did, with the first-floor lunch room reduced in size and the ground-floor café, with its windows onto Montpellier Gardens, expanded. The basement smoking room was converted into a distinct space in its own right, now an extension to the café rather than the haunt of elderly pipe-smokers. One of Jonathan's first lasting marks on the business was to make it into the Spindler Gallery, full of all of the various Spindler marquetry pieces that Frederick had collected over the years and which he and Lesley were adding to. The Spindler collection now became an understated, but integral, part of the Bettys aesthetic and continues to be so today.

The connection with the Spindler studio, which had started when Frederick discovered the work of Charles Spindler in the 1930s, was reborn in the 1970s. Jonathan was aware of Frederick's own collection of small, off-the-peg pieces, and very familiar with the two large landscapes in Cambridge Crescent. (The remaining four were still wrapped up, having languished in storage since before the Second World War.) Those that had been on display were now nicotine-stained and tatty and needed restoration, but they had piqued Jonathan's interest. When he was studying in Oxford, he took an afternoon off to research them more fully in

THE GROVE, ILKLEY
We apologise to our customers for the
inconvenience caused by the recent explosion
at the rear of our premises.
THE SHOP WILL RE-OPEN THIS FRIDAY MORNING.
Repairs to the café have already begun. However, it will be some weeks
before we re-open.

JON BELL, MANAGER

the Taylorian Institute at the Ashmolean Museum. There he
looked through French art and design books from the early 20th
century, looking for – and finding – information on the Charles
Spindler studio and its work. He and Lesley later tracked down
the original village in Alsace where the studio had been based,
where they found that Charles Spindler's son and grandson were
still working and that the studio was still producing pieces – and
was willing to refurbish the Bettys collection. They got on so
well that the Wilds returned to Alsace year after year, becoming
friendly with Paul Spindler's son Jean-Charles and his wife
Beatrice. Beatrice was from a distinguished wine family, the
Mullers. The Wilds camped in their extensive back garden and
later stayed in their house, which was part of the medieval
village wall.

The link was strengthened further a few years later when
Jonathan and Lesley asked the Mullers to supply Alsatian wines
directly to Bettys. Not only were Alsatian wines something of a
rarity in 1980s England, but this was Bettys' first venture into
selling alcohol (outside the bar at Bettys York). The wines were
initially sold only in the Ilkley branch, which was also the first
branch to get a new Spindler. In 1978 the hot water tank
exploded, destroying the back of the building, which housed the
café. Luckily, it was 3 a.m., and no one was injured, although the
copper water boiler ended up on a roof over 50m away. As part
of the reconstruction, and with an eye on Bettys' 60th
anniversary in 1979, the Spindlers were persuaded to supply a

Top Notice to customers from Bettys
Ilkley to 'apologise for the
inconvenience' following the gas
explosion that occurred on 21 June 1978

Opposite The exterior of the rear of
Bettys Ilkley in the aftermath of the gas
explosion

copy of *La Chasse*, the largest Spindler panel ever created, for
one of the new walls. The installation of the Spindler was the
start of a move to make the interiors of the various branches feel
more connected. Bettys was centralising its buying, using
branch-wide suppliers, and ensuring that the overall experience
was consistent. Nevertheless, the Board was united that Bettys
should not become just another chain. Recognising the unique
nature of each site (and their equally unique challenges) was key:
each branch was different, and that was very much a part of the
Bettys experience.

Change was also afoot at Taylors. Most of the business was in
supplying own-brand tea bags, by now mainly to Morrisons. One
of Jonathan's early ventures was to explore the possibility of
expanding Taylors' Pagoda tea, but, despite various promotional
activities, it remained too high end to be really successful in a
very competitive market. The Directors concluded that 'the
Taylors range should be extended to include a medium price pack
suitable for catering and retail'. They needed a tea which would
be high quality but also able to retail at a few pence lower than the
market leaders. Now Victor, Eddie Hardy and a new consultant
tea broker and blender, Warren Ford, together with a very eager
Jonathan, formed a team to create and market a new tea.

La Chasse, (*'The Hunt'*) by Jean Charles
Spindler, which hangs in Bettys Ilkley, is
one of the largest marquetry pictures
ever made in the studio

It would be based on Taylors' established method of blending tea to suit the local water, and be entirely Yorkshire-focused, with a different blend for East and West Yorkshire, and marketing emphasising that this was a specifically regional tea. The name Yorkshire Tea was chosen above various others – Dalesman's Tea was another contender – and from the very beginning its image was one of no-nonsense and good value, with a touch of the individual pride which came from being a very regional product. Yorkshire already had one of the strongest regional identities in the UK, fostered to a large extent by a sense of otherness versus the southern counties and London, and bolstered by a raft of very successful TV programmes set in the north (though not necessarily Yorkshire itself), as the regional TV companies in the north were particularly productive.

Victor designed the packaging, a bright-orange background with stencilled logo and a Yorkshire white rose – orange was one of the few colours not already in use on the tea shelves. Jonathan gave himself a crash course in marketing and enlisted the support of a cub reporter from the local press to write a press release proclaiming that 'there is good news for Yorkshire's tea drinkers thanks to a Harrogate tea company which has revived

Left Taylors Yorkshire Tea original loose leaf tea packaging. This late 1970s box features the original slogan 'Blended in Yorkshire to suit Yorkshire people and Yorkshire water'

Right Eddie Hardy and Jim Raleigh tasting Yorkshire Tea, 1977

the old tradition of blending to suit local waters'. It gained good coverage, and sales started well, with Morrisons the first supermarket to stock it, alongside their own version of Taylors tea. Various promotions followed, including one to get a free Yorkshire Tea tea towel. Consternation arose when, on testing in the Taylors staff canteen, the ink came off, and all 5,000 tea towels had to be baked in the bakery ovens to set the ink properly. However, the tea towel boosted sales, although consumers didn't necessarily understand (or care) about the water-specific blending. They were drawn more to the solid declaration of regional patriotism inherent in the name (and the price, which was extremely competitive), and it remained one of the key elements of the brand, which carried the tagline 'blended in Yorkshire to suit Yorkshire people and Yorkshire water'.

By 1979 Jonathan was firmly embedded in the business and determined that it was his future. Victor was still not convinced that the business should be getting bigger, but found 'you can't put it into a straitjacket without damaging it', and he admitted that Jonathan's joining had given him a new sense of responsibility, adding new life to the business, and that it 'changed a lot of my thinking'. The British economy was still faltering, with the 'winter of discontent' of early 1979 bringing public sector employees out on strike – scenes of piled-up bin bags and unburied corpses (in heat-sealed vacuum-packed bags) were splashed across the press, although the majority of people simply got on with life as normal. In May 1979 Margaret Thatcher became the first female leader of any European country, and immediately implemented policies to curb the unions and reform the

Victor and Kay Wild cut the cake at the Bettys 60th anniversary party, held at Middlethorpe Hall, 26 July 1979

DIAMOND JUBILEE BALL

at

Middlethorpe Hall York

THURSDAY 26 JULY 1979   8 PM - 1 AM

IN THE GARDEN

Barbeque & Buffet · Brass Band · Fairground Stalls · Steel Band

IN THE HALL

Dancing with two Discos and Steel Band · Three Bars · Pool Competition · Wine Bar

TICKETS

Staff -   Guests -
                                   (only one per member of staff)
Staff Tickets Free   *Husband/Wife Free*
                                            Other Guest £3·50

Transport Provided - please sign ticket application list by   JULY 7

Poster for Bettys Diamond Jubilee staff ball, 26 July 1979 at Middlethorpe Hall, York. Designed by Lesley Wild

economy. For three more years the UK remained in recession, while her popularity plummeted. At the worst point, Taylors sold Yorkshire Tea at cost to protect its sales.

Bettys was 60 years old in 1979, and Jonathan decided there should be a proper staff party, with everyone included. Six hundred staff and guests were invited, and there was a jazz band and a fairground put together by Jonathan and Lesley by using their days off to cherry-pick the best of the local fairground attractions. There were other events too. They hosted a 'young café pianist of the year' competition, celebrating the fact that the pianos were playing in the branches once more. Then there was the offer of tea and coffee at 1919 prices, if paid for in pre-decimal coinage (inevitably, many people saw this as a brilliant opportunity to divest themselves of coins which were no longer legal tender, and Bettys was left with a great deal of copper change). Some of Frederick's 1920s French Fancies were revived, briefly, as well. More significantly, Jonathan persuaded Victor to pay a one-off jubilee bonus of 25 per cent of a year's earnings to all the employees, recognising the importance of everyone in making the company a success, especially in challenging circumstances. Later this morphed into a group profit share, and as the 1970s became the 1980s – the decade of the mantras that 'greed is good' and 'there is no such thing as society'– Bettys (and John Lewis) were among a handful of employers that stood out as quietly radical. Jonathan also instigated a formal charity fund for each branch, starting with a diamond jubilee budget, and encouraged the various branch managers to become more active in their own local communities.

Slowly too he tackled the lack of training, still smarting slightly from his early experiences in the bakery, where every baker had his own notebook squirrelled away, and there was no proper guidance – on one occasion, left to make chocolate sponges with only verbal instructions, hastily given, he forgot to add baking powder, making chocolate leather instead, commenting that: 'for somebody who trained and worked as a teacher it was a defining experience. I just wanted to be competent, and yet everything was standing in the way.' Now proper recipes were introduced, and training plans, culminating in the appointment of Lesley Norris in a new role of product controller, specifically ensuring consistency as well as quality across all of the Bettys and separate Kings bakery range.

1979 was a significant year for Lesley Wild too. She was now a qualified lawyer, but she had been increasingly drawn into the business over the previous five years, her combination of skills and practicality making her an ideal foil for Jonathan's creativity and occasional bursts of romanticism. Now, in a shake-up of the Board, Kay, Liz and Antony – usually known as Tony – became non-executive directors, and Lesley joined Bettys formally, soon becoming the lead on a new project to expand Kings bakery. Neither she nor Jonathan were keen to pursue Victor's drive toward wholesale – there was no way of guaranteeing quality, goods were stored incorrectly, and even Victor later admitted that it 'didn't work, partly because of the management of it [and] because they handle it in ways which we have no control over'. Meanwhile, Bettys itself had bought in sandwich bread from Mothers' Pride.

The Kings project was a way to show Victor that there was another approach. Lesley developed three cakes, based mainly on family recipes, all to be made at Bettys but branded Kings – a

Advertisement for Kings Cakes, c.1979

way of innovating without potential harm to Bettys itself. The
flavours – lemon and almond, ginger and walnut and honey and
fig – were modern yet felt nostalgic. The influence of Jane
Grigson, Elizabeth David (now producing scholarly, exhaustive
works such as *English Bread and Yeast Cookery*), and the self-
sufficiency movement exemplified by Richard Mabey (author of
Food for Free) was evident, and the designs, which were gentle,
floral and soft, were hand-drawn by Lesley and based on
medieval woodcuts. They were nostalgic in tone, but, as usual
for Bettys, at the cutting edge of fashion – this was the era of
Laura Ashley and the rediscovery of the Arts and Crafts
movement. The cakes sold very well, both in the UK and abroad,
but there was no real appetite within the business to develop
more lines under the Kings name, once the project had proven
its point. Additionally, it was now apparent that Victor's laissez-
faire attitude toward the bakery and the lack of experience of
mass production were bigger issues than had been envisaged.

1970s exterior of Bettys Harrogate,
before major refurbishment in 1980

However, the success of the flavours and feel of the cakes now encouraged Lesley and Jonathan, increasingly proud to be representing the third generation of the family to be at the head of the company, to fight for a significant overhaul of Bettys. In 1982 the bulk of the wholesale contracts were terminated, making it the first year that Bettys made a loss. Frozen tortes survived until 1984, but then that contract too was ended, meaning another year in which the company recorded an overall loss. However, improvements elsewhere rapidly made up for it. Jonathan and Lesley started at Ilkley, where the manager was more amenable to trying out new ideas than elsewhere, trialling soups and lunchtime specials, the Alsatian wine, ice cream made in-house and freshly squeezed orange juice for breakfast. Most of their ideas were then gradually rolled out (including Sunday opening, from 1982). Jonathan's background as a historian, plus Lesley's sense of aesthetics, saw the couple trawling through old photographs of Frederick's Bettys, looking for inspiration from the past but careful always to keep it relevant. They were delighted when one customer described them as 'witty, sophisticated and fun'. Meanwhile, Lesley tackled the menu, introducing cinnamon toast, based on a historic British recipe, and adding an option of fruit cake with cheese, a (delicious) Yorkshire quirk seen as highly curious by visitors to the county.

In high-end London restaurants, it was the era of nouvelle cuisine, complete with an incongruous kiwi slice on every plate, but elsewhere food writers and cooks were rediscovering British culinary heritage: it was a schizophrenic era, but one in which food was finally being taken seriously – so much so that the word 'foodie' was coined and has never gone away. One of the most popular TV shows of the 1970s, *The Good Life*, centred on self-sufficiency and (gently) mocked the rising interest in returning to the land. As an outsider, Lesley was also keen to bring out Bettys' Swiss heritage, something Jonathan was less keen on – he was a proud Yorkshireman, one of the instigators of Yorkshire's own tea, after all – but even he could see that some of the underlying values of the business came straight from Ida and her proud championing of Swiss values. As she had written to Victor in 1941: 'the foundation of any successful life is regular work. Being Swiss you will soon find this to be true because it is the secret that leads to success, but it will not work without a strong will and tenacious perseverance in every way.'

'They were delighted when one customer described them as "witty, sophisticated and fun".'

As if changing the working culture, systems management and menus weren't enough, in 1980 Bettys in Harrogate finally began a major refurbishment, sweeping away the mishmash of the past 50 years (and the remnants of the Café Imperial) to usher back its late Victorian past (the building dated to 1900, although the Café Imperial itself opened in 1907). Outside, a wrought-iron canopy now extended the full length of the building, with the windows onto Montpellier Gardens made full-length. Inside, the stainless steel was replaced by Brown Bettys earthenware teapots, along with melamine trays with lace doilies, and French heritage porcelain took the place of the generic hotelware. Marble surfaces lightened the room, and the gentle tinkle of the piano now became a fixture at certain times of the day.

The revamped Bettys Harrogate opened in time for the 1982 Eurovision Song Contest, held that year in the town and which started with a lengthy film explaining exactly where Harrogate was (echoes of Frederick Belmont's struggles back in the 1920s). The shop windows were decorated in suitably effervescent style, with Terry Wogan explaining that 'the whole town is alive with the excitement of Eurovision' as the show broadcast footage of Parliament Street to the world.

In 1984 the refurbishment won a regional award for its sensitive nature and use of craftspeople. York underwent the same treatment from 1984, with Victor, Lesley and Jonathan – now known within Bettys as 'the Design Team' – drawing inspiration from the past but creating a recognisably modern environment, the aim being not to sink into pastiche. Inside, the layout was altered. The shop was moved so that the café could occupy the

Bettys Harrogate Architectural Elevation, 1980

MONTPELLIER PARADE ELEVATION

full expanse looking onto St Helen's Square, and a Harrogate-like canopy was added over the entrance. The self-service restaurant in the Belmont Room closed, and the room became staff quarters and storage. The café and restaurant menus became more integrated, and the Oak Room was made into an extension of the café, no longer a separate restaurant. Again, the restoration won awards, as did the updates to the Kings bakery in Ripon, specifically recognised for its value as a conservation project and for its environmental impact.

Meanwhile over on Stonegate, the Kiosk was now rebranded as Taylors of Stonegate, a way to strengthen the heritage credentials of Taylors. Locals thought it a great secret, a sneaky way to get the Bettys experience without the increasing queues on Davygate. With its Georgian frontage and a lot of original features (the

Visualisation of the frontage of Bettys,
St Helen's Square, York, August 1983

interiors were a mixture of medieval, Georgian and Victorian), the site was different from the main Bettys branches, and here Lesley and Jonathan were able to explore a more overtly historic feel. Just as Victor had circumvented Claire by using his coffee shops and delis to play out his ideas, so too his son and daughter-in-law tried out things away from the watchful eyes of Jonathan's parents, before trying to put them into Harrogate or Bettys in York. Victor may have been on the Design Team, but he was still only half persuaded by all the changes, and Kay was even less so, and her unofficial influence was still very significant in the main branches. New cutlery, crockery and tables topped with glass but with French linen and lace cloths underneath all went in at Stonegate, as well as new, branch-specific uniforms of Swiss cotton pinstripe blouses with brooches and full-length café-style aprons. Lesley and Jonathan also started to collect teapots to decorate the walls and, once more, improved the menu. The new, forward-looking Bettys was not one that would serve the previous standards of 'tinned celery hearts wrapped in processed ham with a layer of Welsh rarebit mix on top, and tinned spaghetti on toast'.

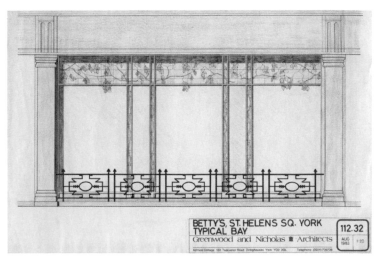

BETTY'S, ST. HELENS SQ. YORK
TYPICAL BAY
Greenwood and Nicholas ▉ Architects
112.32

Increasingly, there was a division of labour. Jonathan summed it up: 'Lesley had the very clear vision about what we should be making and how we should be making it. And I was very clear that I wanted to help people to be able to do that. So, I came at it from the people point of view and she came at it from the product point of view, and together it made sense.' Jonathan was also more involved in Taylors, while Lesley concentrated on Bettys, and Victor had an overview of both. There was an underlying idea that Taylors was masculine – the topless pin-ups in the male changing room, engineers' workshop and foreman's office all suggested so – while Bettys, with its largely female counter staff, was more feminine. All three recognised the need to break down the barriers, and over at Bettys many of the managers and departmental heads in Bettys were women – as they always had been. Taylors was expanding now, giving the company a chance to invest in staff training and recruitment, but improving the gender balance remained an ongoing task.

It was proving hard to get Yorkshire Tea into more supermarkets, as the team were determined to stay regional, both from preference and because they simply didn't have the capacity. Nevertheless, by 1982, armed with better, more efficient teabag machines, they were selling in Asda and Sainsbury's, along with

Bottom 1980s Yorkshire Tea packaging illustrated by Lizzie Sanders and designed by Michael Peters

the significant northern chains of Hintons and Hillards (later subsumed by Safeway and Tesco respectively). The packaging wasn't working properly, though, looking too budget and too amateurish to really compete with the likes of Tetley. As sales grew, Jonathan decided to approach an outside agency, Michael Peters, then one of the UK's most innovative design agencies. The result combined the softer illustrative style already explored on the Kings packaging, with a bold orange wraparound, the overall effect reminiscent of the old waxed paper packages with a decorative branded paper band around them in which the Taylors shops had still been selling loose tea until the late 1970s. The illustrations were nostalgic scenes of rural Yorkshire life, but the overall effect was completely different from anything on sale at the time and proved a winner. Yorkshire Tea expanded into Lancashire, driven by Morrisons' own expansion, with county-specific packaging proclaiming 'tried and tested in Lancashire water. Makes a really good cup of tea.' For the first time an ad agency was commissioned to make some short television adverts for the Yorkshire region. They raised awareness, although the team had reservations: 'We wanted it to be genuine and authentic … [but] when we saw the rushes or the outtakes or whatever, we were always disappointed by our advertising.' Pagoda was quietly rebranded as Yorkshire Gold and gained listings including Asda, while Tesco now agreed to stock Yorkshire Tea as well. By 1985 it was the number two tea brand in Yorkshire, still strictly regional (apart from one shop for desperate Yorkshire types stranded in London), and Taylors tea and coffee became Taylors of Harrogate.

Jonathan had also been intimately involved with another Bettys icon, developed in 1982–3. Aided by Helen Frankel, Bettys marketing assistant, he designed a unique scone-like creation, packed with fruit and with a smiley face picked out in cherries and currants. Lesley Norris, the product development manager, took Jonathan and Helen's home-made version, and made it into something which could be produced in its hundreds (and later thousands). Initially Yorkshire Fat Rascals were sold only in the shops, and Helen recalled that: 'It just took off instantly from what I remember. It immediately became pretty much a top seller.' There were also some attempts to start making chocolates in-house again, starting with Easter eggs. Jonathan remembered

Opposite, top Yorkshire Fat Rascals, developed in 1983 by Jonathan Wild

Bettys

Infants and Childrens Menu

Bettys Doubledecker Stripy Sandwiches £0.90

Choose any TWO of these fillings for your sandwich:

Peanut Butter
Cold Sausage
Wensleydale cheese
Banana and Honey
Cottage cheese
Tomato Chutney
Marmalade
Lettuce and Tomato
Egg
Bacon

Single Deckers £0.50

Bettys Boiled Egg! £0.70

Served with fingers of toast or warm cheese straws.

Round of Buttered Toast £0.30
Round of Cheese Straws £0.40

Eat Bettys Clown! £1.00

Tomato ears and a sausage nose: you can eat every bit of our salad face.

Chips with everything!

Bacon   Sausage   Fried Egg
Tomato   Mushrooms

ONE with Chips £1.00
TWO with Chips £1.30
THREE with Chips £1.60

Raspberry and Strawberry Delight! £1.25

A mountain of Raspberries, Cream, Vanilla & Strawberry icecream.

Bettys Banana Boat! £1.25

An icecream and banana boat, complete with a brandysnap funnel.

Bettys Butterfly! £0.70

Vanilla icecream topped with a Crisp biscuit butterfly.

Icecream Milk Shakes £0.82

Banana, Strawberry, Chocolate.

Orange Juice £0.40

Sparkling Apple Juice £0.55

Cold Milk £0.30

Warm Milk £0.30

Coca Cola £0.55

In addition to these items, half portions of all our normal Menu dishes are available.

V.A.T. included at 15%.

Bettys Infants and children's menu,
February 1985

posing with giant chocolate eggs as a child, and now the moulds were rediscovered, having survived in storage at the bakery. This being the 1980s, the first forays also involved a chocolate Kermit, an Orville and a Basil Brush, perhaps a tad less sophisticated than Bettys' new image (although not entirely at odds with Frederick's carefully lit up gnomes of 1928).

By 1982 a million customers a year were being served across the five Bettys branches. Lesley and Jonathan's first child, Chloë was born, followed by Daniel in 1984. Chloë had sensitive skin and was prone to stomach upsets as a baby, precipitating careful examination of the Bettys menu, already much changed from only seven years previously. The organic movement was then in its infancy, but a new children's menu was introduced, offering 'a range of meatless, preservative- and additive-free foods for small babies'. Artificial colourings were replaced with natural colourings, a process which proved particularly challenging for glacé cherries. No one wanted to produce naturally coloured (dark red) cherries, for 'bright red sells!' Playpens and changing facilities went into the branches, along with high chairs, and the counter staff held a supply of nappies in case of need. In addition to the specific dishes for children – peanut butter or sausage sandwiches, 'chips with everything!' and a Bettys banana boat, among others – every dish on the main menu was offered as half portions, recognising that, while some children needed their own, unchallenging dinner, others were fine with adult flavours, but needed child-friendly portions.

In 1986 the company's efforts were recognised with the inclusion of all five Bettys branches in that year's *Good Food Guide*, which declared its cakes 'famous', the wines 'superb' and that it was 'deceptively unassuming'. The success of the Design Team in bringing the décor back to its roots showed too when the *Guide* stated of York that it 'first opened in 1936, and not much has changed'. It also lauded it for adhering to the principles of what it called 'Real Food', a concept the authors of the *Guide* credited themselves with having helped to spearhead, defining it in the preface as regional, market-led, with much use of relishes and chutneys, vegetables and British traditional food: 'this new style of cooking has an identity of its own. Its symbol is probably the garden'. It also involved 'respect for the craft and skill of the small food producer'.

Bettys was no longer aiming to be among the high-end restaurants that the *Good Food Guide* were promoting and dropped out of subsequent guides (although it was regularly recognised by Egon Ronay), but in its ethos it had certainly caught the zeitgeist. It was also now emphatically a family business, with Lesley and Jonathan a united team, Victor leading with them, and Liz and Tony actively involved (Tony was at this time training as a coffee buyer at Taylors). Bettys and Taylors were still separate but had established identities, based on shared values, including an investment in staff which meant that staff retention rates were much higher than those generally the norm in the catering business. Finally, in 1987 Lesley's work was recognised as she was awarded shares and made a director of the company (part of a wider readjustment to the Board). Many of the stalwarts were starting to retire, and Bettys was now firmly linked to the third generation.

There was still a lot to do, but Victor, recording his memoirs in 1989, was serene as he looked at the business of which he was still the Chair. He admitted he couldn't claim credit for ensuring the continuation of it under 'caring ownership' but felt Frederick would have been delighted with the way it all worked now, that 'business should be a pleasure (as well as a jolly good income)' and that he only hoped the next generation would be 'big-minded enough to put the health of the business above their own personal ambitions and recognise their own limitations and acknowledge the strengths of others'. The British economy was expanding, inflation was low and the world seemed like a pretty good place. Ten years later, in 1999, he would listen back to his words and accuse himself of complacency.

Jonathan and Elizabeth Wild (later
Barnes) with hand-decorated Bettys
Easter eggs, 1953

The rascal machine

I am standing by the rascal machine, one of the newest additions to the craft bakery. It is juddering and whirring and then beeping. A beard-snooded baker stands ready to receive the small pats of soon-to-be rascals which it produces – 480 of them every 10 minutes. Another baker is mixing the dough with which to feed it, while behind me in a separate room a team is busy weighing and checking the raw ingredients before wheeling them through to the mixing area. The machine is a time-saver, scaling (weighing) the rascals out and depositing them ready for finishing. Each rascal is whipped off to be given a final shape and to have the all-important face put on by hand, before being baked in batches. My host, Lesley Norris, cheerfully informs me that, prior to the arrival of the rascal machine, they were being shaped by hand: 8,500 rascals a week. Last year the bakery produced 435,000 Fat Rascals. And that's not all.

Ever since Frederick bought land at Starbeck and opened his small Bettys bakery, it's been producing goods for the cafés and shops, as well as venturing into wholesale and, of course, supplying Bettys by Post. Frederick was clear-sighted and realistic about the labour involved in baking bread and crafting pâtisserie, and an enthusiastic proponent of labour-saving machinery. Conditions in the industry at the time were hard: everything was still very physical, and, although the unrelenting grime of the Victorian era was no more, relatively few

bakeries could afford to invest in machinery. Hours were long, wages low, and the sheer physical effort involved in kneading – by hand – vast quantities of bread dough meant that bakers tended to be men, sweating freely into the troughs as they worked.

Mechanisation meant hygiene, and Bettys menus proudly proclaimed that the bakery had been awarded the Certificate of the Institute of Hygiene. It also meant that Bettys could employ skilled bakers, rather than grunt labour, including some who had been trained in Switzerland. Frederick's early machines were driven by enormous fan belts, potentially lethal, but advanced for their time. Over at Cambridge Crescent, the fridges and freezers were still of the pre-First World War type, cooled with ice

and salt, for, despite having electricity, electric cooling equipment was still in its infancy and very expensive. There was also a steam-heated copper boiler for sugar work, still in use during the Second World War. Consistency was another boon, vital for ensuring Bettys' reputation remained solid.

Frederick's bakery was added to and altered during Victor's tenure. Victor was equally fascinated by the potential of mechanisation but aware of the careful balance to be struck between making life easier and more efficient and losing the all-important craft element which made Bettys so special. As industrialised processes swept through the baking industry in the 1960s, Bettys became more and more unique. Its unequivocal decision not to adopt the

Chorleywood process immediately put it into a small minority of commercial bread makers.

The bakery that I'm visiting replaced the original in 1999. Yet wherever I look there are links to the past, from the battered copper sugar-boiling pans stacked on a shelf in the corner, to the enormous slab of marble used for rolling pastry. The rascal machine frees up staff and stops repetitive strain injury, RSI. The minute books for the 1990s onward have a section for recording any incidents, and it's clear that even then the bakery work remained very repetitive and manual. Lesley notes that further work is needed to mechanise certain tasks – it was only very recently that an enrobing machine arrived, for dipping the thousands of fancy fondants in icing before they are hand-piped with floral motifs.

Many of the enjoyably huge machines are silent on the day I visit, although at peak times when, preparations for Easter and Christmas are under way, the room booms with low-level noise. I peer with glee into a rotary oven, the inside of which holds a set of giant horizontal baking slabs which rotate slowly around a central point. There are retarders so that yeasted goods can be risen as required, enabling the bakers to go home and see their families rather than have their lives dictated to by the dough. For a long time the retarders were known as 'the night shift'. There's a sonic cutter for vanilla slices, much more precise than the human hand, and aimed at cutting waste.

Waste is a watchword here. Things go wrong sometimes, and a whole batch of cakes is ruined. There are offcuts, packet ends, whole packets of biscuits removed for quality control – and, of course, all of the inedible packaging which is produced. It's all tracked. Anything edible goes for staff lunches or to local charities.

But Bettys constantly runs up against the issue of shelf life, for its bakery goods are not designed to last for months and don't have the preservatives or packaging of mass-market supermarket goods. Since the ban on pigswill came in, the bakery cannot dispose of food waste in the time-honoured way, but instead sends it to be processed by a specialist company.

We walk past the cooling tunnels, which remind me of airport body scanners, through the despatch rooms, shelves neatly stacked with cake boxes and spindles of ribbons. The waste cardboard interiors will eventually go off to the Cone Exchange craft community scrap store to be reborn as craft materials and sold in aid of charity. Entering the chocolate room, I breathe in the smell of molten chocolate and get into a conversation about the best way to ensure a consistent chocolate Florentine. Finally, we visit the cake-decorating room, a haven of peace after the main bakery.

Confectionery has always been a more skilled and better-paid trade than baking. When Frederick Belmont, then Fritz Bützer, decided to specialise as a confectioner, it was a calculated decision. In Britain, confectionery was associated with Continental cooks, and, although there were many skilled native confectioners, being Swiss gave him an added cachet. The team working calmly piping royal icing onto cakes are all women today, much as they would have been in Frederick's time, when the bakers tended to be men and the more delicate work fell to women. They show me a sugarwork rattle, designed for a christening cake, which has a dragée inside so that it actually rattles when shaken. I marvel at pastillage flowers so delicate that at first I mistook them for a real bouquet. When I leave, I suspect I have a slight scent of sugar about me, and I don't mind at all.

Back to basics

1986–1996

What's on the menu?

Brunch was introduced at Bettys in 1987, having swept across from America. There, it was strongly associated with upper-class women, but, when it reached London, it was rapidly democratised. Now it came to Yorkshire, where a newly confident Bettys put its own spin on it.

By 1994, when this menu was in use, the Swiss heritage of Bettys was much more obvious to its customers than hitherto, and the balance of two Swiss breakfasts, one Continental and a full English with a solid nod to Yorkshire was typical. The menu here is gently health-oriented, with both a specific health breakfast and the inclusion of granary bread as standard with the full English. Freshness is also emphasised, and the mention of Bettys preserves creates a homely feel.

Taylors is much more integrated than previously, and the wide choice of teas and coffees was backed up with a separate drinks menu in all the branches. At Taylors in Stonegate in the early 1990s, the hot beverages section took up three of the five columns of the menu and included flavoured black teas such as rose petal or jasmine, green tea, varieties including vintage Darjeeling, along with herbal tisanes served with honey. There were also eight different country-specific coffees, along with blends ('French roast' and 'Italian Continental') which were more familiar to British coffee drinkers.

The bakery operated seven days a week from 1992, supplying the breads, croissants, rolls, oatcakes and cake selection listed here, and matching the seven-days-a-week opening of the cafés. High street shopping more generally finally caught up with the passing of the Sunday Trading Act in 1994. St Helen's Square in York and Harrogate were the only two branches which opened for dinner, though, for elsewhere there simply wasn't the demand.

The cafés now had additional seasonal menus: dishes such as salade niçoise appeared in spring, chicken and asparagus rösti in summer and chestnut torte in winter. The rösti was a key dish, appearing here as 'rösti eiger' or just 'rösti', served plain, with vegetables or meats, and as mini rösti. It had been introduced in 1987, the first in a series of overtly Swiss dishes which Lesley brought in and which still form the backbone of the menu today. It coexisted at first with earlier dishes, including the rarebits, which at Stonegate were described as 'the speciality of the house', although gradually the emphasis on them was reduced until they formed only one item on a much larger menu, no longer given a special section of their own.

The cake selection mentioned here now also includes more Continental varieties, such as the rich chocolate Viennese sachertorte, along with Yorkshire curd tart and, from 1988, the Fat Rascal, which had previously been a shop item only.

CELEBRATION BREAKFAST
(12 noon - 2pm only)

Bucks Fizz for Two

(half a bottle of our superior sparkling wine with a jug of freshly squeezed orange juice)

£5.95

Now choose from any of our other breakfast choices

SWISS HEALTH BREAKFAST

Bettys Homemade Swiss Müesli with fresh fruit

Granary Toast with Honey

Pot of Ceylon Tea with Lemon
or
cafetière of Decaffeinated Coffee

£2.75

CONTINENTAL BREAKFAST

The Fresh Juice of three Oranges

Warm Breakfast Rolls
or Croissants
with Bettys Preserves

Pot of Vintage Darjeeling Tea
or
cafetière of Continental Roast Coffee

£2.65

SWISS COOKED BREAKFAST

The Fresh Juice of three Oranges

"Rösti Eiger"
(Golden Swiss Rösti Potatoes Bacon and Egg)

Pot of Ceylon tea
or
cafetière of Continental Coffee

£3.95

ENGLISH BREAKFAST

The Fresh Juice of three Oranges

Bacon, Egg, Sausage, Mushrooms and Tomato

Hot Yorkshire Oatcakes
or Granary Toast with
Bettys Preserves or Marmalade

Pot of Special Rich Assam Tea
or
cafetière of Indian Estate Mysore Coffee

£4.65

SIDE DISHES

Choice of Side Salads	85p
Mushrooms Cooked in Butter	1.22
Chipped Potatoes	60p
Cakes, *from the trolley*	65p-1.45

Poached Eggs, Granary Mushrooms and other breakfast dishes are on the à la carte menu.

Bettys first Sunday Brunch menu, c.1994

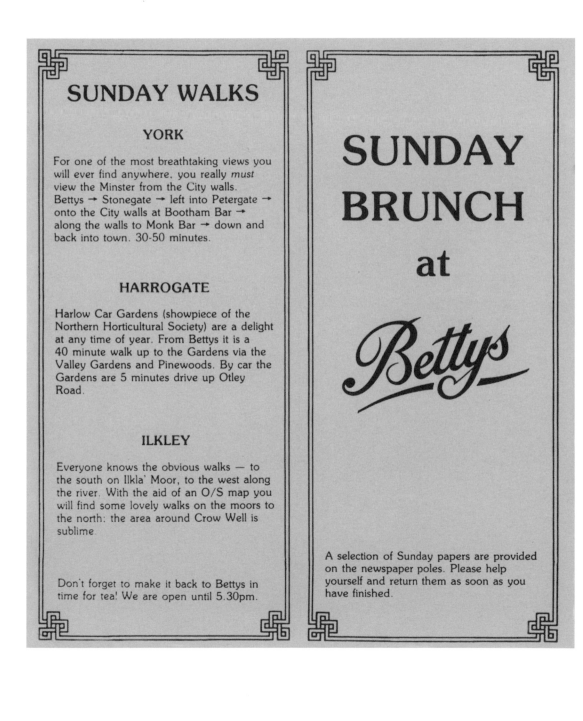

SUNDAY WALKS

YORK

For one of the most breathtaking views you will ever find anywhere, you really *must* view the Minster from the City walls. Bettys → Stonegate → left into Petergate → onto the City walls at Bootham Bar → along the walls to Monk Bar → down and back into town. 30-50 minutes.

HARROGATE

Harlow Car Gardens (showpiece of the Northern Horticultural Society) are a delight at any time of year. From Bettys it is a 40 minute walk up to the Gardens via the Valley Gardens and Pinewoods. By car the Gardens are 5 minutes drive up Otley Road.

ILKLEY

Everyone knows the obvious walks — to the south on Ilkla' Moor, to the west along the river. With the aid of an O/S map you will find some lovely walks on the moors to the north: the area around Crow Well is sublime.

Don't forget to make it back to Bettys in time for tea! We are open until 5.30pm.

SUNDAY BRUNCH at

Bettys

A selection of Sunday papers are provided on the newspaper poles. Please help yourself and return them as soon as you have finished.

Bettys Ilkley, c.1990s

The apparently calm, slowly growing Bettys of 1986 underwent a series of sharp growing pains in the decade that followed, emerging from them shaken, but ultimately more stable than before. Victor updated his memoir recordings in 1999, looking back at a period during which, slightly to his surprise, Bettys had grown significantly both financially and in national – and indeed in global – prestige. He admitted to being slightly bewildered by the sheer number of people now involved – staff numbers had gone up by 69 per cent in a decade, and in 1996 stood at 575, but he was also thinking of the way in which the business had become so actively involved in the wider community. Now Bettys had a direct impact on local schools, charities and community groups, and it also regularly employed outside agencies for marketing and training. Charitable involvement and prioritising employee welfare were 'quite normal and expected', both of them integrated into the way the company operated rather than considered as desirable add-ons if only the Bettys Board wasn't fighting the latest small crisis to crop up. He summed it up as a 'change from a rather homely and in some ways rather amateur business into a really highly professional organisation', adding: 'I stand back sometimes in amazement.'

Many of the elements that came to fruition in the late 1980s and early 1990s were already visible, the results of the frenetic period of activity in the early 1980s: the gradual reintroduction of some of Bettys' earlier aesthetics, the addition of an overtly Continental flavour to the menus, the building of long-term relationships with suppliers and customers, the importance of environmental and business sustainability and the firm stand against the industrialisation and subsequent cheapening of even high-volume goods. Bettys remained a private company, able to set its own dividends, and as such was not beholden to faceless shareholders who expected the profits to go up year on year, and whose main motivation was financial. Victor's policy had been to keep the dividends low, reinvesting profits into the business, its staff and the community, and the shares were still all held within the founding families.

Other Yorkshire firms stood as a warning: Harry Ramsden's, founded in Guiseley in the old West Riding of Yorkshire in 1928, and in 1986 still operating only the original fish and chip shop, was floated on the stock market in 1988, and rapidly expanded across the UK, including into motorway service stations, becoming a generic fast-food chain. The Bettys Board remained convinced that this was not a model they should follow. Instead, they wanted to grow slowly, solidly and organically. 'Prudence', said Victor, 'served us well.' He said he'd been taught the value of careful risk assessment at school in Switzerland, studying the systems by which the Swiss vineyards were supplied with water from far-off glaciers, working in harmony with nature and only changing things when it was certain this would work.

One of Victor's long-held policies had been to insist that all of the various premises paid market rents, even though the company generally owned the freeholds. They also had to pay capital charges and operate, to all intents and purposes, as separate, independent businesses from a financial point of view. In the turbulent economy of the 1970s and 1980s, this made brilliant – if brutal – sense. There was no room for unprofitable parts of the business, and the approach ensured that when the economy took a downturn, Bettys was able to survive. Moreover, both the bakery and the Taylors factory only expanded when they absolutely had to, although when they did, it was generally with extra capacity and therefore (limited) future-proofing. However, the slightly piecemeal approach meant that the bakery in particular was a bit of a mishmash of styles and sections, with sheds and extensions – intended to be temporary – making the whole site into a bit of a maze. In heavy rain the valley gutters between the various buildings leaked, and artful bucket placement was part of the working environment.

In January 1986 Eddie Hardy retired. He'd been instrumental in the expansion of Taylors off the back of Yorkshire Tea, but there was a need now for a younger team, more in step with the forward-looking ethos of the third generation of family owners. There was a new confidence, based on what had already been

Bettys & Taylors Board, c. late 1980s

done since 1975, including a determination to make Taylors more integrated into the business as a whole, with more active family involvement there as well as in Bettys. Gone were the years when Bettys people knew little of Taylors and what went on there. Jonathan had trained at Taylors as well as at Bettys, spending an hour each morning with Jim Raleigh (now officially retired but still a consultant), reading and discussing with him the commodity pages of the *Financial Times*, and learning far more than just the art of tasting tea and coffee. Jonathan later credited Jim with getting him truly excited by the world of tea and coffee. That older generation were used to their managerial privileges, though, often dubious about some of Jonathan's attempts to make the working environment more egalitarian. Victor had found himself fielding comments that it was a shock to see some of the more 'exotically dressed staff' sharing the same entrance to the building that the directors used.

Jonathan had also instigated a free and open-to-all staff canteen, shocked by the way in which the supervisors would eat egg mayonnaise sandwiches in their own cubbyhole, while the staff made do with a basic canteen providing tea, (instant) coffee, toast and jam. Equally irked by the preferential parking provision for the managers, he went out early one morning with an engineer and together they painted over all the proprietary initials and made the car park first-come, first-served.

With Eddie's retirement, Lesley stepped up, formally setting up a Group Design Department, with new staff recruited and a remit to oversee the aesthetics of packaging and menus – among an exhaustive list – going forward. Her keen artistic sense, honed by art school, was vital, but so too was her upbringing, for her father had worked as a builder as well as running the farm, and she was able to work easily with architects, builders and craftspeople as she led the branch refurbishments. She would become Creative Director in 1992. Bettys was gaining a name for itself as a repository for art in an unwelcome manner, though – in June 12 of the Spindlers were stolen during a break-in at Harrogate. (They were eventually recovered after a tip-off from a dealer who'd been offered them.)

In June 1986 Bettys started another new venture, inspired by the Bettys of the 1920s and 1930s. One of Lesley's former art teachers, Mary Godfrey, had applied for a position at Bettys. Jonathan interviewed her, and 'at her interview I asked her whether she knew anything about mail order. She said no; I said neither do I, let's do it.' She was taken on to head up 'Bettys by Post', a catalogue-based delivery service, initially intended to test the waters for national demand for Taylors teas and coffees, with a small section of Bettys cakes and shop goods. It was the latter, however, which proved most in demand, and the second catalogue, for Christmas 1986, was stuffed with rich fruit cakes and Christmas puddings, along with jams and chutneys and Alsatian wine.

Over 1,000 parcels were eventually despatched, 250 of which went overseas (including to Alaska, Hong Kong, Iceland and Hungary), showing the reach that Bettys already had. In the next few years the Board's aim became both to further bolster the bakery sales and to gain Bettys national press coverage, because now everyone in Britain could buy their products. The service made very little profit as the costs of packaging and catalogues was very high, but it was deemed to be an investment. Demand was, inevitably, highest at Christmas and Easter,

Bettys by Post catalogue, 1986

B/22/1

Bettys BY POST

CHRISTMAS 1986

1 BETTYS CHRISTMAS HAMPER

Celebrate Christmas in style. Our hamper has got just about everything you could desire, except the turkey! For Christmas morning there's a bottle of sparkling Crémant d'Alsace. Then to whet the appetite for lunch there are cheese straws and spicy roasted almonds. After the main course the perfect Christmas pudding (to serve 4/6) followed by our Christmas Blend fresh roasted coffee, fresh cream liqueur truffles, petit fours or chocolate coated nuts. For the Children there are bags of chocolate coins, Bettys chocolate guineas and marzipan fruits. To complete the hamper there is a bag of spiced Christmas tea, and of course, a magnificent Bettys Christmas cake.

HAMPER £59.90 REF NO X100

NB Most of the items featured in the hamper are also available individually in this catalogue.

'Jonathan was convinced that one of the key differentials between Bettys and its competitors was the quality of the staff, many of whom were very loyal, and that more should be done to train and inspire them.'

although there was a year-round catalogue as well, with wedding orders a particular speciality – in 1987 an order came in for 300 scones with clotted cream for a wedding in the Netherlands. The first floor at Harrogate was converted into a store and packing room, until it grew large enough to move to Starbeck in 1998. The Easter catalogues offered a large range of chocolate eggs, which proved sufficiently successful that by 1987 the catalogues were promising French chocolate truffles made in-house. Lesley had been quietly outraged that Bettys no longer made its own chocolates, and this was the continuation of the movement she and Jonathan later called 'back to basics'.

Getting back to basics was also the aim over at Taylors, where, with tea doing well, the focus turned to coffee. To date, most of the coffee sales had been through the Bettys shops, and the products now included several different grinds, for percolators (including their own, Taylors-branded system) through to the newly fashionable cafetières. However, the success of Yorkshire Tea was showing that products needed to be sold where customers were doing their shopping – and that was increasingly in supermarkets. Although some still shopped for groceries on the high street, most now did not. If Taylors coffee was not to

Taylors packaging featuring the 'Aromafin' valve, 1987

dwindle and eventually die, it needed to be accessible and convenient for those who wanted to buy it.

But coffee, like tea, was a competitive market, complicated by highly volatile commodity markets and prices that went up and down on a daily basis, making profits almost impossible to predict – a far cry from the relative stability of the Bettys suppliers. If coffee was to survive at Taylors, they needed something which would stand out enough that it would be worth a supermarket taking the risk of stocking a brand which was virtually unknown, especially outside Yorkshire. The smaller, local chains, which enthusiastically stocked Yorkshire Tea, were being swallowed up by the likes of Tesco and Asda, and national chains were less willing to stock regional items. Yorkshire Tea had strong enough sales that its position was established, but a Yorkshire Coffee was never on the cards.

Taylors' coffee business at the time was based on delivering freshly roasted coffee beans to retailers on a weekly basis, for them to grind to order for their customers. Pre-packed ground coffee existed, based on a technology whereby manufacturers would allow the freshly ground beans to 'gas off' before packing. Letting the gases off inevitably involved letting oxygen back in, meaning that the coffee was always slightly stale even before it reached stores. Led by Tony Wild, the coffee buyer at the time, Taylors invested in the first Bosch Aromafin system in the UK. The system included a plastic valve on the front of the foil or plastic sealed packet, which let the carbon dioxide out, but prevented oxygen from getting in. The upshot was that an unopened packet of coffee would last a year, a vast improvement on the current industry norm of four months. It was beneficial right down the chain, from Taylors itself to the stockists, to the customers who usually bought their coffee already quite a long way into the four-month shelf life. The new system was a massive investment, but Tony saw it as a way into the ground-coffee market which would enable Taylors to sustain its reputation for quality against competitors who opted for cheaper and inferior systems. The various competitor valve systems which existed were nowhere near as good at keeping oxygen out. It did the trick, and in 1987 Taylors launched a range of Aromafin-packaged coffee specifically for supermarkets which quickly gained listings. In 1989 Taylors gained a contract with

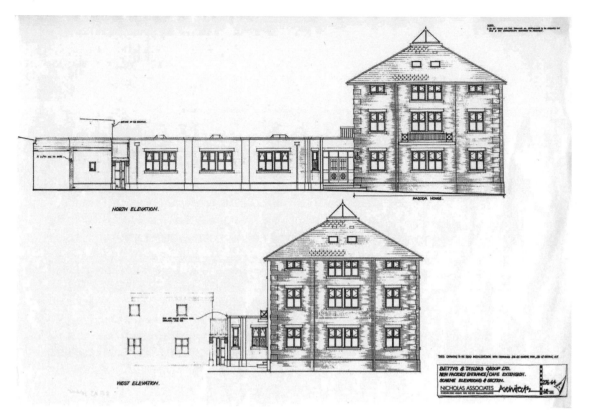

Marks & Spencer to supply its own-brand coffee – quite a coup, for M&S food was sold at a premium, based on its high quality. The partnership gave Taylors much more influence and enabled it to lead in supporting better-quality environmental and social standards on the farms and co-operatives which produced its coffee beans, and the partnership continues to this day. By 1991 all of the various grind sizes had been phased out, replaced by one grind which was suitable for any type of coffee-making apparatus. Omnigrind, as it was known, was a precision process, involving controlling the grind so that the grinder did not produce a mixture of consistencies. Eventually a new slogan was devised for a national sales campaign, stating simply that Taylors made 'coffee to be taken seriously'.

With Taylors becoming a serious contributor to the overall turnover of the business, and needing to expand, its factory at Starbeck needed overhauling. Victor's 1970s warehouse had been three metres high, but as forklift truck technology improved, taller extensions were added, and now plans were drawn up for a warehouse 15 metres tall. A finished goods warehouse was constructed off-site, and new offices were built, christened Pagoda House, after the terraced house in Leeds which Taylors

Taylors Pagoda House elevation drawing, 1994

had occupied for so much of its history. Victor watched it go up, feeling in his heart that this was it: Bettys had 'made it'. Meanwhile, the entire Kings operation was closed, both at Ripon and Bedale. With the end of the wholesale operation in 1984, the two Kings bakeries had been producing exclusively for Bettys as well as for their own shops. However, they were taking internal sales from the Bettys bakery, which could easily take over from them, and with competition in both towns from national chains such as Greggs and Bakers Oven (bought out by Greggs in 1994), and more local vendors such as Thomas the Baker (founded in 1981, and another family-run business, spread across the north), the shops were struggling to remain afloat. Jonathan recorded that he was 'heartbroken', having trained with the Kings staff, and he continued to help out in the bakeries at busy times until the very end. The staff were offered new positions at Bettys, although few chose to make the move.

Jonathan was convinced that one of the key differentials between Bettys and its competitors was the quality of the staff, many of whom were very loyal, and that more should be done to train and inspire them. Already he'd helped instigate company-wide social initiatives, mainly centred on sports and including darts and running, but the 'them and us' feeling remained between Bettys and Taylors, and the branches were out on a limb. Now he became enthused by the idea of 'action centred leadership', a theory of leadership developed in the late 1960s by John Adair, which emphasised teamwork, training and communication, with internal organisation based on small groups working together with close contact between managers and workers on a daily basis.

He instigated a new structure, a much flatter hierarchy than previously, with a top tier of managers and directors feeding down to department heads, who, in turn, fed down to team

Kings Master Bakers' shop, Ripon, 1984

leaders, usually in charge of a small team of 12. Equally, they fed back up, with frontline reports and any grievances conveyed immediately, rather than being stored up or forgotten. Monthly briefings on what the company was up to and how it was doing – and what part each team had played in that – were intended both to inform and to motivate. Jonathan took to 'walking the floor' for most of the week, sitting in the canteens, talking to staff, making himself visible and known: exhausting, not least as he was also conscious of setting an example. He wore a suit and tie at all times, despite admitting to being 'as scruffy as they come' at home, acting out his firm belief that there should be no separate rules for staff and directors. He admitted that 'if I felt trapped in this exhausting regime of being visible to the business, maybe that is why for more than 20 years I carried a fully packed rucksack (including boots) in the boot of my car. I called it my "running away rucksack", and I used to promise myself that one of these fine days, driving over to Ilkley or Northallerton, I would simply disappear into the hills for the day.' He never did.

Lesley Norris, Confectioner of the Year, 1991

More formal schemes were set up too, including an obligatory food hygiene qualification for every member of staff. This was not just for best-practice reasons: it was also intended as boost for those members of staff who had left school with few or no qualifications. First aid training was also offered to everyone, far beyond the legal requirement to have one first-aider at each branch. This followed an incident at the now annual staff ball, where one of the attendees choked on a piece of potato, to be saved by a first-aider performing a timely Heimlich manoeuvre. Victor drew up a new version of the scribbles he'd done for Jonathan when he was agonising over whether to join the business, now called 'Where our customers' money goes', to show how both the business and the individuals who worked within it could feel proud of their contribution to wider society. 'Are we winning?' noticeboards went up, and monthly brainstorming sessions came in, and it all worked to change the culture. In 1988 Bettys won its first National Training Award (one of 80 winners from 1,500 entrants) for its first staff conference, and in 1991 it was one of the first companies to hold an Investor in People award. Within the company, people were encouraged to job swap, spending time in different departments, and to apply for awards – in 1991 Lesley Norris won British Confectioner of the Year. Bettys also won a second National Training Award for an exchange project in which Bettys & Taylors staff spent time shadowing local teachers and vice versa, trying to build links with schools as a potential provider of jobs that were more than just fill-ins. Jonathan gave speeches at business conferences on the importance of training and support. After one such speech in 1992, a woman came up and thanked him for the transformative effect a Bettys waitressing job had had on her teenage daughter: 'I would gladly have paid Bettys … it must be like Swiss Finishing School'.

Charitable engagement was another key area for Jonathan and Lesley. Charitable spending went up by nearly 1,200 per cent between 1985 and 1990, and the first official group charity of the year was the sponsorship of a Red Cross nurse in Sudan in 1986 – Live Aid had brought Africa into the public eye the previous year. Staff feedback was that giving should be focused more on charities directly relevant to Bettys, though, and after that first year staff voted on the charities they wished to support.

In 1989 a pivotal moment came when Jonathan came home one afternoon to find his children distraught. Chloë, then aged six, and Daniel, at four, had been watching *Blue Peter*, which was deeply engaged with environmental topics: deforestation, the ozone layer and the destruction of wildlife habitats for farmland. But the programme wasn't doing a direct appeal, so Jonathan, fired with both idealistic zeal and the desire to cheer his children up, promised that they would help. He came up with an idea, summed up to them as 'if you two plant one tree for me, I will find a way of planting nine hundred and ninety-nine thousand, nine hundred and ninety-nine more'. Making this promise a reality would take the next decade, starting and ending on Harrogate Stray. Chloë, Daniel and primary schoolchildren from across Harrogate ceremoniously planted the first tree, a hornbeam, with a stone plaque next to it reading: 'Trees for Life. Planting Trees around the World. First of a Million. February 1990.' The local press duly photographed the event and then left, while at Bettys Jonathan, Mary Godfrey and Liz Wild (now Liz Barnes) set about organising links with a charity in Ethiopia, which engaged local communities in tree planting and maintenance. Tokens went onto Yorkshire Tea packs which allowed the public to contribute (three tokens sent in meant that the company would fund one more tree), talks were given to local schools as well as to stockists of Yorkshire Tea, with one unexpected knock-on effect being that some supermarkets increased the prominence of the brand in-store, as this upped their own green credentials at little cost. The internal newsletter carried regular updates, including letters sent in with the tokens: 'what a wonderful thing you are doing and so worthwhile in this day and age, it's an exercise that is a must for this world and like the tea I drink, it's simply marvellous', and 'I enclose three "tree" tokens – please plant another tree and accept my congratulations for your far-sighted initiative.'

By the end of 1990 over 100,000 tokens had been sent in, and 120,000 seedlings had been potted up in Ethiopia. By 1993 they were up to 500,000 trees, and the project had expanded, with planting now in India, Brazil and back home on the Yorkshire moors. Victor built a tropical house at Starbeck, slightly crazily sandwiched between two factory buildings and stocked with coffee and tea plants he had grown. It underlined the importance of global agriculture to the whole Bettys & Taylors business, so much of which relied on farmers growing things across the

Top Chloë Wild planting a Tree for Life

Top School children planting the first of one million trees on The Stray at Harrogate, 1990

Right Daniel Wild with the first of a million trees

world. In 1995 the number of trees planted would hit 750,000, but by then the project had diversified into community schemes around trees as well as the trees themselves, and it was not until 2000 that Daniel Wild would officially plant the last of the (first) million Trees for Life, next to the first on Harrogate Stray.

1990 wasn't just notable for the start of Trees for Life. In October that year the latest Yorkshire Tea advert launched, showing not just in Yorkshire and Tyne Tees, but also in Lancashire, continuing Yorkshire Tea's slow expansion. Conceived and produced by Tony Wild, Jonathan's brother, they were finally a set of adverts which felt like a true reflection of the brand. Tony had joined as a management trainee in 1981, became a coffee buyer in 1982 and a director of Taylors in 1990. He was keenly creative and an innovative coffee buyer, introducing kopi luwak coffee to Britain, to a media furore. Better known as civit coffee, the coffee berries have been eaten, and the indigestible beans excreted − whole − by Indonesian palm civits. The berries take on a faint tang from the process and are highly prized, although there are debates about the ethics of the process following a rise in its popularity. Tony was also free-spirited, and he struggled with routine and the lack of creativity inherent in a managerial role.

Tony was passionate about the new medium of video and had started his own production company making arthouse music

Tony Wild (centre) filming a Yorkshire Tea commercial, 1990

videos, so Jonathan suggested he take charge of the next advertising campaign for Yorkshire Tea, hoping he could channel his creativity and knowledge of the business and make the campaign more genuinely representative of what Yorkshire Tea stood for. Previous ventures into advertising had shown that creative agencies rarely fully understood the ethos behind it. Tony's resulting adverts featured a real Yorkshire farming family, the Firths. Each short film followed them on the farm during lambing season, ending each segment with a cup of Yorkshire Tea. The adverts were exactly what Jonathan wanted and were followed by a similar series in 1992 (filming was slightly interrupted by an escapee pet ferret, not shown on screen). The film showing Josie Firth playing cricket in the Nidderdale Ladies League was a particularly lovely tie-in, for Yorkshire Tea was just beginning its long association with cricket, supplying tea and kit to every cricket club in the county. (Cricket is the only sport in which a tea break is a vital part of the game.) The effects on sales were very positive, and with that and a new range of heritage teas, Taylors now edged above Bettys in its contribution to turnover. In 1992 Sainsburys listed Yorkshire Tea nationwide, and in 1993 Prospect Foods was renamed, becoming, for the first time, Bettys & Taylors.

It was a pivotal moment. When Victor had renamed the company, it was to increase its appeal to banks and lenders, as he felt that a generic name felt solid and reliable. Changing it to Bettys & Taylors was a recognition that both companies were now worthy of respect, and that they were names to be proud of.

At Bettys, Lesley still faced challenges. Northallerton had won the first ever Top Tea Place of the Year in 1987, awarded by the Tea Council, and a high-prestige recognition of the work done so far. The decorative schemes were working, and the new, neat, slightly art deco vibe was very much in tune with the times. But the more she saw of the workings of the company, and the more she and Jonathan travelled in Switzerland, staying with his cousins and broadening her knowledge of the culture, the more she felt that Bettys should celebrate Frederick Belmont – Fritz Bützer – and his Swiss roots, along with the ethos which was still – to her – so evident in Victor and Jonathan's way of thinking. Sitting in cafés in Bern, eating biber cake and potatoes made out of marzipan, she said: 'I could see the seeds of where Bettys had

been.' She thrilled as the Swiss went 'chestnut mad' in the autumn, thinking of ways to reflect this in the Bettys menus, but had to argue the point with Jonathan, who was still insistent that 'we're Yorkshire now'.

As recession hit once more in 1990, British food increasingly emphasised the homely and domestic: kitchen suppers over dinner parties and hot buttered toast over carefully turned quenelles. In 1992 Nigel Slater published *Real Fast Food*, full of tantalising descriptions but short ingredient lists, and 'real life' photography with crumbs on the table and spoons on the plate. He was a sharp contrast to the other publishing phenomenon of the time, Delia Smith, who notoriously hated seeing chefs taste things on TV; she made cooking safe and boring – process, rather than pleasure.

Meanwhile, the ongoing decline of the local pub, combined with young chefs who couldn't afford to open high-end restaurants, was responsible for a new wave of 'gastropubs', serving beer and atmosphere along with a modern British menu. This meant eclectic influences, lots of pastry and solidly home-cooked credentials. Inevitably there were large chains trying to copy the format on a bigger scale – the likes of Harvester and Beefeater cornered the market in what one critic called depressingly representative British food with 'none of this foreign commitment to excellence'.

A Bettys Rösti, one of the Swiss specialities introduced onto the menu in 1987

Bettys

SWISS
SPECIALITIES

Adding an openly Swiss influence to the Bettys menus was
entirely in keeping with the trends within British foods and, as
Lesley said: 'it didn't mean we had to be one or the other'. She'd
managed one significant introduction in 1987 in the form of
Swiss rösti. Described on the menus as 'a Swiss speciality: grated
potato with onions [or peppers, or bacon, or vegetables], fried
until golden brown and topped with melted raclette cheese', it
was Swiss country fare, a peasant dish which was filling and tasty
but which could also be a versatile base for many variations,
including seasonal ones, and not necessarily just strictly Swiss.
Rösti showed the direction Lesley wanted to take: relatively
timeless, simple, but reliant on quality ingredients and freshness
for its appeal. The basic mix could also, importantly, be prepped
ahead of time, so that busy cafés could cook from fresh, but still
serve hundreds of customers a day.

Rösti summed up the 'back to basics' approach with regards to
the menu: down-to-earth food, inspired by where Bettys had begun,

but reinvented and reinterpreted for the modern day. In 1990 the first overtly Swiss-influenced seasonal menu was trialled, with a Christmas offering including mushroom and chestnut roulade, spiced Christmas strudel, Christmas stollen slice and a chestnut sundae. By 1992 Bettys was offering a Swiss winter bake, and pork and chestnut sausages with mini röstis, along with pheasant and pistachio terrine, and fruit cake served with Wensleydale. On the main menu, Swiss raclette and ham Florentine and a Swiss harvest lunch joined the omelettes, salads and sandwiches, while the sweets selection now included an Amadeus torte, which consisted of layers of sweet pastry brushed with kirsch and dusted with cocoa and cinnamon, sandwiched with sour cherry cream. In 1995 the Engadine torte was added, a crisp confection of meringue, hazelnut cream and chocolate, served both as an airy sweet and as a cake with afternoon tea. More Yorkshire dishes were also developed, including pikelets, similar to crumpets but flatter – so holding far more butter – and crisper, so they don't go soggy while the delighted diner munches them.

There were still generational tensions, though. With her interest in fashion and skills in tailoring, Jonathan's mother Kay had long led the evolution of the staff uniforms, which constantly needed updating as fashion and technology changed. The brown pinafores which had been so fashionable in the 1970s had already

Bettys uniform, 1980

gone, but their replacements were far from perfect, and Lesley was determined to update them. The 1980s was a decade of chintz and mohair knits, all accessorised with lace collars and neck bows, and the current uniform reflected that. It was an uneasy mixture of streamlined 1920s flapper and 1980s cool: cutting edge mixed with lacy frills. The main elements of the uniforms were a black skirt (virtually all the front-of-house staff were women) and a rather transparent puffed-sleeve broderie anglaise blouse with frilly collar, and tied bow at the neck. Over this went a broderie anglaise apron, and a nippy-like lace headband, known by staff as the 'head-garnish' and which had a tendency to disintegrate when washed. Later, the managers wore a Bettys brooch at the neck instead, made by a local Harrogate firm to Kay's design (they are still in production to the original design). The overall effect was part Victorian servant, part antimacassar. Jonathan and Lesley privately referred to it as the French maid uniform, and both thought it overly fussy and at odds with the new aesthetic.

The whiff of servant was also a problem. This was an era when servitude, in the form of domestic service, still loomed large in many people's backgrounds, and for those whose grandparents had been in service between the world wars, it was often accompanied by notions of shame, misery and anger at the exploitation. A rash of popular memoirs by staff (often cooks) in the large houses compounded the idea that service of any kind was a terrible thing. The black-and-white colour scheme fitted well – but the headband and frills which were so obviously Edwardian-servant-like were a step too far. By the early 1990s potential recruits were giving the uniforms as a reason why they didn't feel comfortable working at Bettys. Gradually Lesley managed to – partially – redesign them, to a compromise version which still forms the basis of the uniforms today.

Although Kay and Victor had already given over almost their entire shareholding to a trust for their grandchildren, they still struggled to let go of control. Kay, in particular, felt that Bettys wasn't a true family business unless she and all of her children were actively involved – although she was not entirely delighted when Valerie approached Jonathan for a part-time job, initially in the Harrogate shop and then at Bettys by Post. Kay's own energies became focused on assembling the growing collection of antique teapots and wooden baking tools and bowls which were used in shop displays and café décor. With her experience of interior design and interest in antiques, she now became an enthusiastic collector, buying several very rare examples. One of the more eclectic was an 1882 Royal Worcester 'Aesthetic' pot, a satire on the movement of the same name, the poster child for which was Oscar Wilde. She had found one up for auction at Sotheby's, and, while travelling to Sussex by train to bid on it, befriended a fellow traveller, who confessed that he too was off to the auction, armed with £6,000 in cash to buy a particular item, but that he had no idea how they worked. Kay took pity on him, talked him through the intricacies and finally offered him a lift from the station to the auction house, as he'd failed to book any transport. Only as they arrived did she ask which item he wanted to bid on. Naturally it was the same pot, and Kay's £1,000 fund was hardly a match. Happily, a few years later she managed to acquire one through another source.

Maintaining family harmony while running a family business was a perennial problem. Victor and Kay were slowly stepping back, but the next generation was not entirely aligned on the future direction of the business. Tony, in particular, felt shut out from decision-making at the top, resenting the established triumvirate of Jonathan, Lesley and Victor and feeling that too much power was concentrated in their hands. He asked questions that were important to face and raised concerns that were crucial to tackle as the business grew and professionalised. He argued the case for increased share dividends, rather than the prioritisation of charitable involvement and staff engagement, and he suggested that Bettys & Taylors would be better off as two separate companies. He raised the question of whether Bettys should open outside Yorkshire, specifically as a joint venture with a French friend of his, in Fitzrovia in London. Victor, mindful of the North British Hotel Trust debacle at Bettys in York, was adamant that franchises were disastrous, and having dropped wholesale because of lack of control over certain products, he saw it as ludicrous to then lose control over the reputation of Bettys itself. The Board considered the question of expansion, but came down firmly against it: Bettys was a Yorkshire firm, embedded in its locality, and, if anything, its members wanted more focus on the Harrogate head office, not less.

Aesthetic teapot, 1881. Part of Bettys' vast teapot collection which dates from 1750 to the present day

The issues being discussed were vital and needed careful thought. The future of Bettys, as a family company, as a Yorkshire business and as an ethical concern, was at stake. Victor commented that 'things were said that I'd rather forget', and, for two years, lawyers and family members were sucked into increasingly acrimonious debate about the stewardship principles on which the business was to be owned and run and prosperity shared fairly between all the shareholders, including a trust which Claire Belmont had set up for Valerie. In 1994 a series of agreements was reached, and the questions were mainly resolved. Tony resigned, but remained active in the tea and coffee trade, publishing several books including *Coffee: A Dark History* and a history of the East India Company.

Having exhausted all other options, the company set about consolidating the shares, and control of the company, into the hands of the existing Board. Victor was badly shaken, and Jonathan, Lesley and Liz Barnes (Jonathan's sister) decided that they needed to understand better the challenges facing family-run businesses in the modern world. They set off for Switzerland, where far more companies remained in family ownership, on a fact-finding mission, to talk to other people in the same situation and to attend a course at the Lausanne Institute of Business Management specifically dealing with the very issues they were facing.

Victor saw himself very much as a father figure, holding family and business together, and he declared that like Uncle Fritz (Frederick) he was going to die in office. Jonathan, however, argued that this 'holding family and business together' was exactly what Victor had failed to do, and that now was the time for him to step down, freeing the next generation to prepare adequately for the future. 'But who will wind the Bettys clock?' was Victor's (rather tongue-in-cheek) response. The clock, whose mechanism was in a cupboard behind Victor's desk, was on a tower arching high above Bettys, and was reputed to be the timepiece by which all Harrogate set their watches. Jonathan did, indeed, regularly fail to wind it, and his secretary found the ancient winding gear too strenuous to operate in his absence. The clock was hardly the issue, and Victor did, eventually, agree that Jonathan was right. In 1996 he resigned. Some years later Lesley had the clock electrified.

Learning to cook

'Well, surely Bettys is the only place to learn to make pastry?' exclaims my neighbour as she explains to me what brought her to sunny Harrogate at 9 a.m. Seventeen of us are enrolled on the viennoiserie course and will be spending the whole of Friday at Bettys Cookery School. Most of the participants are women, but there are several men, including an ex-GP and a gentleman who has newly retired and wants to broaden a long-held interest into a proper hobby. We are a mixture of ages, from a final-year undergraduate for whom the course was a 21st-birthday present, to a proud grandmother of many, who enjoys making things to delight the procession of youngsters who throng her house.

The day starts with coffee, tea and a briefing on what to expect. The room is part country pantry, part catering kitchen, designed to reflect course participants' own homes, but also as a professional environment in which Bettys staff can learn new skills. A bank of eight numbered stainless-steel fridges at one side contrasts with the wooden cupboards and black granite worktops, and we have double ovens with gas hobs and stainless-steel heatproof surfaces to one side. Our tutor, Jenny, has a full demo area with overhead camera and screens showing what she is doing.

We start with making dough, everything explained in short steps, backed up by a course booklet in a wipe-clean folder. We work in sets of three, each making his or her own dough,

A Bettys Cookery School course
in action

seen as particularly vital for working-class girls to learn skills that would enable them to gain employment, and with domestic service the single biggest employer of women at the time, that meant sewing, cleaning and cookery. The term 'domestic science' came into use at the very end of Victoria's reign, coined by women eager to promote cookery as something beyond mere drudgery. The leading chefs were all men, and it was rare for women to work in top restaurant kitchens, or indeed as professional cooks for the very rich, but domestic cookery was very much associated with women. Cookery became an expected part of the school curriculum.

By the 1930s cookery had become part of home economics, still wrapped up with skills such as cleaning and dressmaking. Although by the 1970s home economics was nominally open to boys as well as girls, it was rare for them to take it, being steered instead into metalwork or art. In the 1980s it morphed into food tech, infamous for being more about designing pizzas than actually cooking. By 2000, when the cookery school opened, cookery came under the banner of design technology, not valued as a life skill, but merely as another subject that could be examined. Part of Lesley Wild's motivation to open the school was to help fill this gap locally. Cooking finally came off the school menu in 2014, even though the food tech GCSE had been taken by over 30,000 people the year before. This was despite the decision by the previous government to invest more heavily in cooking skills in schools, seeing it as a way to tackle growing obesity, diet-related ill health and lack of knowledge around food. Bettys, meanwhile, continues to be involved with local educational provision.

but sharing scales and ovens, along with anecdotes and chat as we get to know each other. By the time we break for tea, we feel like old friends. The room starts to warm up, the smell of butter and chocolate mingling with the aroma of coffee as the cafetières come out. I meet the owner of a small tea rooms who is doing the course both for pleasure and for inspiration, and a Scandinavian civil servant who is a regular Bettys Cookery School attendee and a very experienced cook.

Nearly all of us, I suspect, learnt rudimentary cookery skills at school, although the curriculum has changed many times over the years. As the school-leaving age increased to 14 at the end of the 19th century, there was debate over what children should be taught. It was

We break for lunch, an object lesson in quiet, calm catering. We munch on Caesar salad followed by raspberry meringue, all of us eager to get back to our croissants. There's wine, the announcement of which is greeted with cheers, and the afternoon swims by. I'm particularly intrigued by the way in which my fellow bakers have become much tidier cooks as the day has progressed, taking their cues from the way in which Jenny automatically cleans down after each demo. Everyone's babkas, pinwheels and pains aux raisins look fantastic sitting on their proving trays waiting for the right moment to pop them in the oven.

As the day draws to an end, there's a rush to the shop, stocking up on equipment such as dough scrapers and specialist tins. The bakes are in the ovens or already cooling on worktops. I snatch a moment to talk to Jenny about her experiences as a course tutor. Like so many of the people I've met at Bettys, she

started elsewhere, with a holiday job as a washer-upper at Bettys Ilkley. She credits the team there for nurturing her personally and professionally as she gained in skills and confidence, eventually joining Bettys Cookery School because of her communication skills and ability to inspire. Now she's helping with menu development and points to the close links between cookery school and craft bakery as one of the fundamental themes of the work she does.

People are gathering around a carefully displayed set of viennoiserie goods, made by Jenny as she taught us. Now they are set out so that we can have our pictures taken with goodies almost the same as those we have now packed into bags, to be eaten at home. Some, I suspect, won't quite make it that far. I'm pretty certain that that last almond croissant is calling to me as I say goodbye.

Yorkshire and beyond

1996–2009

What's on the menu?

In 1993 the menus for Bettys had been radically redesigned following consultation with the branch managers, moving from a series of large folding single sheets to an A5 booklet which could contain all the various drinks, foods and event listings in one place. The cover was designed by Claire Williams and Lesley Wild under their design department remit, incorporating illustrations by watercolour artist David Holmes of key products (rascals and rösti, plus meringues and ice cream bombes) along with teapots and cafetières. Photographs and adverts from the archive completed the home-made, scrapbook feel, while, inside, the text was clearly set out and easy to read, with a standardised font across the main menu and the stand-alone seasonal inserts.

From 1999 this children's menu joined them, matching the main menu in feel but using visuals drawn from the wider Bettys world. Bettys had commissioned the ceramicist Emma Bridgewater to design a range of crockery featuring the Fat Rascal to be sold in the shops, the result being a typically exuberant mixture of hand-drawn lettering and illustrations of the rascals themselves and which echoed the polka dot design for which Emma Bridgewater was already known. It was a fitting link-up, for Emma Bridgewater, like Bettys, was a family-run business concentrating on high-quality, small-scale products, part of a quiet revolution in British design, with a focus on quirky, personal-feeling visuals, printed onto earthenware made in the British Potteries. (Emma and her partner Matthew later admitted that one of the joys of attending the Harrogate gift fair in the early days of their business was the chance to 'sneak off and spend time at Bettys eating delicious home-baked cakes and drinking tea in stylish surroundings'.) It was a manifestation of so-called Cool Britannia, a slightly nebulous cultural movement which saw London once more positioned as fashionable, amidst regained pride in British manufacturing and heritage. By the 2000s their mugs and teapots would be instantly recognisable, and the company would be one of the biggest British ceramics brands.

The streamlined menu design echoed the approach to the food too. These menus applied, as was usual, across all the branches, but now the dishes were subject to rigorous quality control. The children's menu reads like a Bettys' greatest hits: fish and chips, egg on (a choice of) toast, the bread made in-house, a rarebit, now accepted as an integral part of the Bettys offering, and two slimmed-down versions of the Swiss specialities, the macaroni and the rösti. Ice cream is well represented, and the banana-and-toffee sundae could have come straight from Frederick's 1920s menus. The biscuit animals linked to the constantly changing window displays, which were especially creative at Easter, when Lesley Norris, Ruth Vasey and the confectionery team sculpted chocolate into everything from a tree trunk surrounded by squirrels and owls, to the HMS *Betty* complete with marzipan sails. Other Easter windows included a set of big tops with circus performers, a farm with marzipan animals, a Noah's Ark and a Germanic medieval castle with wizards and princesses in pointy hats which would have made Frederick (and his gnomes) proud.

Bettys

LITTLE RASCAL
— MENU —

*All dishes on our Little Rascal Menu are suitable for children
up to the age of six. In addition, most of the dishes on our
main menu can be served in smaller portions.*

HOT DISHES

HOMEMADE FISH FINGERS IN BATTER	£3.95
Served with chipped potatoes.	
SWISS ALPINE MACARONI	£3.50
Pasta, bacon and new potatoes, in a cream sauce.	
SAUSAGES & CHIPS	£3.50
BACON & CHIPS	£3.25
SCRAMBLED EGGS ON TOAST	£2.60
CHIPS	£1.50
Served with mayonnaise and tomato sauce.	

SANDWICHES

EGG MAYONNAISE	£2.60
ROAST HAM OR ROAST CHICKEN	£2.85

ICE CREAMS & CAKES

BANANA & TOFFEE SUNDAE	£3.25
Organic chocolate and vanilla ice cream,	
sliced banana and homemade toffee sauce.	
ICE CREAMS	£2.50
Two scoops of organic rich vanilla,	
strawberry or chocolate ice cream.	
WITH RASPBERRY, TOFFEE OR CHOCOLATE SAUCE	£2.95
LITTLE RASCAL	£2.00
A plump fruity scone packed with chocolate chips	
and orange peel.	
CHOCOLATE BROWNIE	£1.80
GINGER BISCUIT ANIMAL	£0.95
BUTTER BEAR BISCUIT	£0.85
CARAMEL SLICE	£1.55
FONDANT FANCY	£1.55

DRINKS

SMALL HOT CHOCOLATE WITH CREAM	£1.70
Made with Bettys rich dark chocolate.	
SMALL ICE CREAM MILK SHAKES	£1.80
Fresh banana, rich dark chocolate or raspberry.	
COCA COLA	£1.60
SMALL FRESHLY SQUEEZED ORANGE JUICE	£1.95
PURE COX'S APPLE JUICE	£1.95
CHILLED MILK	£1.00
SMALL FRESH HOMEMADE STILL LEMONADE	£1.50
ORGANIC BLACKCURRANT CORDIAL	£1.00

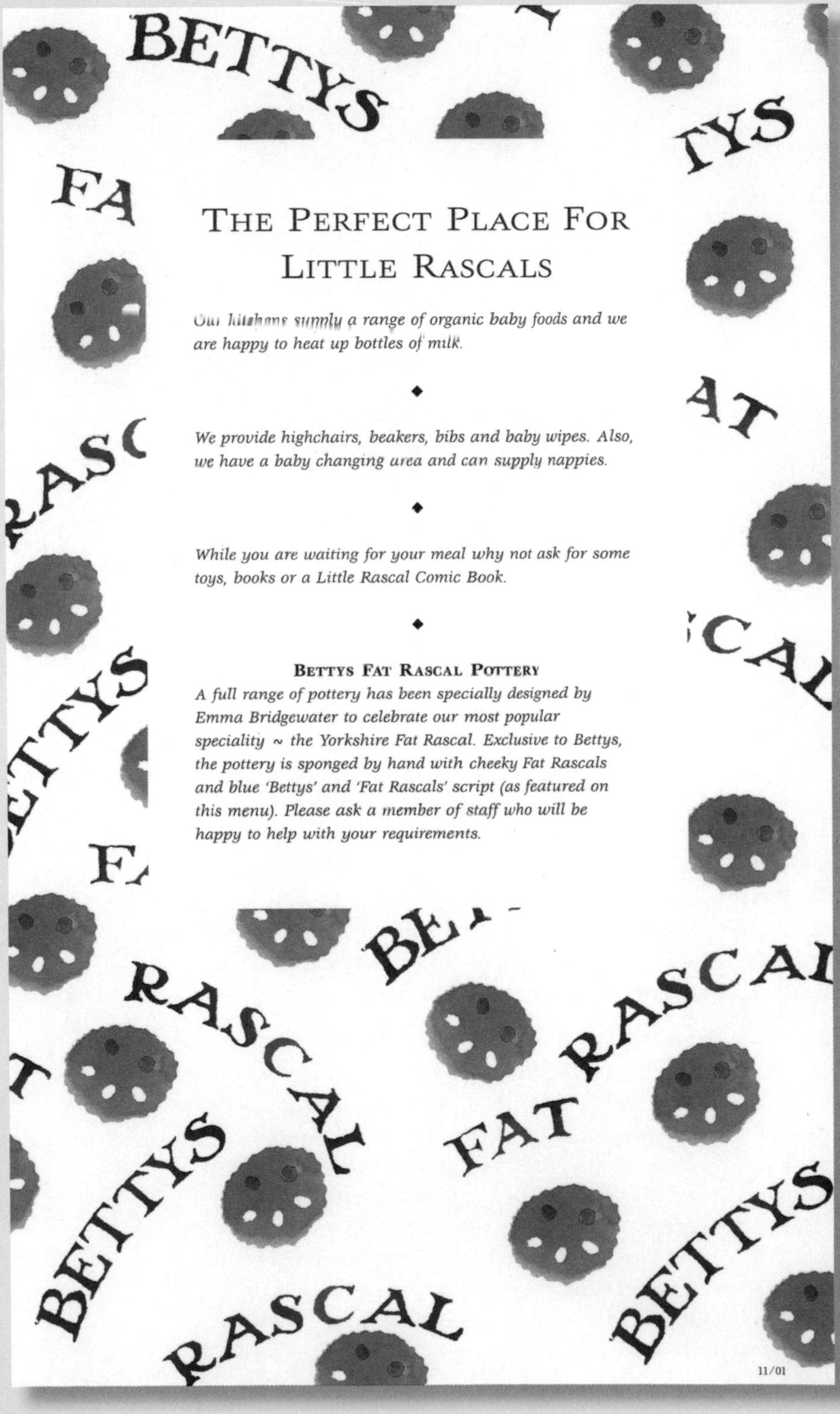

THE PERFECT PLACE FOR LITTLE RASCALS

Our kitchens supply a range of organic baby foods and we are happy to heat up bottles of milk.

◆

We provide highchairs, beakers, bibs and baby wipes. Also, we have a baby changing area and can supply nappies.

◆

While you are waiting for your meal why not ask for some toys, books or a Little Rascal Comic Book.

◆

BETTYS FAT RASCAL POTTERY

A full range of pottery has been specially designed by Emma Bridgewater to celebrate our most popular speciality ~ the Yorkshire Fat Rascal. Exclusive to Bettys, the pottery is sponged by hand with cheeky Fat Rascals and blue 'Bettys' and 'Fat Rascals' script (as featured on this menu). Please ask a member of staff who will be happy to help with your requirements.

11/01

Bettys Little Rascal
menu, 2001

V ictor officially retired as Chair on 30 October 1996. The minutes recorded that 'Victor hands over a professional Board and management which provides a strong foundation for the future' and praised him for his 'knack for making good decisions, of making bold decisions and his willingness to experiment and try new things'. The Board declared that the theme for 1997 would be 'building on success'. Kay and Liz stood down at the same time, Liz formally recognised for her role in leading environmental awareness and Kay for setting a personal example in 'how to care for staff, maintain meticulous standards of housekeeping and be aware of beautiful things and craftsmanship'.

For Victor, stepping down as Chair did not mean slowly slipping into dotage, however. He had been involved in Bettys since he was 13, and now, at 73, life without it was unthinkable. He and Kay were hardly the types for a golf-filled retirement. The previous five years had forced the Board to think hard about succession planning and the role of family members within a business which was increasingly complex, with a set of brands which were known across the UK. The questions of how to balance the needs of a thriving, modern business with those of the family who owned it, and what role the family should play going forward, were difficult.

Codifying the values that underlay the whole business was a start – currently they were unwritten, and, while evident to most, open to interpretation. Jonathan, Lesley and Liz – 'generation three'

Victor Wild with Kay Wild and Liz Barnes receiving one of his retirement gifts, 1996

260

'how fortunate – how lucky – we are that previous generations have enabled us to have a shared inheritance which gives us the opportunity to create a better, more secure world for our family, for the staff in the business and for the wider community'.

The Family Constitution

as they were informally known – had done a great deal of work on this in the months leading up to Victor's retirement, recognising that they needed a forum through which the family could resolve family issues away from the boardroom, and a formal mechanism to enable the family to work with the business without necessarily relying on individual family members having a direct managerial role. Through trips to Switzerland, they discovered the international Family Business Network, founded in 1989 precisely to help families work through their issues in a fast-changing world with more opportunities – but also challenges – than ever before. It was in Switzerland, at the Lausanne Institute of Business, that Victor turned slight bewilderment at being suddenly retired from the Board into a solid commitment to change. He reported that he and Kay found the course they went on to be a deeply rewarding experience, and with gorgeous surroundings: the mountains which he loved so much.

The result of all of this was the 1996 Family Constitution, a document which, for the first time, articulated the values of the

company and then set forth the terms under which the family, the Board and the company directors would henceforth operate. Although it would evolve over the years, its basic tenets continue to underlie everything Bettys & Taylors does – for all the shareholders had to sign up to it, and changes had to be agreed by all. Key to the whole was the list of values, which started with a reminder of 'how fortunate – how lucky – we are that previous generations have enabled us to have a shared inheritance which gives us the opportunity to create a better, more secure world for our family, for the staff in the business and for the wider community'. Both the Swiss and the Yorkshire heritage were explicitly recognised, with a commitment to 'exceptional quality products and exceptional quality service in an exceptional quality environment'. The Family Constitution encompassed rules for shareholding, and a new system of governance which included an independent non-family member, intended to ensure that no one would again hold total power in the way that Frederick and Victor had done. Family members, while encouraged to work in the business, would no longer automatically be entitled to the top jobs and would henceforth compete with all other candidates for positions.

There was now to be a Family Council, headed by a Chairperson, whose role was to represent the views of the shareholders, all

Bettys & Taylors
Family Council

of whom were family members (or their partners), to the Bettys & Taylors Board, and to act as an important advisory and decision-making part of the company. The Family Constitution looked forward to the future, recognising that a time might come when no family member was actively involved in the daily running of the business, but ensuring that the family would still be involved. The role of the Family Council, and by extension of the wider family, was now one of stewardship, of keeping the business focused on its codified values and of acting as a guarantor for future generations, as well as representing the heritage of Bettys. In keeping with the latter, Victor was appointed the first Chair of the Family Council.

Bettys & Taylors was now entirely under the leadership of the third generation. In 1997 Lesley became Deputy Chair at the same time as a new set of divisional directors was appointed. This was a recognition that, while the ideal was for as flat a hierarchy as possible, the number of staff and the complexity of the company were growing, which meant recognising areas of expertise and dividing people into teams. In the 1960s and early 1970s Victor had been everything – finance director, head of personnel and in charge of sales and marketing – but this had been changing since the 1970s. Now the group employed over 600 people, and governmental regulations, as well as methods of communication, were constantly changing, making certain areas – notably marketing and communications, as well as quality control, health and safety and finance – much more important than they had once been. However, what could have been the end of an era was actually a period of apparent continuity – Victor had been preparing for his retirement for a year, and the impact of the Family Constitution, so significant for the Wilds as a family, was very low-key for their staff. Staff experienced it mainly in the form of a set of new publications: a staff handbook, customer communications manual and recruitment manual.

The focus was on strengthening structures and developing written materials that would support the work done at shareholder level, further enabling the business to continue to modernise. Taylors, in particular, was growing off the back of Yorkshire Tea, which was slowly gaining national supermarket listings. Although the team had long assumed that the core market for it was older traditional tea drinkers, it was becoming apparent that there was also a flourishing market among younger tea aficionados, who appreciated its quality and regional specificity. When a promotional gold-coloured tea caddy was brought out in 1997 it became an icon, appearing not only in the north-set soaps *Coronation Street* and *Emmerdale*, but also in the background of the New York-based comedy *Friends*. Sponsorship of ITV's popular Yorkshire drama series *Heartbeat*, together with Yorkshire County Cricket Club, meant that the tea caddy's colours crept into people's living rooms, associated with leisurely afternoons and gentle Yorkshire accents.

In 1999 Yorkshire Tea for Hard Water packs were launched, specifically aimed at London, the Midlands and the south-east, and underlining the company's continued commitment to different blends for different areas. There had always been different blends of Yorkshire Tea for the areas in which it was sold, and in the early days of supermarkets, when distribution was direct to the stores, it had been easy to deliver the right blend to the right area. Now, however, national distribution warehouses were the norm, and clearly marked packs were necessary so that consumers could make their own choice. Yorkshire Tea was now a national name, and in 1998 the *Independent on Sunday* newspaper even somewhat unexpectedly listed it as one of ten things that made Britain cool, stating that 'the inventors of the round bag, the pyramid bag and novelty granules should all bow down before this giant of simplicity and cool'. This was the peak of Cool Britannia, a reactionary cultural movement which emerged from the liberal left, who were feeling sidelined by nearly 20 years of Conservative Party rule, albeit latterly with a slightly softer edge under John Major. The last half of the 1990s saw an upsurge in British culture, from film to the arts, and especially in music, where Blur, Pulp, Oasis and the Spice Girls all proudly sang with regional accents. While the movement itself was seen as passé by the end of the decade, its legacy was to contribute to the ongoing renaissance in British food and drink (among other things), as the country continued to wake up to its own rich cultural heritage. In 1997 the Tories finally fell, and Tony Blair's landslide victory was immediately hailed as ushering in a new age of diversity and liberalism, and as the end to a government which had been increasingly derided for inner division, scandal and sleaze.

Top Yorkshire Tea caddy, 1997

Bottom Yorkshire Tea for Hard Water packaging launched in 1999

In 1999 Taylors' new 'Fauves' coffee range became the best-selling roast and ground coffee range in the UK. Launched only three years before, it exemplified the new spirit of optimism and determination to be different in Britain at the time. The concept emerged from a visit to the opera by Jonathan, who came out so enthused by the all-encompassing drama of the performance that he determined to do something different with the coffee range Taylors was developing at the time. The name was from the term given – disparagingly – to a group of painters centred on Henri Matisse, and who had exhibited their work in Paris in 1905. *Fauves* is French for 'wild beasts', and the movement was characterised by non-naturalistic colours applied loosely, often from the tube, with the result an emotive, slightly abstract set of works. Now Jonathan urged: 'If we don't become "Fauves" – unafraid to immerse ourselves in an idea, and a wild, colourful personal expression of it, then there is little chance of creating something compelling.'

The market at the time was based on roast types and country of origin, and the new range was completely different, each blend named for a moment in time, or an emotion, with a clearly numbered strength rating making it easy for would-be consumers to tell at a glance how punchy it was. The packaging, designed in-house, was colourful and flamboyant, reflecting the names: Hot Lava Java, Lazy Sunday, Dinner Party, Rich Italian

Taylors 'Fauves' Coffee Range, 1996

The Belmont Room, Bettys York

and Café Imperial ('our classic house blend'). The new coffees were immediately successful and were followed up with a decaffeinated blend as well as a selection of the then highly fashionable flavoured ground coffees and a range of SOS coffees, sold specifically to raise funds for areas needing aid in the aftermath of natural disasters. The so-called 'second wave' of coffee was just hitting the UK, with the American chain Starbucks buying out the Seattle Coffee Company to launch in the UK in 1998. Both companies had started as small coffee shops, reacting against the commodification of coffee (especially instant granules) and emphasising the idea of a cup of coffee as an experience, not just a caffeine hit. They were part of a new boom in coffee shops – similar to the 1960s iteration but with a more profitable business model. British competitors included Costa and Caffè Nero, and over the next two decades they would open on almost every high street. With them came a new vocabulary, of lattes, espressos and cappuccinos. Bettys quietly installed espresso machines (which also made cappuccinos) in its branches in 1997. However, they remained convinced that the best way to serve their carefully sourced and blended speciality coffees was in a cafetière, which was the standard form a pot of coffee took in the Bettys cafés.

Both Bettys and Taylors were gaining fame. Such was the success of Yorkshire Tea that Safeway announced it planned to bring out its own version. Rather belatedly, the team started the process of applying for trademarks for Yorkshire Tea and Yorkshire Fat Rascal. Both marks were accepted by the examiners, having been devised and exclusively used by the company for over a decade. Some years later, Fat Rascal was also registered as a trademark in its own right.

Meanwhile, in 1997 the Bettys logo was upgraded and tweaked to its current iteration (the 'est. 1919' was added in 2002). The focus for Bettys remained Yorkshire, with branch improvement the aim rather than new openings. Ilkley expanded into the building next door, with a new glass canopy added in a similar style to that of Harrogate and York. York was now Grade II listed in recognition of its architectural significance. In the year it turned 60, the first-floor Belmont Room was reopened, intended both as a function room and as an overspill area for the main

café, which had queues around the corner in the summer (which was not only off-putting for would-be customers outside, but also blocked the views for people seated within). Now the marquetry was restored, and the storage boxes were removed, with the first big event being the opening party for staff and local dignitaries. Once more, the Belmont Room became popular for wedding receptions, and was also used for a brief experiment in a Bettys Sunday Roast.

1997 was remarkable for another key milestone: the first Bettys and Taylors websites. Fewer than 10 per cent of households in the UK had internet access at the time, but Jonathan had been inspired by a talk about the world wide web (the term itself only coined in 1990) and saw a potential market for Hot Lava Java in the world of nerds (Java being a programming language). And so the computer team set up hot-lava-java.com. Bettys by Post, meanwhile, was part of a Microsoft online Christmas promotion, and also joined the internet revolution. Gradually, the other parts of the company would join in.

The way in which commodities were bought and sold was changing too, and in 1998 the London Tea Auction, which had been at least a weekly event since 1679, closed. Sales through the auction had been declining for years, with brokers buying tea direct from producers or through local auctions in the countries that produced tea. The tea market had moved from hundreds of blenders buying through brokers to a few big tea companies buying their own supplies. Taylors still nominally used Warren

Jonathan Wild buying the last tea chest at the London Tea Auction, 1998

Ford as an outside broker, but in 1998 it too finally brought buying in-house, with Warren staying on as a consultant as it sought to forge new relationships with coffee and tea growers who matched its ethics. The last London auction had something of a celebratory atmosphere, and Jonathan was deputed to represent the company, bidding on the final chest of tea to be sold. Later he admitted that 'what with all the TV cameras and photographers there, I'm afraid "auction fever" possessed me. Anyway, I was absolutely convinced that the rightful home for this treasure was in Yorkshire. It was all for charity, so how could I be blamed if I kept on bidding?' When the gavel came down, he'd set a new record for the highest price ever paid for a single chest of tea: £18,315. He was not allowed near an auction again.

As the millennium approached, the company newsletter, now renamed the *Yorkshire Rascal*, recorded the highest-ever total for the charity pot and updated readers on the work of the coffee and tea buyers as they travelled across the world. The company was now working with Oxfam as part of the Trees for Life project, and Taylors was a founding member of the Tea Sourcing Partnership (now the Ethical Tea Partnership) dedicated to improving conditions for workers on tea plantations. Charitable work was an integral part of the way Bettys worked – as was the incentivising of staff on an equal basis. Jonathan wrote a short article commemorating the 20th anniversary of the annual group staff bonus, noting that 'what started out as a birthday present has become part of the company's way of life'.

The newsletter gave details too of the new-look menu, launched in 1999 as a small booklet, with a confident emphasis on the dual Swiss–Yorkshire nature of the dishes and the introduction of a full afternoon tea. Then there was Taylors of Stonegate, which was renamed Little Bettys (ostensibly for the 80th anniversary of Bettys as a whole). Harrogate won 'loo of the year', a significant accolade given the importance of the toilets (one staff member at Ilkley remembered one customer being so excited at the prospect of being pregnant that she did a pregnancy test in the loo – it was positive, and she gave her daughter Betty as a middle name). In December, Swiss wine, virtually unknown in the UK, was added to the Bettys menus, sourced, like its Alsatian counterparts, from a family-run vineyard in Swiss Valais. There were also regular updates on the

latest major project: the purchase of extra land at Starbeck and subsequent replacement of the bakery with a new, purpose-built building, which would become known as Bettys Craft Bakery.

In December 1999 a film crew was commissioned to follow Jonathan around the old bakery as part of a Nostalgia Day. He and Victor interviewed staff (Shirley Fell and Marion Jones also interviewed Victor in a mock job interview based on their own experiences when applying, including asking him to draw something and arguing over his weekly wages) and reminisced about the changes they'd seen. Jonathan recalled his own primary school visit to Bettys where one child had burst into tears as Victor declared he was 'going to divide them into two' (the child took this rather literally). They were filmed peering at a huge marble slab, bought as one enormous sheet and then dropped. The resulting halves were still in use – and moving with the bakery.

The old bakery was a total mishmash, the original 1922 structure having long since been subsumed by additions, which inevitably leaked at the joins. There was little logic to the layout, and it was full of twisty corridors and rooms built for one thing and converted to another. Still, the staff talked of it with great affection, although they agreed that working methods had improved – 'it's more like teamwork now' and that the needs of health and safety

Lesley and Jonathan Wild with Tony Watts, Project Manager, on the site of the new Bettys Craft Bakery, 1998

270

Top Jonathan and Victor Wild at the opening of Bettys Craft Bakery, 12 July 2000

Bottom Bettys Craft Bakery, 2000

Overleaf Inside Bettys Craft Bakery

were somewhat at odds with the existing building. Many of those interviewed had been with the company for decades, having joined from school or shortly after, and spoke of the family atmosphere, the camaraderie and the pride they took in their jobs. Several had met their spouses at Bettys; others had children working there.

The new bakery opened in May 2000, its design winning both an award for environmental excellence and a RIBA award for its architecture. It was deliberately reminiscent of a Swiss chalet, with cedar cladding and an overhanging roof, while the terraces around it were landscaped with appropriate plants. It was full of light, with large open-plan spaces, in keeping with Jonathan's philosophy of creating vistas, about which he commented:

'it may sound somewhat mystical (and even weird) but I really did believe that uninterrupted views the length or width of a building and on out into the landscape opened up energy flows and connectivity'.

Average bread consumption in Britain was now 800g per person per week, half its 1950s levels, but Bettys had ridden out the general trend toward industrialised bread and now was able neatly to harness the interest in artisan bread, which was just emerging. While nationally sales of economy bread dropped (by nearly a quarter in 2004–5 alone), sales of craft breads, in which Bettys specialised, rose. In 1999 Bettys had already introduced its first sourdough loaf – mouse bread. It was named for Robert Thompson, a York-based furniture maker of the 1930s, whose signature had been a small, carved mouse. The new bakery sported a French wood-fired oven alongside top-of-the-range retarder-provers, and mouse bread would now be part of a range of nearly 30 different items. Many of these were organic, although market research later showed that customers cared less about a label they saw as fairly arbitrary and more about provenance, preferring to support local small businesses with decent ethics, including (but not limited to) the environment. Since the regulations surrounding organic food were difficult to manage in a bakery that produced both organic and non-organic goods, the range was later reduced.

Lesley Wild, hosting a class at Bettys Cookery School, c.1990s

The craft bakery wasn't the only new building taking shape at the Starbeck site – now known as Plumpton Park – for Lesley had pitched plans for a project of her own, a 'dream I'd had for years'. Staff training remained a crucial area for the company, and to date aspiring cooks had been trained off-site at a local catering college. However, the only day the college wasn't in use was a Saturday – the busiest day at the branches – and the college facilities were not the same as those at Bettys. Lesley had asked for space at the new bakery, but this wasn't possible. Additionally, she had been harbouring a growing sense of outrage at the axing of cookery from the national curriculum, seeing it as a valuable skill for all children, without which children would potentially grow up not only unable to cook, but also lacking understanding of where their food came from and how to balance nutritional needs against the blandishments of the fast-food and snack industry. Jonathan had drawn up plans for the demolition of two cowsheds-turned-temporary-drawing-office left over from the previous occupants. Now Lesley argued persuasively that a better idea would be to turn the building into a new Bettys Cookery School, which could be used both for in-house training when it suited the company and for schools' workshops, engaging the next generation of potential Bettys bakers and confectioners as well as equipping local children for the future. External courses for the public, led by Bettys own staff, would help subsidise the schools work. Bettys Cookery School duly opened in 2001 and was highly commended in the National Training Awards two years later.

By 2003 Bettys was well enough known to feature in *The Times*, reviewed by food critic Giles Coren, who amidst lamenting the decline of tea in London ('a polystyrene sconce of boiled rat bile') and the generally sad standard of tourist tea shops outside it, found space to describe Bettys as 'a wonder to this day – as heart-warming a venue for eating and drinking as you could ask for'. He gave it 9 out of 10 for charm and suggested London caterers hasten to the cookery school and cafés to learn about 'cooking, coffee-making and tea-buying. And, above all, about service. Let this be the next big gastro-trend to hit the capital. Please.'

Bettys in Northallerton was just about to move two doors further
down the street, to a much better location, with a bigger and
more manageable interior space. Lesley had to fight hard with a
dubious Board for the funds, arguing successfully that the existing
location was really not fit for purpose: it was too small, too open,
too hot, and it just couldn't match the high standards of the
other branches. Eventually the Board agreed to buy 189a High
Street, an elegant Georgian townhouse, latterly occupied by a
bank (the bullion safe was still *in situ* in the cellar). As was now
the established pattern, local craftspeople were used to restore
and extend the building incorporating key elements of the Bettys
identity such as the carpet, carved wood panelling, Lloyd Loom
furniture and careful use of light. The carpet had long since
changed from Victor's 1950s design, and the present incarnation

Bettys Northallerton, 2004

BLENDED AND ROASTED IN HARROGATE

was a bespoke design subtly incorporating almonds and cherries, contained within geometric squares. This was no identikit Bettys, though, but instead its look was unique to the building and to the town – in this case taking inspiration from the elegant proportions and symmetry of the Georgian frontage to create a series of top-lit rooms stretching back from the shop at the front.

In Harrogate, Prince Charles came for tea, one of the few customers not to have to queue, having personally requested a visit. Security was tight, and preparations including redecorating a loo on the top floor, which was duly security checked. Unfortunately, when the time came, he opened the door to a store cupboard instead – but it had an old urinal in the back, which did the trick – so he never saw the pristine new wallpaper. He didn't seem to mind, and in 2008 Taylors was awarded a Royal Warrant to supply tea to Clarence House (the official residence of the Prince of Wales). Prince Charles planted the two millionth Tree for Life outside the Harrogate branch.

Charitable involvement was further integrated into the Bettys way of working with the opening of the Cone Exchange, initially in a shed at Springwater School in Harrogate. Springwater was a special needs school with which the company worked closely, and the Cone Exchange was a community scrap store, enabling the upcycling of business waste such as cardboard packaging or fabric offcuts. The name came from the suggestion that started it all – from a young child on a visit to Taylors, who had asked for one of their waste cardboard cones to take home and make into an angel for the Christmas tree. The Cone Exchange was championed by Chris Powell (aka Captain Rummage), and in 2008 he received an MBE for his work there. By 2009 it was so successful that it moved closer to the Plumpton Park factory site and opened officially to the public (previously public access was by appointment). It remains an important community hub and an excellent source of knitting needles and craft supplies.

Trees for Life remained the most nationally significant charity campaign, and in 2007 the three millionth tree was planted, now in an entirely new location: RHS Harlow Carr. In 2004 Bettys had opened its first new branch in 33 years, taking over the catering contract for Harlow Carr's main tea rooms and summer kiosk. The minutes recorded two years of talks and negotiations, evolving from sponsorship of a kitchen garden through to a full, all-new Bettys.

This page Bettys at Harlow Carr Gardens

Opposite The Cone Exchange

In order not to neglect the other branches, a new creative marketing team, led by Ian Jackson, took on some of the remit of the old design department, notably the look and feel of the branches – interiors, exteriors and window displays. Harrogate expanded into the building next door, with the shop to one side, as at York. The area previously occupied by the shop now sported the new Montpellier Café, where the waiting staff wore ties and waistcoats, with ankle-length Continental-style aprons, and customers could feast their eyes on a wall of wine as well as the glass stands of cake. The full-height windows of the rest of the building did occasionally cause a flutter – one of the waiting staff recalled a heady moment when the queue in front of her became distracted as an amorous couple leaning up against the window took things just a little too far, given the view the whole of Bettys had of their tryst from behind. In 2008 the Harrogate equivalent to the York Belmont Room opened, called the Imperial Room, and like York it quickly made Bettys a popular party and wedding venue once more.

Ten years after Victor's retirement, the Jonathan–Lesley duo had truly come into its own. The work they were doing, especially Lesley's work on the branch refurbishments and expansion, was explicitly about their legacy, about leaving the business premises in the best possible state for the future, a far cry from the underinvestment of the 1970s. In 2008 the *Sunday Times* listed Bettys & Taylors as one of the top 100 companies to work for, *Caterer and Hotelkeeper* recognised it as the Best Place to Work in Hospitality, and the company was awarded Investors in People for the sixth time. However, the couple's interests were diverging:

Montpellier café bar,
Bettys Harrogate, 2009

Jonathan was devoted to Yorkshire Tea, which he'd helped devise, and saw himself as a Taylors person, while Lesley looked after Bettys.

A new Pagoda House was built for Taylors, with the wide-open spaces and views of the distant countryside that typified the Starbeck site. At the same time, a teapot-shaped clock was erected on the outside of the factory, set to pour as the Harrogate to York train passed by. (The line is notorious for being late: eager passengers looking out of the window are sadly rarely rewarded with a timely movement.) Yorkshire Tea was still growing fast, with its first fully national TV campaign in 2006 and special export packs. Taylors always used natural bergamot oil in its Earl Grey, rather than an artificial substitute, but it quickly melted the glue on the export packs, so initially only a green tea was launched. Most of the marketing was still done in-house, with only occasional recourse to consultancies, and it was still relatively low-key and ad hoc. There was a series of branded vans giving out samples at festivals, including, from 2005, Little Urn, a converted ice cream van, which garnered a cult following.

In 2001, meanwhile, Taylors launched a range of Yorkshire Tea-branded food products, starting with a tea loaf. The recipe was based on one of Lesley Norris's family recipes, and had been tested in the cafés before being altered to meet the requirements of supermarkets, who wanted it to be long-life rather than the preservative-free standard fare of Bettys. The range included T-shaped biscuits ('ideal for dunking'), and a ginger loaf cake. A marmalade cake followed.

But Taylors wasn't a food company, and, despite good sales, the range proved problematic. All the issues that had beset Bettys' forays into wholesale came back, including lack of control over the product and capacity issues. The problems were compounded by the power of the supermarkets to enforce discounting and by their habit of playing suppliers off against each other, always fighting for the best shelf space.

Additionally, the different supermarkets had very different consumer groups: Booths, the first to list the Yorkshire Tea Loaf, was an upmarket northern chain whose ethos matched that of Bettys & Taylors: 'to sell the best goods available, in attractive stores, with excellent assistants'. Elsewhere, customers shopped predominantly on price and were less interested in whether their cakes used real butter or the industrial fat of the day: trans fats (artificially produced hydrogenated fats, increasingly recognised as contributing to heart disease and subject to a voluntary agreement not to use them by most major producers from 2012). When the UK went into the worst recession since 1929 following the American sub-prime mortgages scandal and the UK banking crash in 2008, price became even more of an issue. Wages were too – both Pizza Express and Café Rouge (founded by an ex-Bettys employee) were fined for failing to pay staff the new minimum wage.

Jonathan was doing more and more public speaking. He was moving into an ambassador's role, promoting the Bettys & Taylors way of doing business, from its stance on environmental issues to its staff training programme. He was also trying to organise the wealth of collected material into a proper archive, in order to better trace Bettys' history. A paragraph, together with Frederick's picture (taken when he was still Fritz), already appeared on the menus, and now Jonathan, together with Sarah Wells, the first full-time (albeit temporary) archivist, pulled together some of the material for a Bettys book, *Hearts, Tarts and Rascals.*

Lesley, in addition to leading Bettys to its first yearly turnover of £10 million in 2003, also had outside interests of her own which she was eager to pursue. She sat on the University of York Council from 2005 and became pro-chancellor in 2008, a recognition of her significance in Yorkshire and her ability to contribute meaningfully to businesses beyond Bettys. Following the success of Bettys Cookery School, and her own work on menu and dish development, she decided to write a cookery book, which would come under the Bettys name but be a book of home cooking. *A Year of Family Recipes* was written in a year, based on seasonal produce from the Wilds' own garden. (Jonathan was a devoted fruit-and-vegetable grower.) Her writing had to be juggled around commitments to the business as everything always was, and when the book was published in 2007 she was immensely proud of it. It sold over 15,000 copies in the first year, testament to the Bettys name and the quality of the recipes within it.

The book project was a relief, in many ways, from a somewhat frustrating situation at Bettys itself, for, with Jonathan representing

the family in the business – a very visible presence due to his habit of walking the factory floor – it was hard for her to gain recognition. He prided himself on knowing all of the more than 1,000 employees' names and was the face of the company at talks and conferences. He later commented: 'I worked (and argued) with my father for many years, and never thought I would be good enough to replace him. It was only the combination of Lesley and I, standing back to back (with complementary skills, although often armed with duelling pistols), that was able to take his legacy forward through a period of renaissance.' But he also acknowledged that he was the maverick, sometimes driving his staff nuts with his 'meddling and impossible perfectionism', while Lesley's contribution was steadier, calmer and more long-term, that she was able to 'cut through the clutter'; that, going forward, was needed more and more. In 2009 she celebrated 30 years with the company, and the pair took a sabbatical, returning refreshed to announce a new shift in emphasis. Henceforth, Lesley would be non-executive Chair, taking over at the top, with Jonathan stepping sideways to become group chief executive. His operational responsibilities were now devolved, as the position was explicitly one concerned with future strategies and direction.

Left *A Year of Family Recipes* by Lesley Wild, 2007

Right Jonathan and Lesley Wild in their garden, July 2004

A family business

2009–2019

What's on the menu?

As Bettys turned 100 in 2019 the company geared up for a year of celebrations. A '100' logo and centenary illustration was commissioned, to be used on limited edition teapots, mugs, tea caddies, cake tins and bags. It also formed the cover for the tearoom menu, which was standardised across the bigger branches.

The menu is much slimmed down from a decade before, with no need now for side tabs, and with seasonal dishes integrated into the main menu rather than on separate sheets. There is no differentiation between eating occasions, with sections now called 'Breakfast Specialities' (served all day), 'House Specialities', 'Lighter Dishes', 'Side Dishes', with sections for sandwiches, cakes and pâtisserie, ice cream sundaes, teas and coffees and hot chocolate. At the back is a full page for wines, champagnes and Pimm's, plus ales and finally soft drinks.

Breakfast includes the breakfast rösti, the most popular dish in this section, along with Bircher muesli, hot buttered pikelets, cinnamon toast and viennoiserie. Yorkshire and Switzerland rub shoulders right from the start, and breakfast also includes muffins and poached eggs, along with two newer dishes: kedgeree, and crushed avocado on toast, one of the most emblematic dishes of the decade. House specialities are, likewise, the established mix of Swiss and British, with local producers to the fore. The fried fillet of haddock and chips is as popular now as the fish and chips was in the 1960s, but it is joined by chicken schnitzel, Swiss alpine macaroni

(both a family and a staff favourite), various röstis, and the Yorkshire rarebit, an updated version of a dish which has been a menu constant since the 1930s.

In a typically understated, yet firm, nod to the latest popular food trend, that of plant-based diets, the aubergine schnitzel is served with oat crème fraîche, and every section contains one entirely vegan dish, along with fish and vegetarian options. Mixed salads, introduced to the menus over the preceding 20 years, and very much a Swiss tradition, are well represented, not least in the side salad of carrot, coriander, cucumber and fennel with mixed beans and cashew nuts. The cakes section ranges from the now iconic curd tart, another dish which dates back, in essence, to the 1920s, and the ever-popular Fat Rascal (the biggest-selling shop item), to French bombes and Swiss tortes, the Engadine still earning its place. Ice creams are made by a small Yorkshire company, who make a brown bread ice cream to a Bettys recipe. Meanwhile, the tea and coffee menu reflects Taylors' heritage, still without actively pushing the name. The classic tearoom blend is the most popular, although coffee aficionados can now choose to drink a flat white as well as a cappuccino or latte, for Antipodean coffee culture has swept through Britain, causing another quiet change to the way Brits consume their coffee. Swiss wine is now a firm fixture, and includes a special centenary wine, made by the Bonvin family specially for Bettys.

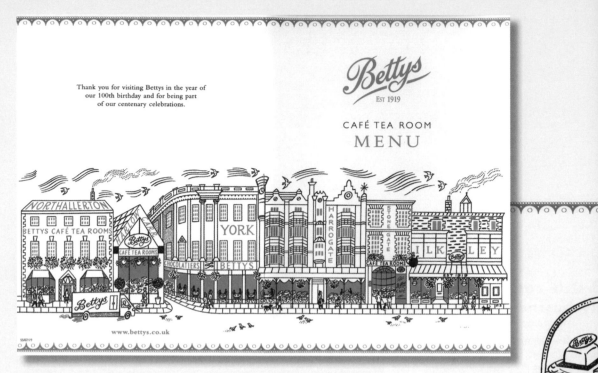

Thank you for visiting Bettys in the year of
our 100th birthday and for being part
of our centenary celebrations.

Bettys
EST 1919

CAFÉ TEA ROOM
MENU

www.bettys.co.uk

A Century of

Important
Announcement
In view of the considerable
number of patrons not taking
cream with tea, we have
DECIDED TO REDUCE
THE CHARGE FOR
AFTERNOON TEA
TO 6D.
ORCHESTRA DAILY

Betty's Ltd

Please inform your server if you have any allergies, int
*(V) suitable for vegetari

Bettys Centenary Café Tea Room
Menu, 2019

Centenary Afternoon Tea

Afternoon Tea and Yorkshire Cream Tea
are served all day.

Traditional Afternoon Tea

Sandwich selection
Cucumber, dill and cream cheese
Coronation Yorkshire chicken
Ham and wholegrain mustard
Scottish smoked salmon

A sultana scone with strawberry preserve and clotted cream.

Miniature cake selection
Chocolate cube
Lemon tart
Engadine slice

A teapot for one of Tea Room Blend tea.
£19.95

Pink Champagne Afternoon Tea

Traditional Afternoon Tea with a glass
of Moutard Rosé Prestige champagne.
£27.95

If you would prefer a vegetarian selection of sandwiches, please let us know.

Yorkshire Cream Tea (V)

Two freshly baked sultana scones from our Craft Bakery,
strawberry preserve and clotted cream,
with a teapot for one of Tea Room Blend tea.
£9.95

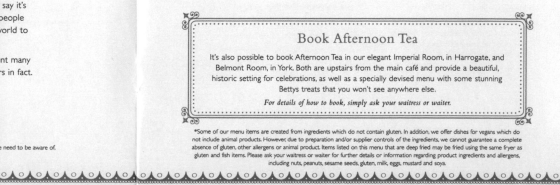

Book Afternoon Tea

It's also possible to book Afternoon Tea in our elegant Imperial Room, in Harrogate, and Belmont Room, in York. Both are upstairs from the main café and provide a beautiful, historic setting for celebrations, as well as a specially devised menu with some stunning Bettys treats that you won't see anywhere else.

For details of how to book, simply ask your waitress or waiter.

*Some of our menu items are created from ingredients which do not contain gluten. In addition, we offer dishes for vegans which do not include animal products. However, due to preparation and/or supplier controls of the ingredients, we cannot guarantee a complete absence of gluten, other allergens or animal product. Items listed on this menu that are deep fried may be fried using the same fryer as gluten and fish items. Please ask your waitress or waiter for further details or information regarding product ingredients and allergens, including nuts, peanuts, sesame seeds, gluten, milk, eggs, mustard and soya.

In March 2009 Lesley wrote a piece for the internal newsletter, reflecting on the changes she'd seen since she first joined the business and on the challenges facing Bettys & Taylors in the middle of one of the worst recessions for eight decades. She wrote of the uncertainty of the 1970s, with catering out of fashion as a career, and fast and frozen foods seeming to threaten everything that formed part of Bettys' core business. She recognised the importance of the work she and Jonathan had done as a team: 'the combination of Jonathan, a teacher and historian, and myself, an art student turned lawyer, brought up in a household where good food was a vital part of daily life, was serendipitous – a happy accident which meant that between the two of us we had the skills the business needed at the time'. She stated calmly: 'The world's current financial crisis is different from any we've lived through. One thing is for sure – no business will remain untouched. Old strategies are no longer appropriate in an uncertain world – we need to regroup and reorganise ourselves to face the struggle ahead.' The key, she concluded, lay in teamwork and the strength of the Bettys & Taylors family – that of the Wilds themselves but also the wider body of staff, which now numbered nearly 1,200.

Times were indeed uncertain. The 2008 recession lasted until July 2009, and it was not until 2013 that the UK economy reached its pre-downturn size. Unemployment reached its highest level since 1995, and the combination of a public sector pay freeze, subsequent pay cap and slow private sector wage rises meant that earnings lagged behind prices until 2014. Prime Minister David Cameron declared that Britain was now in 'the age of austerity' and introduced a raft of measures which aimed to reduce public spending, cut the budget deficit and promote 'big society', wherein grassroots charities and non-governmental organisations would fill any subsequent

Lesley Wild, 2012

gaps in public services more efficiently than a top-down approach could. Social services were cut, and household spending dropped.

Bettys & Taylors was further hit by an increase in raw material costs – affecting not just food but also tea and coffee, along with sharp rises in gas and electricity prices. When the Leeds-based family-owned bakery chain Ainsley's folded in late 2009, administrators cited as reasons energy and materials prices, along with the recession and fierce competition on the high street. A new wave of mid-range, casual dining restaurants – such as Prezzo, Zizzi, Jamie's Italian and Carluccio's – were expanding despite the recession, open all day and edging into the spaces previously occupied by pubs and cafés. That they were often (if loosely) Italian was not coincidental, for the pizzas, pastas and sauce-based dishes they offered were cheap, quick and easy to make with healthy profit margins.

The steady expansion of national bakery chains and coffee shops, especially Greggs, Starbucks and their rivals, also continued. Patisserie Valerie, a Continental-style shop and café founded as a family business in 1926 but sold off in the 1980s and now owned, like many of the other chains, by a private equity group,

A present-day view of the shop at Bettys Harrogate

was also opening new outlets, with windows full of anglicised versions of Continental pastries. Bettys launched its version of the French-style macaron, which was busy taking over the pâtisserie world at the time. Lesley Norris and her team developed a range of French pâtisserie classics as well, including an Opéra cake, which were showcased in the Montpellier café at Harrogate.

In the supermarkets too competition remained cut-throat. Twinings launched its Everyday Tea as a budget offering. Yorkshire Tea remained at number three in a market dominated by Tetley and PG Tips. The market for black tea as a whole was slowly declining, and Yorkshire Tea was the only brand showing steady growth within it. Prince Charles wrote to congratulate the company on its 90th anniversary, praising it for 'showing that it is indeed possible to be both a responsible and profitable business'. Anniversary activities included an outing to Whitby (a nod to Frederick's 1930 staff trip, also at peak recession), staff

A colourful stack of Bettys' famous macaroons

dressed in quasi-1920s uniforms and a tree protected in Peru for
every customer on the anniversary day itself. The Yorkshire
Rainforest Initiative was launched, a new pledge as part of Trees
for Life, with Bettys & Taylors working with the Rainforest
Foundation to save an area of rainforest the size of the Yorkshire
Dales. Independently, Jonathan was a founding member of the
United Bank of Carbon, a wide-ranging initiative partnering
businesses with environmental scientists to study and support
projects concerned with forests and climate change. It was based
at the University of Leeds, and he remains the Chair.

2009 was not a year for major capital projects, though; rather, it
was one of consolidation. Bettys by Post revamped its website,
and Yorkshire Tea joined Twitter with the simple post 'drinking
tea!' Initially the account was intended to be responsive, allowing
customers another means to reach the customer services team,
while also enabling the team to engage with conversations
already happening. It took some years before a dedicated social
media 'voice' was established. The following year Yorkshire Tea
launched on Facebook, discovering a number of existing fan
sites, which were merged to give it an instant following of
around 10,000 followers. The interactions on social media
resulted in the idea for the next advertising campaign, which
followed the 'Little Urn' van, complete with a cast drawn from
within the business, across America, on a quest to save the
British abroad from a bad brew. Both Facebook and Twitter
became an active part of this, with behind-the-scene stories and
a level of interactivity that saw Yorkshire Tea become the most
talked about tea brand on social media, with a very committed
group of fans. Bettys launched its own social media presence in

Yorkshire Tea on tour of America, 2011

2011 with a more understated approach, developing its own voice, quirky and very warm. Again, from the very beginning it punched above its weight, and the team discovered legions of dedicated fans, often from across the world, whether ex-pats or devotees who had visited while on holiday and fallen in love. Bettys lovers wanted to share their stories, which often had a romantic bent or centred on special occasions, and the Facebook site, in particular, developed a community feel.

In the cafés, meanwhile, the work continued. Having developed an aesthetic which reflected all the company values, each branch needed to be kept at its best, which meant continuous small changes, small tweaks to paint colours or toilet fittings to ensure that the cafés still felt modern and fresh, despite their apparent timelessness. The window displays were also important, especially at Easter, but throughout the year there were teams dedicated to developing new confectionery items and working out how best to display them. The surprise hit of 2010 was the milk chocolate badger, which joined the ever-increasing (and delightfully eclectic) range of Bettys creatures – previous ventures having included praline starfish, ganache bumblebees and a milk-chocolate otter.

In June 2010 the 300th consecutive monthly team briefing took place. The internal newsletter congratulated the 38 of the 1,208 staff members who could feasibly have attended all of them, and announced bursaries for the best team suggestions – whether business or community related. While it may have seemed a strange thing to celebrate to those outside the company, who were probably more interested in the new range of teatime cakes at Bettys by Post, inside it was a mark of real pride. It proved that Jonathan's business approach was not only working but a totally accepted part of the way the company ran. Customers only saw the results, not the workings.

The commitment to working with like-minded companies was in evidence too with the launch of a significant new range of chocolates. The basic chocolate (couverture) was made by a small Swiss company, Felchlin, which, like Taylors, sourced its ingredients ethically and worked closely with its global producers to improve standards in an industry as prone to poor conditions and low pay as the tea and coffee industry.

Overleaf A scene from Yorkshire Tea's 'Brewtopia' advert, 2015

Jonathan and Lesley, meanwhile, had been on sabbatical, taking time away from the business to plan for the future without the daily concerns of running it on the ground. They were in their late fifties, aware that it might be nice to retire, but equally aware that over three decades of joint work to stabilise and build the business needed to be safeguarded. The Family Constitution had been a start, and the Family Council was flourishing, now chaired by Liz, Jonathan's sister, but there were other, more specific areas that needed addressing: who would lead the business if they stepped away; could one person take over from their collaborative way of working; and how would the relationship with the family really work in practice if there wasn't a strong family member at the helm? They'd built a thriving business, with modern, fully refurbished premises, and strong sales, but now they wanted to ensure that the structures of governance were equally strong, creating a 'genuine sense of permanence and legacy'.

When they returned, in 2010, Jonathan announced that he was retiring the following year, stressing that 'Lesley will remain as Chair, providing continuity and a close connection between the family and the business. Meanwhile, the family shareholders, myself included, are committed to the values and vision that have

Top Bettys Café Tea Rooms in Harrogate, 2019

Bottom Liz Barnes, Family Shareholder

made our business so successful – quality, service, craftsmanship, attention to detail, fairness, sustainability and all the things that make Bettys & Taylors a unique and special place to work.' Characteristically, he added: 'I will be out and about in the business over the next few weeks, so please take the opportunity to come and have a chat,' and he subsequently went out to the branches and onto the factory and bakery floors, to gather views and reassure his staff. Jonathan, Lesley and the Board agreed that Lesley's legal background and organisational skills made her the best person to lead this vital structural work, while Jonathan concentrated on his interests away from Bettys.

The fourth generation of the family were now all adults, forging careers of their own. Chloë, Jonathan and Lesley's daughter, recalled that they were all encouraged not to feel beholden to Bettys, although equally they all knew it was there, a family responsibility and, hopefully, a source of satisfaction and joy when they felt ready to be part of it. Chloë and her brother Daniel had both gone to university in Bristol, and Chloë now worked in market research in London, while Dan was a designer for a food-and-drink magazine, with a successful sideline as a DJ. Liz's children Madeline, Antony and Rowan were all shareholders, part of the wider Bettys & Taylors family ownership. Liz's daughter Maddy

Bettys York, 2019

went north to study philosophy at Durham, and ultimately settled on the Northumberland border, opening a craft gallery. Except for short forays away to study and work, Liz's two sons, Antony and Rowan, remained Harrogate-based, working with their father to start an internet gift-and-bookmark business. Both Antony (who described the Swiss alpine macaroni as the only dish he'd risk his life for) and his wife Hannah would also work at Bettys & Taylors, both eventually moving on to new roles outside the company. All would later sit on the Family Council.

Other members of the family were also around, working alongside the staff but no longer appointed merely through their connections. Victor's great-nephew Timo Walt spent six months as an intern, breaking hearts as a Bettys waiter and achieving a long-held goal of spending time in Britain, before returning to Switzerland to study at the University of St Gallen, Victor's birthplace. Val's son Richard had joined Taylors as a school-leaver without mentioning his family connection and continued to work for the team as an engineer for over 30 years. Generation five was on its way as well: Madeline Barnes (now Bennett) had two children, and Chloë had one: in 2010 she became Chloë Benest when she married Andy with celebrations at Bettys Harlow Carr and in the Imperial Room at Harrogate. Her son Dylan cheerfully talked of going 'to Betty's house', personifying

Shop at Bettys Harrogate

the business in much the same way that the early-1930s press had talked of Frederick's cakes being designed by Betty herself. He later described Lesley as 'the captain of Bettys'.

In April 2011 Jonathan officially retired, going from being 'in charge of everything' to 'in charge of nothing', as he cheerfully put it in a closing statement to the company, thanking the staff who 'have brought out the best in me, and for that I am truly grateful to you all'. Lesley, still the Chair, as well as the sole family member on the Board, commented that 'he leaves behind a values-driven business where people and planet matter just as much as the bottom line. The people in the business will especially treasure Jonathan "the person" – his leadership, enthusiasm and sense of fun. They might also recall his determination (some might say stubbornness!), tempered by his ability to laugh at himself. He has always had time for people,

Bettys Harrogate centenary mosaic

been willing to chat over a cuppa in the staff cafés, and, most amazing of all, remembered the names of pretty much everyone who is involved in the business.' Staff were asked to share their memories of him – from his childhood visits until his last trips around the business – and they commented on his appreciation for people, his personal connection to every team member and his willingness to pitch in.

Bettys & Taylors was now continuously winning recognition for its ethics, working practices and products. There were Craft Business awards, environmental awards and awards for the cookery school. And, of course, the Bettys branches were also recognised. For the lucky few, there were even trips to Buckingham Palace: Katy Squire, who like so many people had worked across many areas of the company, including leading Trees for Life, editing the newsletter and heading up the communications department, had been one of three people representing Bettys & Taylors when it had won the Queen's Award for Enterprise in 2007 (Jonathan and Chris Powell, still championing the Cone Exchange, were the others). She commented that while meeting the Queen was a huge honour, it was even more exciting spotting Daniel Craig when they went for a meal at The Wolseley to celebrate later. The maître d' treated the group like VIPs, not because they'd been talking to Her Majesty earlier but because he'd heard that they were 'Bettys'. Summing up a general feeling, Katy commented on her own long service: 'for me personally – and I'm sure for many – it's the values of the company and the fact that it's a family business. It's grown and changed enormously in the years I've been here, but the commitment to do things properly and to be

Jonathan and Lesley Wild with Chris Powell receiving Bettys first Queen's Award for Enterprise for Sustainable Development, 2001

a decent, caring business – whether it's for our customers, our people, our suppliers or the jobs we do – has stayed the same.'

Jonathan was still a shareholder, and remained close to the business, as well as pursuing his environmental and business leadership interests beyond Bettys. He was recognised for his role as a local employer and significant community figure by Harrogate Borough Council, who awarded him the Freedom of the Borough in 2012 – one of only 29 such awards in the 128-year history of the council. He was also awarded an Honorary Doctorate from the University of Leeds in recognition of his environmental and social efforts regionally and

The Queen and Prince Philip as they ride past Bettys York on a Royal visit in 1971

internationally and named a Prince of Wales Ambassador for Business in the Community.

The new leadership structure was still a work in progress – a new CEO was appointed, but Bettys & Taylors was moving away from being a business with one autocratic leader, and it didn't work. It was now that the Family Constitution really mattered, as its underlying principles were rewritten as the 'six Ps', a simple statement of values, which were not only circulated within the management but became part of the basic training of every member of staff. The Ps were prosperity, people, product, process, planet and passion, with one-line explanations emphasising the importance of family ownership, long-term sustainability, exceptional quality and service and a Swiss level of attention to detail. The final P, passion, summed it up: 'the deep love and belief in what we do is the pounding heart of the family business. It lifts the spirit of all around us and creates our uniqueness. For the family shareholders, this pride and passion are valued as highly as prosperity.'

Newly reinvigorated by the work on what the business really stood for, Lesley now put in place a new, overtly collaborative leadership structure, which resulted in a collaborative CEO (CCEO). It soon consisted of five executives, working closely alongside Lesley. Rachel Fellows, the Chair, commented: 'Having a group of people with complementary skills filling the Chief Executive role means you get decisions informed by wider thinking. We're also able to be flexible and, between us, take the CCEO perspective into our functional roles and the many groupings in which we work. It boils down to the age-old adage that many heads are better than one.'

The group now put together a future plan, which would take the business to 2020, demonstrating the workability of the new structure, and that it would be able to function – and thrive – in a future when Lesley would eventually retire, leaving the business to be led entirely by non-family members on a daily basis. The building of a professional Group Board, comprising both executive and non-executive directors, with members who had the knowledge to genuinely contribute to the business going forward, was another key move. The non-executive directors were, for the first time, recruited specifically for what they could

contribute to the business, and, as Lesley commented: 'when I took over as Chair, I had to start from scratch to populate the Board with non-executive directors with the necessary skills and experience'. She appointed on merit, and the resulting Board was not only balanced in terms of gender but also had a generational mix.

The British recession ended in 2010, but trading conditions remained tough. VAT rose to 20 per cent, while business rates and raw-materials costs also remained high. The effects of austerity were being felt: there were many contradictions and competing sets of figures, but it was generally agreed that poverty, especially child poverty, was increasing, that crime was up, homelessness had increased and that government policies had added to the UK mortality rates (in 2019 a UN report would blast the government for 'massive disinvestment' in social welfare). Food bank usage doubled between 2013 and 2017. At a branch level, many of the Bettys charity initiatives concentrated on these areas, including the provision of freezers and toasters for a Harrogate homeless charity, which wanted to take Bettys' unsold bread but could not store it without a freezer because, being preservative-free, its shelf life was short. Food items past their sell-by date or other waste products (offcuts from bakery goods, for instance) that were not sold or consumed by staff went to such charities now as a matter of course.

Bettys was continuing to quietly innovate. Bettys Cookery School celebrated its 10th anniversary in 2011 and was

Bettys & Taylors Group
Board, 2019

303

Bettys York, 2019

flourishing. A new wedding cake range was launched, along with a bookable afternoon tea in the Belmont and Imperial Rooms – otherwise the egalitarian queuing system remained a fixture. Little Bettys was renamed once more, finally becoming just Bettys Stonegate, although the menu remained slimmer than elsewhere because of the restrictive kitchen space and the challenges of working in such an old building. Prince Charles provided the foreword for a short book of cartoons and stories – *Who Was Betty?* – with contributions from various well-known figures, which was sold in aid of the Yorkshire Rainforest Project.

Bettys asked if it could contribute a cake to the Queen's Diamond Jubilee celebrations at Buckingham Palace in 2012, just as it had for the silver and gold jubilees. When it received royal assent, the decorating team created a cake based on designs submitted by local schools. A range of jubilee bakery goods was also produced, including a lebkuchen corgi. Lesley, meanwhile, was asked to continue in her role as pro-chancellor at the University of York, making sure that student needs and concerns were heard at the governing level. As part of this she chaired a focus group looking at the catering and became involved in careers provision, commenting that 'my understanding of the complexities of running a business (particularly catering and retail) was appreciated, as was my commitment to improving the overall student experience'. The relationship with the university now included an internship programme as well as various links with academic departments, including a study to look at the feasibility of using waste coffee grounds as a replacement for peat in compost.

As part of the process of guaranteeing that Bettys & Taylors' heritage would continue to inform the business, in 2012 Mardi Jacobs was made the first permanent long-term archivist. Her remit was to professionalise and increase accessibility to the archive. She found herself in charge of a rich collection of documents, photographs and objects which had built up over the years, and which included everything from 1920s chocolate boxes to bits of cornice and door frames from various branch refurbishments – and Frederick's office chair, still with a faint whiff of cigar smoke about it. She commented: 'I never quite recovered from opening a box and discovering a loaf of bread. It turned out that it was Jonathan's first ever twist loaf, made while he was training in 1975.' She would act as a conduit between the business and its heritage. Bettys now had a thriving events programme, which included concerts and talks, and the various books and events that covered its heritage were very popular.

At Taylors, Yorkshire Tea now had a 12 per cent market share, and was growing at 17 per cent a year. A new finished-goods warehouse was opened in Harrogate, and the company introduced a 'supplier of the year' scheme for its coffee and tea growers. Winners were invited to Harrogate, to meet the team there and see how their raw products were blended roasted, ground and packaged. The aim was to build long-lasting, strong relationships, based on mutual understanding of the businesses involved, their ethics and their needs. The UK news sporadically reported on the often terrible conditions for workers on chocolate, tea and coffee plantations, and the social media team took time to respond to the occasional hostility on Twitter with measured articles about the work that Taylors was doing on the ground with suppliers, partners and charities. All Taylors teas and coffees were Rainforest Alliance certified from 2014. Meanwhile, the struggling Yorkshire Tea food range was quietly pulled, for, despite a 2010 relaunch, it simply wasn't profitable. Despite this, Taylors was now turning over more than £150 million a year,

Tea production in Rwanda. Plucking tea on a hillside on the Kitabe tea estate where the steep slopes, acidic soils and high altitude make it unsuitable for growing food crops, but ideal for the cultivation of tea

Lesley Wild tea tasting in the tasting room at Taylors, Harrogate

popular both for its high quality and quirky, no-nonsense image. On YouTube the Yorkshire Tea 'tea song' managed almost 500,000 hits when Russell Crowe shared it with his million or so followers, declaring it 'refreshingly insane'. As with so many of their non-famous aficionados, the relationship deepened via social media, culminating in Crowe's 2017 surprise visit to Taylors, when his band performed in the offices to crowds of staff as part of Yorkshire Tea's 40th birthday celebrations. In 2016 a YouGov survey put Yorkshire Tea in as one of the most highly regarded brands in the UK, alongside Ikea and M&S. It was the only food brand to make the cut.

In 2014 Yorkshire was put on the global map once more when the annual Tour de France staged its Grand Départ and first three stages in Britain. Three billion people watched the Tour on television, with around 15 million spectators live across the entire 3,656km race. The first leg, Leeds to Harrogate, and

The peloton passing outside Bettys
York as part of the Tour de France
Grand Départ, July 2014

the second, York to Sheffield, both took in Bettys towns, including Ilkley on both routes. Yorkshire rose enthusiastically to the occasion, far outshining most of the southern towns on the route, with yellow-painted bicycles hanging from shops and tied to hedges along the whole route, bunting, and shop (and house) windows all joyously celebrating the race. The Bettys newsletter asked for anyone with language skills to join in teaching counter and shop staff basic phrases in foreign languages, and Taylors brought out 'Allez! Allez!' a special-edition Tour coffee. Yorkshire Tea, meanwhile, was an official supporter of the race, promoting the tie-in with a glorious yellow-banded Yorkshire Thé packet and running two tea vans as part of the entourage, giving out samples, in the party atmosphere that always accompanied the race. On the race days themselves, the route went past both Bettys York and Bettys Harrogate. (The British cyclist, Mark Cavendish, the 'Manx Missile', collided with another rider outside the latter, injuring his shoulder, and was forced to pull out of the race). Keen cyclists of Bettys & Taylors celebrated with the 11th annual Fat Rascal Ride, a sponsored bike ride between the branches, which raised money for charity and enabled the riders to consume a great number of cakes and bacon sandwiches without fearing for their waistlines.

Taylors' growth was driven both by new customers discovering its existing range and by continued innovation. Although black tea consumption was still in slow decline. Yorkshire Tea remained in growth, and edging closer to taking the number-two slot. It finally took over from Tetley in 2017, achieving a 22.6 per cent market share. Nevertheless, as its competitors sought to exploit the market for green and herbal teas, Taylors also looked beyond its core range. In 2015 the company partnered with Kew Gardens for a range of herbal infusions, and in 2016 Bedtime, Breaktime and Breakfast Brews launched. (Breaktime was later pulled, but Biscuit Brew rose from its ashes, the subject of fanatical comments across the web).

Coffee was a slightly different story, appearing to be a burgeoning market, with coffee consumption rising to 95 million cups a day from 80 million between 2008 and 2018. But this disguised a marked difference between older and younger consumers: coffee drinkers were an ageing market, as millennials bought into health messages around caffeinated beverages and

expressed concern over the ethics of the trade by choosing not to buy into it. The rise of the so-called 'third wave' of coffee, influenced by both Antipodean coffee culture and the hipster movement, which championed craft, environmental sustainability and ethical business practice (along with the more easily lampooned beards and tattoos), saw independent coffee shops offering a bewildering range of coffee-making methods, grinds and blends, finally ousting some of the ubiquitous chains. Older drinkers who had long been satisfied with instant coffee, still around 42 per cent of the overall coffee market, now started to look for easy delivery methods in-house, a gap filled by systems such as Nespresso (and a few rivals such as Dolce Gusto). Coffee pods and capsules became a huge area for growth, and Taylors launched a Nespresso-compatible pod in 2015. An experimental cold brew and tonic was possibly too cool for the UK market, although by 2019 Caffè Nero would be selling a version. Coffee bags came out in 2016 for those people who wanted a better result than instant but did not wish to invest in a machine.

Bettys, meanwhile, was also continuing to grow. It was a different business, ostensibly more Yorkshire-focused and facing the challenges of the changing high street, rather than having to fight for space on a supermarket shelf. However, its reach was global, and when the social media team released a short video of the making of that year's Imperial Easter egg, which weighed 5kg and was hand-piped with iced decoration, it unexpectedly

A fifth-generation Tadpole Tour introducing younger family members to the business went viral. Over 6 million people watched it, and nearly 90,000 people commented (the phrases 'wow', and 'do you ship worldwide?' were common strands). Easter egg sales rose by 37 per cent. Both the range on offer in the shops and the café menus were constantly evolving in line with the trends of the time. In 2015 the bookable afternoon tea was revamped, becoming the Lady Betty Afternoon Tea, named, and gently designed, to echo Frederick Belmont's Lady Betty chocolate fancies.

There were new tills, new ways of managing stock and dealing with waste. The bread range was also overhauled, making the sourdough offering more explicit and bringing in seasonal breads, as sourdough became trendy. The continuing success of BBC2's *The Great British Bake Off* (made by C4 from 2017) resulted in a sharp rise in interest in all things baked. In 2017 Lesley received a double vindication of the Bettys & Taylors approach when she went to Buckingham Palace to collect a Queen's Award for Sustainable Development. This was Bettys & Taylors' third Queen's Award, this time for their approach to sourcing tea and coffee and explicitly recognising the impact the company was having on lives and livelihoods around the world. At the reception afterwards Lesley found herself approached by one of the royal footmen, a former Bettys Northallerton team member, who told her he was convinced that his Bettys training had got him the footman's job. She said: 'he was a perfect example of someone whose life had been changed by Bettys'.

As the 100th anniversary of Bettys approached, together with Lesley's 40th year leading the business – and nearly a decade fully in charge – a new Future Picture was compiled by the CCEO team, Lesley and the leadership teams. It was clear now that the radical change in leadership structure initiated by her was working, and that the relationship between family shareholders and appointed directors within the business was established. The fundamental issue of how the business could transition smoothly from the third to the fourth generation had been addressed. The collaborative CCEO team, the professional Board and the instigation of a culture where more people were accountable and decisions were made more deeply within the organisation were all now embedded in the way Bettys & Taylors worked. It was no longer an owner-led company, but one in which both family and leaders within the business worked together for the good of all. The 'six Ps' were integral to the whole ethos going forward, and additional changes such as the removal of a performance-led bonus in favour of a more egalitarian scheme highlighted the value placed on every person who worked there.

Meanwhile, the fifth generation was gradually being introduced properly to the business, via Tadpole Tours. They were so-named because one of the regular ways in which the family stayed engaged with the business was via the FROG forum – Family, Relationships, Organisation, Governance – which brought together the CCEO, wider family beyond the Family Council and the Bettys & Taylors Board. Lesley's nephew Jonah commented on the first Tadpole Tour: 'I knew it was going to be fun, but I didn't know it was going to be that amazing.'

In July 2018 Chloë Benest, Lesley and Jonathan's daughter, took over as Chair of the Family Council, having spent the previous two years learning about family businesses and their workings and preparing herself for what was now a formalised, paid, three-day-a-week position. She commented that hers was the first generation not to feel that their personal life was subservient to the business and that she was proud to represent a new way of working, while being very aware of the challenge of keeping a family business feeling like one, when a future would come with no family member working directly within the business.

Victor Wild looking up at the lettering falling off the frontage of the old Pagoda House at Plumpton Park, before it was demolished to make way for a new blending warehouse

Bettys was a founder member of the Institute of Family Businesses in the UK, actively helping others to work through some of the challenges they had faced in the previous two decades.

Meanwhile at Starbeck the old Pagoda House was demolished to make way for a new blending warehouse. Victor and Jonathan sat down to be interviewed for a video a few days before the bulldozers moved in, with Victor expressing his sadness that his beloved building, the marker of success for him, was going, saying: 'I hope they'll think twice before knocking it down.' Jonathan pointed out that even the name above the door was falling off: 'I think they've thought twice, Victor, I think the writing is on the wall. As we walked in today, the D was hanging down, the G and the S were missing … if ever there is a clearer sign that they've thought, once, twice and made a decision, then that's it.'

Bettys centenary celebration for family and staff in the grounds of Ripley Castle, Yorkshire, May 2019

The centenary window display at
Bettys Harrogate

As Bettys entered its 100th year, there were obvious challenges once again looming. The 2016 Brexit vote had already affected the British economy, and it largely crippled the government for much of 2019 as MPs failed to agree on anything around the issue; every business was busy preparing for a still very unknown future relationship with Europe. The high street was changing, with stalwarts such as Debenhams and House of Fraser (the owner of many of Bettys' former department store wholesale clients) closing stores, and the era of chain restaurants seemed to be ending. The collapse of the Jamie's Italian chain in May was just one among many such casualties, and Bettys once more found itself in the position of watching as former rivals closed their doors. The Luke Johnson-owned Patisserie Valerie chain had already fallen, its expansion into motorway service stations along with alleged fraud having caused many of its branches to stop trading overnight. There were others coming up to take their place – The Ivy, Côte, Bill's – all also driven by the private equity model to expand before being sold on.

At 2019's Bettys & Taylors AGM, as the risks ahead were being discussed, the minutes recorded Victor's contribution to the debate: 'This discussion of risk reminds us of what Frederick faced in 1919 when he established this business. The social history of the time was far more dramatic, impacted by the end of the First World War and its aftermath. Frederick, with little resource and no support, started this business in such difficult times. He would be both delighted and staggered at its success, as a £200-million business a hundred years later, particularly as the ethos behind his original business remains as strong.' Victor went on, expressing 'his admiration and gratitude to all, the Board, the CCEO and everyone who has contributed to the success of the business. It is a business to be proud of, one hundred years on, continuing to give pleasure to many people.'

He wasn't the only person looking back – and forward – with pride. Jonathan tried to sum up what made Bettys unique, concluding that it was a business which was 'family, Swiss, Yorkshire, craft, aesthetic and thoroughly modern'. Meanwhile, Lesley added that from her point of view: 'each leader has built upon and developed what has gone before, and I hope that's what I've managed to do too. But our business is not just about its leaders – it's the people who make a business – and we do have wonderful people working in our business, people who care about our values and who want to be a part of making a difference in the world.' Victor was the longest-serving family member, but Lesley had now beaten Frederick's 33 years and Jonathan's 35 years. She recognised herself that, given that she had joined the business by marriage, her understanding of its ethos, emphasis on it rediscovering its Swiss roots and ability to forge new governance structures for the future were all the more remarkable.

Bettys centenary was celebrated in style. There was a range of new commemorative items, from teapots to bags, with a specially commissioned illustration of the branches, which also featured on the menus. For Easter, the Imperial Easter egg became a glorious, shiny pink Centenary Imperial Easter egg, weighing in at 5.8kg, decorated with handmade pastillage flowers and piping, and costing £495. It, and the other products sold fast to Bettys

'it's our constancy of purpose
and spirit, our commitment to
quality and service, that's
ensured we've made it to the
end of our first century'.

adoring fans. On 31 May Bettys held its official staff Centenary
Celebration, closing the branches early, so that the over 700
members of the team who had signed up to attend could gather
at Ripley Castle Showground for a celebratory party. There was
Swiss raclette, Swiss wine and a film featuring the family talking
about the business of which they were so proud. Lesley summed
up the family vision: 'to work together to create a great Yorkshire
business, inspired by our Swiss heritage; one that creates pride
and prosperity by doing what we believe in'. As the firepits
glowed, and the band brought people to the dance floor, the
Tadpoles – the fifth generation – joined in enthusiastically as
staff ate and drank and queued up to have their photographs
taken dressed up in top hats and tiaras. Lesley announced a
one-off £500 bonus to all staff members, regardless of seniority
or length of service, or whether they were full or part time. It
was a continuation of Frederick's determination to recognise
and thank the Bettys staff, without whom the business would not
thrive. The evening ended with a spectacular fireworks display
which lit up the faces below. Many of them would be back at
work the next day, doing what Bettys & Taylors does best. Lesley
summed it up in her opening speech: 'it's our constancy of
purpose and spirit, our commitment to quality and service, that's
ensured we've made it to the end of our first century'.

Overleaf Bettys family and staff raising
a toast to the next 100 years, 2019